THE LAST
BLASKET
KING

PÁDRAIG Ó CATHÁIN, AN RÍ

This book is dedicated:

To Michael J. Carney who, at ninety-four years of age, is the oldest of seven living natives of the Great Blasket Island and is currently a resident of the Springfield area in Massachusetts. Mike is my father-in-law and he introduced me to the story of the Great Blasket when I met his daughter Maureen almost thirty years ago. I was inspired by Mike's deep and abiding love for the island and his fervour for preserving its legacy. Our collaboration in the publication of his memoirs, *From the Great Blasket to America – The Last Memoir by an Islander*, only deepened my own fascination with this very special place. This work is a salute to Mike's monumental commitment to the Blaskets and to his to his lifelong celebration of his Irish heritage.

GERALD HAYES

To my three dearly adored John Kanes who, each in a unique way, have made their lives a tribute to the Kanes that came before them. Papa, Dad, brother – you are all Kings of my heart.

ELIZA KANE

THE LAST
BLASKET
KING

PÁDRAIG Ó CATHÁIN, AN RÍ

GERALD HAYES
WITH ELIZA KANE

The Collins Press

First published in 2015 by
The Collins Press
West Link Park
Doughcloyne
Wilton
Cork

Paperback ISBN: 978-184889-237-8
PDF eBook ISBN: 978-1-84889-886-8
EPUB eBook ISBN: 978-1-84889-887-5
Kindle ISBN: 978-1-84889-888-2

A CIP record for this book is available from the British Library.

Maps by Dómhnal Ó Bric, Dún Chaoin, Contae Chiarraí
Typesetting by Carrigboy Typesetting Services
Typeset in Garamond Premier Pro 11.5pt/14pt

Printed in Poland by HussarBooks

Contents

Introduction   ix
The Ó Catháin Family Tree   xiv

1. A Kingdom and a King   1
   The Kingdom: the Great Blasket Island   1
   The Last Island King: Pádraig Peats Mhicí
     Ó Catháin   12

2. Kings in Irish and Blasket History   17
   Ancient Irish Kings   17
   Local Kings in Ireland   20
   Kings of the Great Blasket Island   28

3. The Last Blasket King: a Profile   36
   The King's Role   39
   The King's Character   41
   The Wealth of Blasket Kings   43
   Tomás Ó Criomhthain and the King   44
   The King's Voice   47

4. The King's Lineage   51
   The King's Great-grandparents   52
   The King's Grandparents   53
   The King's Parents   55
   The King's Birth   56
   Máire (Ní Chatháin) Uí Chriomhthain   57
   Cáit (Ní Chatháin) Uí Conchúir   61
   Mícheál 'Bofar' Ó Catháin   62
   Muiris Ó Catháin   67

5. The King's Youth   70
   The King's Education   70
   The Joys of Youth   80
   Competition   85

6. The King's Family 89
   A Proposal of Marriage........................... 89
   The King's Children 91
   The 'Palace' 93

7. The King's Stewardship 97
   Leader.. 97
   Decision Making 97
   Rent Collection Crisis 99
   Land Ownership and the Reorganisation of the
        Fields..................................... 100
   Yellow Meal from Government.................. 106
   Lobstering..................................... 109
   The Salvage of the Quebra 111

   Postman 114
   Intermediary 117
   The Great War (the First World War) 119
   The Easter Rising 1916........................ 123
   Ventry Regatta 126
   Transporter 127
   Muiris Ó Súilleabháin Returns to the Great
        Blasket 127
   Muiris Ó Súilleabháin Joins the Garda
        Síochána................................. 130
   Adviser and Counsellor 132
   Religion...................................... 132
   Méiní Elopes.................................. 132
   Host-in-Chief................................... 137
   Visitors...................................... 137
   The King's Bed and Breakfast 138
   Courting 139
   Arbitrator...................................... 140
   A Man for all Seasons 141

Contents

8. Island Visitors and The King 144
    John Millington Synge 149
    Carl Marstrander 165
    Eibhlín Nic Niocaill 171
    Robin Flower 177
    Brian Kelly and Pádraig Ó Siochfhradha 191
    George Thomson 194
    Marie-Louise Sjoestedt-Jonval 199
    Plácido Ramón Castro del Rio 201
    Other Visitors to the Great Blasket. 204
    Visitors and the Last Blasket King. 206

9. The King's Passing. 209

10. The Kingdom Evacuated 217

11. The King's Descendants in Ireland 229
    Máire (Ní Chatháin) Uí Ghuithín 230
    Cáit (Ní Chatháin) Uí Chathasa 244
    Seán Ó Catháin 250

12. The King's Descendants in America 262
    Mícheál Ó Catháin (Mike 'The Fiddler' Kane) 262
    Making it in America 272
    Family Relations. 277
    Life after Mike 'The Fiddler' 279
    The Famous Kane Fiddle 283

13. The King's Legacy 295

Endnotes 304
Acknowledgements 325
Photo credits 327
Bibliography 329
Index 338

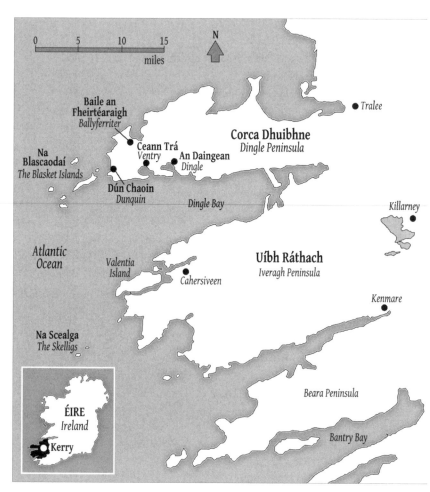

Map of West Kerry

Introduction

For such a small community, that of the Great Blasket Island is the subject of a surprisingly large number of books, more than eighty in all, not to mention countless newspaper and journal articles. The first five Blasket books – *Island Cross-Talk, The Islandman, Twenty Years A-Growing, Peig* and *An Old Woman's Reflections* – were written by Blasket Islanders, with the encouragement and assistance of non-islanders. These books have now become classics of Irish literature – with *Peig* even attaining the status of mandatory school reading in Ireland. These books were written in Irish and then later translated into English, with some eventually being translated into as many as six other languages, including French, German, Polish, Italian, Danish and Swedish. The most recent generation of Blasket books have been written primarily, but not exclusively, by non-islanders in both Irish and English. All these books have enjoyed broad readership and their widespread popularity has given the Great Blasket a fairly high level of recognition in both Ireland and the United States.

The continuing allure of the Great Blasket is a reflection of a natural human interest in several compelling dimensions of the island's story: a shared struggle against great hardship in an isolated environment; a quintessentially Irish folk culture that is manifest in storytelling, music and dance; the strong and emotional tug of emigration on islanders and their families; the gradual decline and eventual evacuation of the Blasket community from the island; and the various stories of the

Great Blasket's diaspora as the islanders resettled far and wide around the globe.

Why is yet another contribution to the Blasket library important?

From the perspective of the members of island community, the Ó Catháin (Keane/Kane) family was clearly one of most prominent on the island. Two members of this family are among the three persons who are recorded to have served as 'King' of the island during this period and, through marriage and otherwise, the Ó Catháins had direct personal connections with most other island families.

The last island King was Pádraig Ó Catháin, known on the island as 'Peats Mhicí,' who served for about twenty-five years until his death in 1929. To the islanders themselves, Peats Mhicí was arguably the most important citizen of the island during twentieth century. Island authors Tomás Ó Criomhthain, Muiris Ó Súilleabháin and Peig Sayers have enjoyed far greater fame beyond the island, for the most part because of the publication of their timeless Blasket books. But most of their well-deserved renown occurred after their passing. Peats Mhicí Ó Catháin, the last King, was the central figure on the island itself during their shared lifetimes.

For example, the King helped the islanders to understand and navigate their way through national and world events such as the Easter Rising in 1916 and The Great War (the First World War). A hands-on leader, the King also collaborated with his friend Tomás Ó Criomhthain and other island 'elders' in planning the transition of the ownership of the island land from the Earl of Cork to the Congested Districts Board in 1907 and, in turn, to the islanders themselves. They also participated in the reorganisation of the island's meagre field system that took place between 1907 and 1917. These were important economic and social reforms, although they did not address the fundamental problem of the island's isolation and they were insufficient to staunch the downward spiral of emigration, particularly to the United States, that ultimately led to the island's demise as a community.

While the King is referred to frequently in many of the books about the island, to date there is no single work that compiles the entire story of his extraordinary life. This book now tells the very special tale of this unique man, his many contributions to the island and his extensive legacy.

And, of course, there is something almost magical about the notion of a king. Today, even the concept of a king invites curiosity. It conjures up images of a largely bygone era and, perhaps, of great material affluence. The juxtaposition of such a grandiose title with such a small, isolated place beset with hardship seems incongruous. Few people would look upon the humble ruins that now remain on the Great Blasket and imagine that a king had ever lived among them. And yet, a distinguished king was very much a forceful presence on this storied island.

This work has been undertaken in collaboration with the King's descendants in the United States and in Ireland. The Kane family in America has been particularly supportive of every aspect of this project and sees it as a complement to their own efforts to illustrate the King's life and legacy in a documentary film called *The Crest*.

Eliza Kane, the great-great-granddaughter of the King, has taken the lead in writing the portion of this book that chronicles the emigration of the King's descendants to the United States and their efforts to preserve their island heritage. She also provided thoughtful and invaluable input throughout the book. Thus, this work is a unique collaboration by the son-in-law of Michael J. Carney, the oldest living native Blasket Islander with a direct descendant of the main subject of the book, the last King himself.

A couple of editorial comments are in order: Irish can be a challenging language, particularly with respect to matters of translation. Every effort has been made to convey the meaning intended by the original sources of information. In addition, we have tried valiantly to include the Irish spellings for names, places, artifacts and selected expressions that seem closest to the local Irish convention in West Kerry. The Irish is presented in parentheses immediately after the first use of a particular name, word or expression.

In the instance of names, we have used the version that was commonly used during the subject person's lifetime, either Irish or English, unless a person was known two ways at different times in their lives in which case both versions are given at first mention. Nicknames are presented in single quotation marks, e.g. Pádraig 'An Rí' Ó Catháin. Patronymics and matronymics are given without quotation marks, e.g. Pádraig Peats Mhicí Ó Catháin. Thus Seán, the King's son, who was not himself King, is referred to as Seán An Rí Ó Catháin rather than Seán 'An Rí' Ó Catháin because it is a patronymic (Seán, son of the King), not a nickname. Maiden names are indicated in parentheses to keep the lineage clear.

In the various source documents, the word 'King' is sometimes capitalised and sometimes not. In quotations from other works, the case of the 'k' reflects its treatment in the source. Otherwise, the 'k' has been presented in upper case out of respect for the centrality of the role of King on the island.

Finally, writing this book has involved synthesising information from multiple sources, both written and oral in nature, into a single coherent story. Though known for his way with words, the King was not an author himself so we are without autobiographical material. At the time of writing, the King has been deceased for about eighty-five years and virtually all of his contemporaries are also deceased. Detailed information about him is sparse and dispersed among many other works. Nevertheless, by weaving together snippets of information from various sources, we were able to construct an in-depth and detailed biography of this truly intriguing man. The endnotes are an essential part of this book, assuring proper attribution of information to these sources.

We hope this book is worthy of a truly great man, Peats Mhicí Ó Catháin, the last Blasket King, and a valuable addition to the Blasket library.

GERALD HAYES & ELIZA KANE

First Ó Catháin on The Great Blasket Island		Mártan Ó Catháin Graigue/Great Blasket (*c.* late 1700s)
First Ó Catháin King		At least 2 siblings: Mícheál & Tomás Great Blasket
Spouse		
Last King's Parents:	Pádraig Ó Catháin Great Blasket (1862–Unknown)	Mártan Ó Catháin Great Blasket (1835–1863)
		Máire Ní Chriomhthain Uí Chatháin Great Blasket (Dates Unknown)
Last King/Siblings:	Máire Ní Chatháin Uí Chriomhthain Great Blasket (1859–1901)	Cáit Ní Chatháin Uí Chonchúir Great Blasket/Muiríoch (1860–1932)
Spouses:	Tomás Ó Criomhthain, The Islandman Great Blasket (1855–1937)	Seán Ó Conchúir Muiríoch (Unknown–1896)
Children:	Sean I, Pádraig, Eibhlín, Tomás, Cáit, Máire I, Domhnall, Mícheál I, Muiris Sean II, Mícheál II, & Máire II	Seán, Mícheál, Nell, Tomás, Máire, Muiris, & Peats
Last King's Children:	**Michael 'The Fiddler' Kane Great Blasket/Springfield, MA (1881–1949)**	Máire Ní Chatháin Uí Ghuithín Great Blasket/Dunquin (1882–1970)
Spouses:	**Mary Foley Ventry/Hartford, CT/Springfield, MA (1886–1982)**	Mícheál 'Léan' Ó Guithín Great Blasket (Unknown–1926)
Last King's Grandchildren Great Grandchildren and Great Great Grandchildren	**Helen, James, Michael, Mary, Kathryn, Agnes Dorothy, Theresa, Joseph, Eileen**	Eibhlín Ní Ghuithín (1906–1923)
	John Patrick Kane (1910–1997)	Mícheál Ó Guithín (1906–1906)
	Catherine Veronica O'Connor (1917–1981)	Pádraig Ó Guithín (1908–1908)
	John (Jack) Anthony Kane, Sr. (1952–)	Máire Ní Ghuithín Uí Chiobháin (1909–1988)
	John Anthony, Patrick Joseph & Caroline O'Connor (various)	Seán Ó Guithín (1911–1999)
	Eliza Catherine Kane (1981–)	Mícheál Ó Guithín (1913–Unknown)
	Maple Eliette Avery Spurr (2013–)	Muiris Ó Guithín (1920–2007)

Family Tree

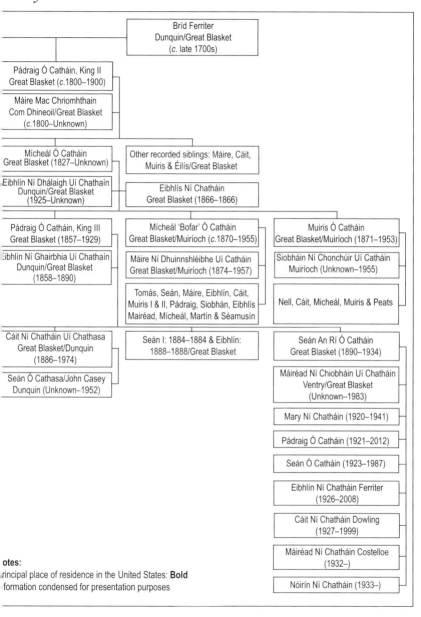

Bríd Ferriter
Dunquin/Great Blasket
(*c.* late 1700s)

Pádraig Ó Catháin, King II
Great Blasket (*c.*1800–1900)

Máire Mac Chriomhthain
Com Dhineoil/Great Blasket
(*c.*1800–Unknown)

Mícheál Ó Catháin
Great Blasket (1827–Unknown)

Other recorded siblings: Máire, Cáit,
Muiris & Éilís/Great Blasket

Eibhlín Ní Dhálaigh Uí Chathaín
Dunquin/Great Blasket
(1925–Unknown)

Eibhlís Ní Chatháin
Great Blasket (1866–1866)

Pádraig Ó Catháin, King III
Great Blasket (1857–1929)

Mícheál 'Bofar' Ó Catháin
Great Blasket/Muiríoch (*c.*1870–1955)

Muiris Ó Catháin
Great Blasket/Muiríoch (1871–1953)

Eibhlín Ní Ghairbhia Uí Chathaín
Dunquin/Great Blasket
(1858–1890)

Máire Ní Dhuinnshléibhe Uí Cathaín
Great Blasket/Muiríoch (1874–1957)

Siobháin Ní Chonchúir Uí Cathaín
Muiríoch (Unknown–1955)

Tomás, Seán, Máire, Eibhlín, Cáit,
Muiris I & II, Pádraig, Siobhán, Eibhlís
Mairéad, Mícheál, Martín & Séamusín

Nell, Cáit, Micheál, Muiris & Peats

Cáit Ní Chatháin Uí Chathasa
Great Blasket/Dunquin
(1886–1974)

Seán I: 1884–1884 & Eibhlín:
1888–1888/Great Blasket

Seán An Rí Ó Catháin
Great Blasket (1890–1934)

Seán Ó Cathasa/John Casey
Dunquin (Unknown–1952)

Máiréad Ní Chiobháin Uí Chatháin
Ventry/Great Blasket
(Unknown–1983)

Mary Ní Chatháin (1920–1941)

Pádraig Ó Catháin (1921–2012)

Seán Ó Catháin (1923–1987)

Eibhlín Ní Chatháin Ferriter
(1926–2008)

Cáit Ní Chatháin Dowling
(1927–1999)

Máiréad Ní Chatháin Costelloe
(1932–)

Notes:
Principal place of residence in the United States: **Bold**
Information condensed for presentation purposes

Nóirín Ní Chatháin (1933–)

1. A Kingdom and a King

The Kingdom: the Great Blasket Island

The earthly domain of the 'King' of the Great Blasket Island *(An Blascaod Mór)* was exceedingly modest by almost any measure. It was a tiny 'kingdom' indeed, an island of only about 1,100 acres of steep and rocky land situated in the often raging Atlantic Ocean 5km (3 miles) off the Dingle Peninsula *(Corca Dhuibhne)* on Ireland's southwest coast in County Kerry *(Contae Chiarraí)*. Its population was just 176 at its maximum in 1916.[1]

But there was much about this small and isolated kingdom that makes its cultural and historic importance to Ireland and the world vastly disproportionate to its size. The Great Blasket was fertile ground for the development and advancement of a whole genre of Irish folk literature. At least three island authors of great stature described the unique life of this vibrant Irish community in great detail for posterity.

The Blasket Islands are among the westernmost points of occupied land in all of Europe. This archipelago includes six principal islands: the Great Blasket Island, Beginish *(Beiginis)*, Inishnabro *(Inis na Bró)*, Inishvickillane *(Inis Mhic Uileáin)*, Inishtooskert *(Inis Tuaisceart)*, and Tearaght *(An Tiaracht)*.[2] Each of these islands is actually a mountain sitting on the ocean floor and sharply jutting up out of the water within eyesight of the mainland.

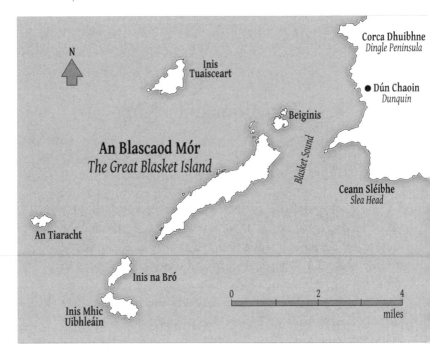

The Blasket Islands with Dunquin to the east (right) on the mainland.

The Great Blasket Island is the largest of the Blaskets by far: about 6km (3½ miles) long and 1km (half a mile) wide. Its highest point is a peak called 'the Crow' *(An Cró)*, rising 292m (958 feet) above sea level. The only relatively level land on the entire island is its beautiful white sandy beach *(An Tráigh Bháin)* which faces the mainland on its eastern shore just north of the small island village.

The Great Blasket has been said to resemble a huge whale basking in the Atlantic Ocean. Its landscape is totally treeless and is often shrouded in fog and mist, sometimes creating an otherworldly feeling on the island. Winter days are very short with the sun positioned low in the sky and disappearing behind the island's long central east–west ridge for months, creating a kind of gloom in the village until occasional sunshine returns each year on or about St Bridget's Day, 1 February.[3]

According to *National Geographic Traveler*, this whole area is 'the most beautiful place on earth.'[4] Together with the dramatic coastline along the adjacent mainland from The Three Sisters *(An Triúr Deirfiúr)* in the north to Slea Head *(Ceann Sléibhe)* in the south, the natural beauty of this stretch of Ireland's west coast is breathtaking. But it is not always tranquil. Between the Great Blasket and the mainland lies Blasket Sound *(An Bealach)*. These waters are often treacherous and gale-force winds and heavy rains are commonplace.

In fact, there is ample evidence of the inherent danger of navigating in these turbulent waters. Many unfortunate ships were wrecked here over hundreds of years, including a vessel from the Spanish Armada, the *Santa Maria de la Rosa (Our Lady of the Rosary)*, that sank after striking a rock during very bad weather on 21 September 1588 with the loss of about 175 lives.[5] Other ships that met their fate here include the *Lochie*, the *Commerce*, the *Caroline* and the *Quebra*.[6] The word 'Blasket' itself is generally thought to be a derivative of the Norse word 'brasker' meaning sharp reef.[7] This is an entirely appropriate descriptor.

The always challenging and sometimes impossible 5km (3 mile) journey between Dunquin *(Dún Chaoin)* and the Great Blasket only exacerbated the isolation of the island. The trip from the Dunquin harbour of *An Fhaill Mhór* over to the island harbour of *Caladh an Oileáin* typically took forty-five minutes to an hour even in good weather. In bad weather, the crossing was simply postponed. This physical remoteness proved to be a major factor in the eventual decline and demise of the island community.

Turbulence in Blasket Sound.

Transportation between the mainland and the island was almost always by way of *naomhóg*, a local version of the currach, a versatile ocean-going canoe sometimes fitted with a sail if conditions allowed. *Naomhóga* were built by the islanders themselves and were essential in maintaining contact with the mainland and in supporting the island's fishing economy.

The Great Blasket was the only one of the Blasket Islands to be occupied on a sustained basis over time. The first inhabitants probably arrived during the Iron Age and they left behind stone beehive huts *(clocháns)* later used by monks and possibly others. Vikings followed, although they were primarily raiders and probably used the island only as a base of operations for brief periods. They either built or at least utilised the promontory fortification that once stood at 'the Fort' *(An Dún)*, another high point on the island.[8]

In 1736, the Earl of Cork wrote of the Great Blasket 'I saw some tillage and a few cabins from whence some poor wretches entered into a boat with rabbits for sale.'[9] These first long-term inhabitants were fishermen and farmers who had migrated to the Great Blasket from the mainland, probably settling on the island sometime in the late seventeenth century. Writing in the mid-1900s, Seán Ó Criomhthain, the son of the famous Blasket author Tomás Ó Criomhthain, tells us that these settlers:

> '... went there from the parish of Ventry [*Ceann Trá*], from Dunquin, and from the parish of Ballyferriter [*Baile an Fheirtéaraigh*], not because of high spirits nor on holidays. It was the very opposite. Want, hunger and poverty caused them to go there.'[10]

According to historian Charles Smith, there were 'five or six' families living on the Great Blasket in the mid-eighteenth century. Smith's extensive history of County Kerry, written in 1756, referred to these few residents as 'strong, lusty and healthy.'[11] Smith reported that no one had died on the island during the previous forty-five years. Certainly, however, islanders had died on the mainland during this period, probably crossing Blasket Sound to the mainland with the onset of serious illness.

By implication, it appears that at least some permanent settlement of the island occurred during the late seventeenth century.[12] The population grew during the early eighteenth century as people fled to the island seeking a better way of life and, perhaps, in an effort to escape increasing land rents on the mainland. The population reached 153 in 1841. There was then a population dip during the Great Famine in the mid-1800s, yet the decline was proportionately somewhat less than

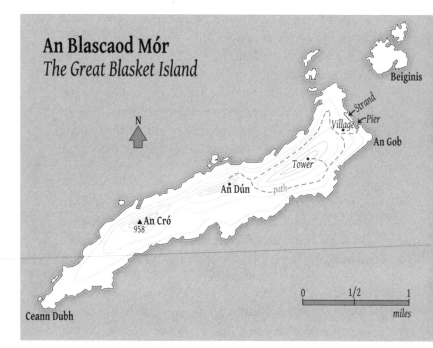

Map of the Great Blasket Island.

that on the mainland. For example, the population of the Great Blasket fell only to 141 between 1841 and 1851, while the population of Dunquin parish was roughly halved during the same period.[13] Thereafter, the number of inhabitants began to grow slowly again. The island's peak population of about 176 was reached in 1916 after a brief period of relative prosperity on the island. By 1947, however, the population was down to only fifty people as emigration to the mainland and to America gradually took its toll.[14]

Even in the best of times, the islanders endured difficult physical conditions and scarce resources. It was a tough life that continually tested the human spirit. Shelter consisted of about thirty small one- or two-room, whitewashed homes, built of stone, and clustered in a village *(An Baile)* on a gradual slope facing the mainland – each dug into the rising hill along their west wall so that the floors would be level. The first homes were constructed just above the pier and, as the village grew, it gradually expanded up the hill in a seemingly random pattern. Most of the houses were oriented to the south to avoid the north wind and to catch the intermittent sun on the front side. The primary heat source was a fireplace that burned turf or peat, which was harvested on the island for cooking and warmth. Fresh water was derived from two spring-fed wells.[15]

The Earl of Desmond owned the Great Blasket during the thirteenth and fourteenth centuries. During this period it was leased to the Ferriter family for the annual rent of two hawks. After the Desmond Rebellion was put down, the island was granted to two 'English adventurers' by the British Crown in 1586. They sold it to Sir Richard Boyle who was later named the Earl of Cork.[16] In turn, the land was rented to its occupants.

In November 1907, the island was purchased by the Congested Districts Board, an agency of the British government, for £500. Subsequently, parcels of land were transferred to the island families over a period of years. At the same time, the limited and barely arable land was reorganised and reallocated among the families to address the inefficiencies of the rundale system of organising the communal land (see Chapter 2).[17]

These land reforms were seminal events in the history of the Great Blasket. The islanders were no longer tenants; they were now landowners. And they now had a stake in the island's future, whatever that might bring. But, as significant as these changes were in a social and economic sense, it may have been an unfortunate case of too little, too late.

The economy of the Blasket kingdom was based primarily on fishing with some sheep raising as well. In the early twentieth century, harvesting lobsters became a quite profitable venture. Potatoes and vegetables such as cabbage, turnips, parsnips, wheat, oats and corn were grown in the rocky soil, but the cultivation of edibles was primarily for consumption on the island because of the relatively limited tillable land.[18] Only a modest amount of produce was sold on the mainland.

All these economic activities proved difficult given the island's isolation, persistent adverse weather conditions including frequent rain and high winds, relatively poor soils, and increasing competition in the fishing business that pitted the small and nimble island *naomhóga* against larger boats from around the coast of Ireland.[19] The island actually utilised larger seine boats in earlier years, but they were not very practical since they were difficult to manoeuvre around the rocks and required eight men to operate. The agile *naomhóga* were better suited to the conditions around the island and could be effectively operated by a crew of as few as two.

The Great Blasket was certainly a stunningly beautiful place to live, but as Tomás Ó Criomhthain (pronounced 'O-krih-hin'), the famous 'islandman' himself, once said ruefully, 'You can't live on scenery.'[20]

Despite the spare conditions, the islanders enjoyed a lively and tight-knit community life that was based on mutual reliance, shared responsibility and cultural celebration. Most of the islanders were Roman Catholic and their faith helped them to deal with adversity, which seemed to be ever-present.

The education of the island's youth was a priority and the island school, established in 1864, did its best with scant resources. As per government decree, the English language was an important subject for the students.[21] Amongst themselves, the islanders spoke a pure form of the Irish language on a virtually exclusive basis and were fully immersed in their own special brand of Irish folk culture. Storytelling, music and dance were not only pastimes, they were the cultural soul of the island community.

Because of its rich manifestation of the Irish language and culture, the Great Blasket attracted a series of 'cultural tourists' during the early twentieth century. This was a dimension of the popular movement to preserve and revive the Irish language. These scholars and other visitors were fascinated by the distinctive stories they heard and they encouraged several islanders to commit their tales and life experiences to writing, a practice unheard of for an oral culture such as that of the island.

The product of these efforts include five classics of Irish folk literature in what has been referred to as the 'literary flowering'[22] of the Great Blasket. These books include *Island Cross-Talk (Allagar na hInise)* and *The Islandman (An tOileánach)* by Tomás Ó Criomhthain (Thomas O'Crohan), *Twenty Years A-Growing (Fiche Bliain ag Fás)* by Muiris Ó Súilleabháin and *Peig* as well as *An Old Woman's Reflections (Machnamh Seanamhná)* by Peig Sayers. In the aggregate, these books constitute critically important contributions to 'The People's Literature' *(Litríocht na nDaoine)* of Ireland.

These five Blasket masterworks, all written by islanders with help from 'visitors', were published in the ten years between 1929 and 1939 and brought considerable attention to the island from the world beyond.[23] These were the 'golden years' of Blasket literature.

These books also represented an important transition or evolution from the oral storytelling tradition of the Great Blasket to a written form of communication. This transition to a portable medium was a huge milestone. Now the folklore of the Great Blasket could be shared far and wide.

Despite a flourishing cultural environment and a strong sense of community, island life was nearly always a struggle. Ninety-four-year-old Michael J. Carney (Mike Carney), in 2015

Aerial photo of the village on the Great Blasket Island taken *c.* 2003. The pier is in the bottom centre. The Congested Districts Board homes (the east-facing 'new houses') are visible on the upper right.

the oldest surviving native of the Great Blasket and a fount of information about its history says: 'The island was a bare-knuckle place. There was no police department, no courthouse, no post office, no general shop, no doctor, no running water, no electricity, no church and no pub. The islanders had to make do with what they had, which was not much.'[24]

It would be unfair to say that life on the Great Blasket was primitive, but as historian Malachy McCourt says, it was 'untouched by modernity'.[25] It was a place frozen in time.

The difficult conditions made the relocation of island residents to the mainland and even to the United States fairly common even at the beginning of the twentieth century. Times were especially tough on the island during the First World War. The exodus from the Great Blasket accelerated after the war as American legal restrictions on immigration eased and more islanders emigrated to pursue opportunities on the other side of the Atlantic.

With greater exposure to the advantages of life elsewhere, the youth in particular were increasingly inclined to seek a better life off the island. Those remaining behind on the island were older and as they aged further, they were less able to cope with the rigours of island life. This downward spiral continued and by the middle of the twentieth century the island had reached a point where, as a practical matter, a viable community was no longer sustainable.

After desperate pleas from the remaining islanders themselves and much debate in Dublin over many years, the government evacuated a group of hearty souls from the Great Blasket on 17 November 1953 with a few remaining stalwarts leaving shortly thereafter. There were only twenty-two inhabitants left on the island on the official date of the evacuation (see Chapter 10).[26]

Today, over sixty years after the evacuation, the old village on the Great Blasket is in ruins. On an annual basis, about 8,000 tourists with a penchant for adventure take an always-exciting motorboat trip over to the island when weather and water conditions allow.[27] These modern-day visitors walk among the remains of the island homes, imagining a distinctive way of life that has long since disappeared.

Since it opened in 1993, the Great Blasket Centre *(Ionad Bhlascaoid Mhóir)* in Dunquin has provided another 40,000 visitors a year with a keen insight into life on the Great Blasket and its legacy through a series of multimedia exhibits.[28] The Centre is an invaluable resource for understanding this unique dimension of Irish history.

As for the future, the Irish government, which already owns most of the land on the island, is investing in the preservation of the ruins of the village. There is also a pending proposal to designate the Great Blasket Island as a national park. This would mean additional resources to care better for this precious historic landscape and to share the island's singular story in an enhanced fashion.

Yes, the tiny kingdom of the Great Blasket Island is no longer inhabited, but it is certainly not forgotten.

The Last Island King: Pádraig Peats Mhicí Ó Catháin

For about twenty-five years in the early twentieth century, the Great Blasket Island, was 'presided over' by Pádraig Peats Mhicí Ó Catháin (pronounced 'Pats Vicky O-Ca-hawn' and anglicised as Patrick Keane or Kane). Ó Catháin was the 'King of the Island' *(Rí an Oileáin)* and was referred to on the island simply as 'Rí', meaning 'King'. The 'Mhicí' in his name was a reference to his father's first name, a common naming practice on the island (a patronymic or matronymic as the case may be – adopting a parent's first name as a middle name for identification purposes).[29]

English scholar George Thomson, who frequently visited the Great Blasket in the 1920s and 1930s, tells us that life on the island involved a kind of subsistence existence within a largely egalitarian framework: 'The Islanders were all poor, though some were better off than others. However there were no distinctions of rank apart from the esteem earned by individual merit.'[30]

Peats Mhicí was certainly deserving of the esteem of the islanders based on his meritorious service on the Great Blasket. He was a man truly worthy of the abiding loyalty and admiration of the island's residents that he enjoyed for over a quarter of a century. While the term 'King' may overstate Peats Mhicí's position in a broader historical sense, there is no doubt

The last Blasket King, Peats Mhicí Ó Catháin, with his mailbag outside the Dunquin post office in the mid-1920s.

that he played the central leadership role on the island during his 'reign'.

Peats Mhicí was the last of the three known Kings of the Great Blasket Island. There may have been more island Kings in earlier times, perhaps as a concomitant of the rundale system for organising the land (see Chapter 2), but there is no way to know for certain. Regrettably, the tenure of the first two known Kings occurred before even rudimentary records about life on the island were maintained. Thus, information on these earlier Kings is either sparse or non-existent.

Between each of the three known Kings, there were gaps in time where there was no King on the island. For example, there was a gap in Kings between Peats Mhicí and his grandfather (i.e. neither Peats Mhicí's father not anyone else was named King during the intervening period of indeterminate duration). This pattern seems to reflect the absence of an urgent need to name a King until a person with just the right combination of skills and personality emerged from the island population.

Peats Mhicí was clearly just such a man in the early twentieth century.

The three known Kings of the Great Blasket were:

- **Pádraig Ó Guithín (tenure: early 1800s):** The first known King was Pádraig Ó Guithín (Patrick Guiheen). According to Tomás Ó Criomhthain, Ó Guithín preceded the first Pádraig Ó Catháin to serve as King. Since the latter served sometime between the middle and end of the nineteenth century, Ó Guithín must have served in the early nineteenth century or even before. The only other corroborating information is Ó Criomhthain's statement that he personally knew Ó Guithín's grandchildren. Ó Criomhthain was born in about 1855, so there is a practical limit to how far back in time Ó Guithín was King.[31] With respect to why Ó Guithín was named King, it is known that he rented the largest amount of land on the island from the Earl of Cork, so the title may have been a reference, at least in part, to his economic resources relative to other islanders.[32]

- **Pádraig Mhártain Ó Catháin (tenure: mid-1800s):** The second known King was Pádraig Mhártain Ó Catháin (Patrick Martin Keane), known on the island as 'Peaidí Mhártain'. He is not to be confused with the third King of the same given name, but with a different patronymic name. The third King was Peaidí Mhártain's paternal grandson, born to his son Mícheál. While the second King's birth date is unknown, he was probably born in the very early nineteenth century. Peats Mhicí Ó Catháin said that his grandfather reached the age of 100.[33] Muiris Ó Catháin, another Peaidí Mhártain grandson and a cousin of Peats Mhicí, also tells us in his book *Ar Muir is ar Tír* that he lived to be over 100 years old which would mean that the span of his life roughly coincided with the duration of the nineteenth century.[34]

- **Pádraig Ó Catháin (tenure: 1900/1905 to 1929).** The third known Blasket King, and also the last and best known of the three Kings, was Pádraig Ó Catháin, known as Peats Mhicí. He was baptised, appropriately, on 17 March 1857, St Patrick's Day. When Peats Mhicí was named King sometime after 1900 and before 1905, he was in his mid-forties and had been a widower for over ten years. His youngest child, Seán, was between ten and fifteen years old at the time. Peats Mhicí continued to serve as King until his death at the age of seventy-three in 1929. His son Seán, nicknamed Seán An Rí as a patronymic, helped his father perform his duties as postman in the King's later years and took over these duties after his death. Seán, however, was not subsequently named King and, sadly, died unexpectedly only five years after his father's passing.[35]

After the King's death, there was no successor King on the Great Blasket. Perhaps because of the changing social dynamics, the phase-out of the by now obsolete rundale system for organising the land, the shrinking population on the island and the absence of a dominant personality who would have been an obvious successor, the title of King just fell into disuse. Ironically, this was the very period when the need for strong and effective indigenous leadership was arguably at its greatest. Mike Carney tells us: 'After Peats Mhicí Ó Catháin died ... the island went without a King. I guess the population was going down and those remaining never got around to naming an official successor. If the islanders needed a spokesperson, the oldest male did the job.'[36]

For example, Muiris 'Mhuiris' Ó Catháin, a member of another Ó Catháin family on the island and the first cousin of the by then long deceased King, acted as official spokesperson for the islanders during Taoiseach Éamon de Valera's reconnaissance visit to the island in 1947. Muiris was regarded as a 'good speaker' and thus was chosen by the islanders to perform this role.[37]

Regrettably, the island's fate was sealed without even the informal leadership of a King when, after years of steady decline in population and the erosion of living conditions, the remaining twenty-two islanders were evacuated in 1953 (see Chapter 10). After hundreds of years, the hardscrabble kingdom of the Great Blasket had vanished and the line of Blasket Kings had lapsed, this time forever.

2. Kings in Irish and Blasket History

Ancient Irish Kings

Irish history is replete with kings. From the Middle Ages forward, there were a very large number of kings throughout Ireland. According to *Irish Kings and High Kings*, '... there were probably no less than 150 kings in the country at any given date between the fifth and twelfth centuries. Since the total population was probably well under half a million, this multiplicity of royalty is all the more remarkable.'[1] For the most part, kingdoms were fractious and fluid with frequent infighting among kings at all levels resulting in a constantly changing landscape of loyalties and territorial boundaries.

Generally, there were three levels of king in Ireland: the local king of a clan or a tribe (*tuath*), a regional or provincial king to whom the local kings reported and owed some degree of fealty, and the High King, or the '*Ard Rí*,' to whom regional kings reported.

The history of High Kings in Ireland is imprecise at best, with fact interwoven with legend over many centuries. Various members of the powerful Uí Néill clan held the position of High King for over 500 years. They trace their lineage to Niall Noígíallach *(Niall of the Nine Hostages)* who is said to have reigned from 378 to 405.[2] Traditionally headquartered in Tara in what is now County Meath, these and other High Kings tended to exercise power primarily in their own home province

Etching depicting Brian Bórú, High King of all Ireland, *c.* 980.

and, surprisingly, did not see themselves as countrywide in their scope of influence.[3]

Brian Bórú *(Brian Bóroimhe)* is often regarded as the first true High King of all Ireland. Bórú displaced Máel Sechnaill mac Domnaill *(Malachy II)* of the Uí Néill dynasty as High King 1002. Seated in Cashel in what is now County Tipperary, Bórú achieved for the first time – through a combination of battles won, negotiation and intimidation – sovereignty over Ireland's four regions of Connacht, Leinster, Munster and Ulster. But at least some level of regional unrest continued throughout his twelve-year reign as High King.[4] Some historians even question whether Bórú wielded any more authority than his Uí Néill predecessors.[5]

In fact, the position of High King should not be confused with a traditional monarchy in the classic European sense. Historian Francis J. Byrne tells us that: 'Neither Brian Bóruma [Bórú] or any other kings exercised governmental authority over the whole island [of Ireland]. They reigned, but they did not rule. It never occurred to any high-king that they should abolish the provincial kingships, or even the petty kingdoms.'[6]

Ironically, Bórú is also considered by some to be the last true High King of Ireland.[7] Just twelve years after becoming High King, Bórú was killed in the Battle of Clontarf on Good Friday in 1014. Bórú's forces actually won the all-day battle decisively, defeating the Dublin-based Vikings and Máel Mórda mac Murchada, the regional King of Leinster. But Bórú himself was killed as the battle wound down when a retreating Viking stumbled upon him praying alone and unguarded in his tent and promptly sent him to his death.[8]

Thereafter, Máel Sechnaill mac Domnaill was restored to a somewhat diminished position of High King, but royal fragmentation soon resumed as infighting among regional kings persisted. Post-Bórú High Kings were generally weaker and were sometimes referred to as the 'High King with opposition,' an open admission that a stable all-Ireland kingdom was beyond reach.[9] Alliances among kings tended to be temporary and evaporated after an imminent danger passed. Rory O'Connor *(Ruaidhrí Ua Conchubhair)* of Connacht was the last High King, serving at the time of the Anglo-Norman incursion in 1170 that would eventually bring Ireland under the control of a much different monarch, the King of England.[10]

For the most part, the history of kings at the regional and local levels reflects the evolution of the position of High King. In West Kerry, for example, there was a succession of Kings of Corca Dhuibhne dating from at least the eighth through the twelfth centuries. The Annals of Inisfallen, which track the history of medieval Ireland, cite the death of Échtgal the 'King of Corca Dhuibhne' in 785. On the other end of the timeline, the Annals of Four Masters, another chronology of medieval Ireland, cite the 'killing of Ua Fáilbe, 'lord of Corcu Duibne' in 1158. During the intervening four centuries, there was probably considerable infighting and intrigue among regional kings in West Kerry reflecting the pattern of kingships throughout Ireland as a whole.[11]

Local Kings in Ireland

Leadership at the very lowest level of Irish society was often provided by indigenous leaders who emerged from within the community itself. According to Irish folklorist Caoimthín Ó Danachair '... in the 18th and 19th centuries some small communities, entirely independently of the central government of the country, selected local leaders – usually known as An Rí [the king] who had very definite and very necessary powers and functions'.[12] This practice was fairly widespread, particularly on the islands along the west coast of Ireland where the relative isolation of these communities may have encouraged this custom. Ó Danachair even suggests that '... the selection or election by the members of a community of the Rí from among their own number was in effect a primitive exercise in democracy'.[13]

In this context, the title of 'King' is somewhat akin to the designation of a 'chieftain' or 'headman,' terms that have been used in other cultures throughout the world to describe a comparable leadership position. The term 'King' may have been used to label the role of this indigenous leader simply because it was familiar. The members of the community shared a rough concept of the role of a king if from no other source than from folklore. It is possible that communities simply borrowed the term when the need arose to designate the local leadership position to be filled by one of their own.

The existence of so many kings in rural Ireland may be attributable to the utilisation of the so-called 'rundale' system for organising shared land within a given village. Rundale is essentially a communal approach to the management of land that prevailed for centuries throughout Ireland and Europe, probably beginning in the Middle Ages.[14] Under this system, specific plots of leased arable land were assigned to particular village families and then periodically reassigned to other families by casting lots in a manner that was deemed fair and equitable. 'Each family was given a piece of the best land, a piece of the mediocre and a piece of the worst.'[15] But, with the ongoing rotation of the various plots of land, there was no sense of proprietary interest in the land as the plots were eventually reassigned to new caretakers. Accordingly, there was no incentive to take the long-term productivity of the plots into account when making short-term decisions about its cultivation.

According to Ronald H. Buchanan, the word 'rundale' may be derived from the Irish word '*roinn*', meaning to divide or share and the word '*dáil*', 'an assembly'.[16] Under rundale, the common land of the community was held as a kind of 'divided assembly', as the term suggests.

This communal approach to the cultivation of land permeated other dimensions of community life as well. According to historian Tom Yager, 'It is safe to assume that co-operative work ties were cemented by a strong sense of neighbourly affiliation and a lively evening social life ... Rundale was more than a technical arrangement; it was a way of life.'[17] He tells us further that 'Rundale is best understood, not as an Irish peculiarity, but as an integral part of European culture'.[18]

Essential to the effective operation of the rundale system was the village King who, among his other responsibilities, played a pivotal role in its administration, specifically in the casting of lots in connection with the periodic reassignment of land. Civil engineer Peter Knight, in his 1836 survey of the barony of Erris in northwestern County Mayo (*Contae Mhaigh Eo*), wrote:

> There is a headman, or *king,* appointed in each village, who is deputed to cast the lots every third year, and to arrange with the community what work is to be done during the year in fencing, or probably reclaiming a new piece, (though, for obvious reasons, this is rare,) or for settling the 'bin', as it is called; that is, the number of heads of cattle of each kind, and for each man, that is to be put on the farm for the ensuing year, according to its stock of grass or pasture; – the appointment of a herdsman also for the whole village cattle, if each person does not take the office himself by rotation – a thing not infrequent. The King takes care generally to have the rent collected, applots the proportion of taxes with the other elders of the village; for all is done in a patriarchal way, '*coram populo*'. He is generally the adviser and consultor of the villagers, their spokesman on certain occasions, and a general man of reference on any matters connected with the village.[19]

According to Ó Danachair:

> He [*the King*] had very positive and definite functions. The regulation, division and apportioning of fishing and shore rights and the allotment of tillage and pasture land was left to him, and in some cases he appointed subsidiary officers such as herdsmen.

He was expected to maintain traditional laws, to adjudicate disputes and quarrels, to receive complaints and to advise in time of trouble, and it appears that there was willing submission to his decisions and rulings, while, in some instances, we are specifically told that he punished wrongdoers. He was expected to speak for his community in their relations with the outside authority.[20]

In his early nineteenth century 'observations' on community life on Tory Island *(Toraigh)*, Daniel Dewar wrote: 'the inhabitants are still unacquainted with any other law than that of the Brehon code [the earliest known Irish laws]. They chose their chief magistrate from among themselves and to his mandate, issued from his throne of turf, the people yield a cheerful and ready obedience. They are perfectly simple in their manners, and live as their fathers had done three centuries ago.'[21]

Publisher Samuel Lewis wrote in 1837 that on Cape Clear Island *(Chléire)*: '... the islanders had a resident king chosen by and from among themselves, and an ancient code of laws handed down by tradition [Brehon], which it was his duty to administer; and though the king had neither funds for the maintenance of his dignity, nor officer to enforce his authority, the people generally submitted voluntarily to those laws, and were always ready to carry out his judgments into execution.'[22]

But while there was some commonality among the role of the various local kings, it is apparent that there was no specifically defined 'job description'. Nor were there any laws that governed the manner of a king's selection or election. Further, the unique personality of any given king inevitably gave rise to an expansion, contraction or evolution of the role of a particular king, depending on the local situation.

One of the king's roles is a reflection of the fact that the rundale system seemed to give rise to frequent disputes. According to Desmond McCourt, 'The least trifle is a cause of disagreement. They were formerly perpetually quarrelling about their share of stock, and about what ground should be tilled, and who should occupy the different parts of it. The fences round the cornfields are made in the most temporary manner because the fields would be pastured in common after it was let out in tillage.'[23] It was the king who had the delicate responsibility for resolving these issues when they arose.

Ó Danachair tells us that:

'As to the qualities desired in the King, we are not left in doubt. Stature, strength, comeliness of person are mentioned, as are justice, wisdom and knowledge. Literary attainment is desirable; a good talker, a good storyteller, knowledge of two languages, the ability to read and write, all of these were laudable in the King. A degree of economic well-being or independence was also thought fitting.'[24]

Some local kings were elected by the people such as in Claddagh *(Chladaigh)* and Port Urlainn *(Port Durlainne)* and some were hereditary such as in Inishkea *(Inis Gé)* and Inishmurray *(Inis Muireadheach)*. Some served finite terms and some served indefinitely. Some had substantial authority, some had very little. In some places, there were kings continuously and in others there were gaps of time where there was no king.[25] In the absence of any clear parameters, the role of king and the method of his selection appears to reflect purely local circumstances and preferences.

In many locales, it appears that the new king just gradually insinuates himself in to the role over time. Referring to the king,

Knight wrote that 'He finds his way to the "kingly station" by imperceptible degrees, and by increasing mutual assent, as the old king dies off.'[26] Such is the casual informality that reflected the leadership succession custom in many of these locales.

There are other anomalies as well. This local leader was sometimes referred to as the mayor or *maor* in some instances, as in the case of Claddagh outside Galway.[27] There is also one reference to a 'Queen' who played this leadership role in Erris, although a female leader was clearly the exception rather than the rule.[28]

It also appears that the King did not function unilaterally. In most communities there was a formal or informal 'council of elders' that provided advice and counsel. According to Eamonn Slater and Eoin Flaherty, 'There is evidence to suggest that within each commune there was a council of elders, headed by a local "King".'[29]

According to political scientist John M. Maguire, 'The various functions that the local king performs in this account underline the importance of the fact that his "office" and the council of elders comprised a form of self-government, which "is simply the particular part of the whole social system which deals with general questions".'[30] Summarising this approach, Edward Wakefield tells us that '... the elders of the village are the legislators, who establish such regulations as may be judged proper for their community.'[31]

Eventually, however, the fundamental flaws of the rundale system became apparent. There were no incentives for long-term planning and the land failed to achieve its full potential in terms of productivity. Accordingly, rundale was very gradually phased out over a period of years, primarily in the early twentieth century. In several communities, this was accomplished with the assistance of the Congested Districts Board.

Nevertheless, several local communities that historically designated a 'King' continued to do so long after more formal regional kingdoms in Ireland disappeared. Among them were:[32]

- County Cork *(Contae Chorcaí)*: Cape Clear Island
- County Donegal *(Contae Dhún na nGall)*: Gweedore *(Gaoth Dobhair)*, Inishtrahull Island *(Inis Trá Tholl)* and Tory Island
- County Galway *(Contae na Gaillimhe)*: the Aran Islands *(Oileáin Árann)*, Inishark *(Inis Airc)*, and the fishing village of Claddagh
- County Kerry: the Great Blasket Island
- County Mayo: Inishkea Islands and Port Urlainn
- County Sligo *(Contae Shligigh)*: Inishmurray Island

In 2015, many of the islands among this group of communities that once boasted a king are, regrettably, uninhabited. These include the Great Blasket Island, Inishtrahull, Inishark, Inishkea and Inishmurray. The combination of economic and social circumstances that led to the evacuation of the Great Blasket were at work in all these other island communities as well (see Chapter 10).

One notable exception is Tory Island located off the northwest coast of Donegal which still boasts a king even today. Tory is the most remote of Ireland's remaining inhabited islands.[33] The King of Tory, Patsy Dan Rogers *(Patsaí Dan Mac Ruaidhrí)*, is Ireland's last surviving king.[34] According to Rogers, there has been a king on Tory Island for about 1,400 years since St Colmcille named Tory's first king and charged him with protecting the islanders from attacks from marauding pirates.

Rogers first gained stature on Tory Island as one of the leaders in the successful effort to block the government's plans

Patsy Dan Rogers,
King of Tory Island.

to relocate the Tory Islanders to the mainland after severe storms isolated the island for seven weeks and three days in 1974. Rogers says that, over a period of years, he and the then King 'begged and pleaded' with officials in Dublin and with the Donegal County Council to keep the island alive. The eventual result of their efforts was the construction of new pier facilities on the island and on the mainland along with the establishment of a regular ferry service. But, despite their commendable efforts, half of the 260 Tory residents elected to relocate to the mainland over time.

When the previous King of Tory died after serving for a remarkable forty-five years, Rogers was a natural choice as his successor. In 1993, the islanders selected Rogers as King not by election but by general consensus. He has served faithfully since.[35]

A thoroughly modern King indeed, the affable Rogers maintains his own website on the Internet. According to his website, the King 'revels in his position as a representative of Tory Island and carries out his ambassadorial duties with great aplomb'. Rogers 'greets each passenger ferry and welcomes visitors "*Fáilte romhat*"'. Likewise, those departing the island are bade a personal farewell '*Slán go foill*.'[36] Up to 17,000 visitors per year the journey to Tory to experience the island and to meet its always gregarious King. Rogers is also an accomplished artist and musician. His distinctive straightforward artwork featuring the Tory Island landscape and other Irish themes is on sale in galleries throughout Ireland.

Perhaps Ireland's last remaining King is a throwback to earlier times. But he clearly relishes the use of the title of 'King,' as does his island constituency, and he continues to play a highly constructive role in the life of the Tory community today. Rogers even hopes that some day a younger person will succeed him as King. He says with deep conviction that there is a lot of work to do in advancing the cause of his kingdom and that a successor King should keep up the tradition.[37]

Kings of the Great Blasket Island

It appears that the local kings on the Great Blasket were 'named' by some general consensus of the community. Exactly how this consensus was generated is not known, but the elders of the community must have been involved in some informal way, if only by acquiescence.[38] It may well have been a case of 'imperceptible degrees of increasing mutual assent' as described by Knight (see above). It seems that a person demonstrating

The King of the Island (*Rí an Oileáin*), Peats Mhicí Ó Catháin walking along a path above the island. Photo taken by John Millington Synge in 1905.

precisely the right combination of qualities emerged from the community at some point during a vacancy and he became known as the 'King'.

Officially, the King of the Great Blasket held no real power in the governmental sense, only the power of persuasion when needed and doubtless the force of his personality. These qualities were apparently sufficient to meet the limited expectations of the island community in terms of the day-to-day role of the King.

While there is no documentation that the rundale system of casting of lots for plots of land occurred on the Great Blasket, it is entirely possible that such a system was employed. And it is equally possible and even probable that the King of the Great Blasket at any given point in time was responsible for conducting this process.

The third King, Peats Mhicí Ó Catháin, served simultane-ously as King and postman after postal service to the island was instituted and this task was added to his portfolio. It is clear, however, that the postman was not automatically named King, because Peats Mhicí's son Seán succeeded him as postman, but not as King.

The Blasket King was a member of a very informal group of elders who discussed major issues of the day and tended to make decisions by consensus.[39] The King continued to 'hold office' indefinitely by the implied consent of this group as well as the other islanders. There is certainly no indication in the literature of elections, much less other modern concepts like performance evaluations or term limits. After all, there was no defined regal power to take away as a consequence of under-performance by the incumbent.

Furthermore, as previously indicated, the presence of a King on the Great Blasket was not continuous over time. And, neither was the title of 'King' hereditary, although two of the known Kings were Ó Catháins with a vacancy in the position and the skip of a generation of Ó Catháins between these two Kings.[40]

There is some suggestion that the title of King on the Great Blasket was just a nickname, perhaps a tongue-in-cheek or even a mocking reference to the King's stature. Scholar and frequent island visitor George Thomson gives us a self-contradictory view of the position of King. He says that 'no special significance was attached to the title', but quickly adds that 'all this gave him a measure of authority'. The truth of the situation is probably somewhere in between.

According to Thomson:

> We are told here that the grandson and namesake of this Pádraig O'Keane [the second King] was known as

the King [the third King]. No special significance was attached to the title, which was regarded as a tribute to his fine physique and dignified bearing. Most of the old men had nicknames, and this was one of them. However, his position was an important one ... He had good English, and on the mainland he represented the Islanders in any dealings they might have with the civic authorities. He was their accepted spokesman in the reception of strangers [visitors], and in earlier times, when visitors to the Island were few, they usually stayed at his house. He was the only one, apart from Tomás [Ó Criomhthain], to read the newspaper, which he brought in with the post; and the old men used to meet in one of the houses (known for that reason as Parliament House) to hear the news and discuss world affairs. All this gave him a measure of authority, which must have owed something to the prestige enjoyed by the family as one of the longest-established in the Island, reminding us of the village chief or headman in primitive communities in other parts of the world.[41]

Robin Flower, the English scholar who had the longest relationship with the Great Blasket and who was perhaps in the best position to describe the role of the King with objectivity, wrote 'He is the King of the Island, Pádraig Ó Catháin, the diplomatist and chief man of authority in the village, who holds his office by sheer weight of character.'[42] This clearly indicates that the title was more than a mere nickname.

Irish author John Millington Synge seemed to enjoy emphasising the royalty theme as he described various aspects of the King's household in his 1905 letters to his benefactor, Lady Augusta Gregory in Dublin, a prominent supporter of Irish theatre.

'I have been here for a week today,' he wrote Lady Gregory on August 20, 'and in some ways I find it the most interesting place I have ever been in. I sleep in a corner of the King's room and in the mornings – on state occasions – the princess' (he meant the King's younger daughter, Cáit; he never grew tired of such winking references to island 'royalty') 'comes in when we awake and gives us each a dram of whiskey and lights our pipes and then leaves us to talk.' They talked mostly in Irish – his being better than the king's English. In the evenings the house filled up with sometimes twenty or thirty people, talking, drinking and dancing.'[43]

Mícheál De Mórdha, the long-time director of the Great Blasket Centre and the author of *Scéal agus Dán Oileáin (The Story and Fate of an Island)* writes with respect to the Blasket King that: 'The title of King was more a public recognition than a seat of power or control on the Island and there is no evidence to suggest that his judgment was given in any quarrels or issues of control.'[44]

Probably the definitive statement on the status of the King comes from Tomás Ó Criomhthain who clearly acknowledges that Peats Mhicí Ó Catháin was either the 'chief man'[45] or the 'leading man' on the island. Thus, there is evidence that at least one of the King's key contemporaries, and a distinguished personality in his own right, openly acknowledged Peats Mhicí's elevated position among islanders.

Clearly, a position of leadership does not derive from a nickname. It flows from a status that is either earned or ascribed or both. At least in the instance of the Great Blasket and Peats Mhicí Ó Catháin, the title of King was unquestionably more than a nickname, but not a great deal more. The very limited documentation shows that there was a consistent pattern of reliance on the King for leadership and at least some deference to his judgment (see Chapter 3).

That the King felt some responsibility for the welfare of the islanders is evident in his bragging to Synge about the relative safety of the island. On Synge's very first night on the island in 1905, the King tells him that "'There has been no one drowned on this island," he said, "for forty years, and that is a great wonder, for it is a dangerous life.'"[46] His sincere concern for the safety of the islanders is apparent.

Despite his stature on the island, the King did not hold any monopoly on political views. Tomás Ó Criomhthain, plainly another person of considerable prominence on the island during the King's 'reign,' disagreed with the King on a number of key issues of the day.[47] There appear to be no consequences of holding different views – and a diversity of opinion did not seem to have been regarded as a negative and was perhaps even valued.

Like other local kings throughout Ireland, the Great Blasket's King enjoyed none of the trappings usually associated with royalty. There was no crown, no throne and no royal robes. And there were certainly no riches associated with the position. Although the home of the last King was sometimes referred to as the 'King's Palace' *(Pálás an Rí)*, this was a nickname formulated at least partially in jest.[48]

Being King certainly lent a measure of stature and respect to the incumbent, but just as one cannot live on scenery, esteem alone does not support a family. In this egalitarian society, the King had to work for a living like everybody else. Peats Mhicí's earnings as postman were modest. Like all the men on the island, the King remained primarily a fisherman throughout his life. And he also operated a modest bed and breakfast in his home, catering to island visitors.

Mike Carney was only seven years old when the King died, yet he clearly remembers the role of King and the admirable reputation of the last incumbent. These recollections spring from his early years growing up on the island and his conversations with his family and other islanders after his departure at the age of sixteen in 1937 for Cahersiveen, Dublin and eventually America:

> In my time, the Ó Catháins were the most prominent family on the Island. Pádraig 'Mickey' Ó Catháin was the King or the 'Rí' of the Island. He was not a king in the traditional sense of royalty, but he was the unofficial leader of the island people. He was more like an unelected mayor. The King had the job of going over to the post office in Dunquin by *naomhóg* to get the mail ... Ó Catháin was named King because he was a good talker and he had good judgment about things. He was very easy to get along with. My father got on very well with the King. Of course, it always helped to have a good relationship with the King.[49]

One way to view the position of King is that it was a practical solution to a practical problem. The members of the community understood that they needed some type of leadership, yet they were fiercely independent people and had no tolerance for autocratic leaders. So instead, they adopted a loose approach that seemed to fill the need without running the perceived risks involved in a more structured form of leadership that might not serve their interests well.

Nóra Ní Shéaghdha, the schoolteacher on the island from 1927 to 1934, which included the time of the King's death and five years thereafter, summarises the situation as well as the vacancy in the position of King after Peats Mhicí's death as follows:

> For a period the island had a king – a big hearty strong man, able to carry himself in every way, able too and fluent at talking to any stranger he met, and imparting knowledge. This was Padraig Keane. He died on June 11, 1929 ... The islanders chose not to have another King. The wave of independence is rolling over them like other countries across the world.[50]

In many ways, the naming of a 'King' was a reflection of how the islanders approached life on the Great Blasket in general. If there was a need in the community, they addressed the need in a practical, low-key manner and simply moved on. In this context, the naming of a 'King' is a fine example of all that was good about life on the island. It reflected the community achieving a consensus about how to deal with the challenges of everyday life in an uncomplicated, straightforward fashion. It is part of the charm of the Great Blasket to have had a 'King,' but it was also a seemingly effective approach to island governance that was appropriate to the situation and it carried on a time-honoured island tradition.

3. The Last Blasket King: a Profile

A review of the Blasket literature yields a fairly robust profile of Peats Mhicí Ó Catháin, the man and the King. But many of the usual historical details are difficult and sometimes impossible to establish.

For example, there is no documentation to determine, with certainty, exactly *when, how* or *why* Peats Mhicí was named King of the Great Blasket. In fact, his 'naming' may have been as simple as the islanders gradually beginning to call him 'King' informally because of his demonstrated natural leadership capability carried out in the tradition of his predecessor Kings. And thereafter, the title of King just stuck with him throughout the remainder of his life.

The only way to estimate *when* Peats Mhicí was named King is to interpolate among the dates of other known events. The earliest contemporaneous written reference to him as King was by John Millington Synge in 1905,[1] but he was King for some undetermined period before that date. Referring to the year 1878, Tomás Ó Criomhthain wrote 'though he hadn't got the title of King in those days or for long after'. Referring to Peats Mhicí's marriage in 1880, Tomás again says 'He hadn't the style of *King* at that time ...'[2]

If Peats Mhicí's grandfather, the second King, lived to about 1900 (as indicated by his grandson Muiris Ó Catháin)[3] and if there was a gap in Kings of some undetermined duration between his grandfather and himself, a reasonable assumption

Five islanders in 1897 in a photo taken for an anthropological study by Charles R. Browne. Islanders were very seldom hatless. Peats Mhicí Ó Catháin is thought to be at the lower right. If so, this is the oldest known photo of the King.

is that Peats Mhicí was named King some time after the turn of the twentieth century and before 1905.

As to *how* Peats Mhicí was named King, again there is no documentation of the process, if there was one. The informal 'council of elders' probably played an unofficial catalytic role. It probably involved some level of consensus of the group and others based on Peats Mhicí's proven competency. The elders may have just started using the designation themselves and it persisted. This distinctly informal process is consistent with the very gradual elevation into the position of King over time that was apparently employed in other communities elsewhere.[4] Certainly, the title of King was not bestowed with great fanfare or even fanfare of any description. There was surely no coronation ceremony or anything resembling something so formal.

As to *why* Peats Mhicí was named King, Leslie Matson suggests that it may have been as a result of 'a combination of different attributes' including his common-sense wisdom, his natural inclination to leadership, as well as his strong and effective communications skills, including his unusually forceful voice.[5]

As Tomás Ó Criomhthain wrote:

> So it's little wonder that when knowledgeable people came our way and thought that there ought to be someone in the style of King in the Island, they chose out the man fit to take the title and to carry it with credit.[6]

Furthermore, according to Tomás, the reverse is also true:

> 'An eejit nor a foolish person,' he said, 'has never been King, and if he were not suitable for the task, he would not be the King.'[7]

Author Cole Moreton tells us that leading islanders were expected to prove their worth, and surely Peats Mhicí must have been held to this standard:

> The big men of the Island achieved their status by character or deed; otherwise, there was equality among, if not between, the sexes. There was no leader, but that man whose nickname was 'The King' served as postman and judge.[8]

Another important contributing factor in the naming of Peats Mhicí as King was probably his simultaneous role as postman. There is some uncertainty about the timing here, because it is not clear whether his role as postman preceded his being named King, but in any case, this appointed position established him as the island's only effective and continuous link with the world beyond the island. His command of the English language was critical in this function.

In addition, Peats Mhicí was generally acknowledged to be a man of great personal integrity, as indicated by his ongoing stewardship of the money repeatedly entrusted to him in the mail. Funds and gifts were often sent to islanders from relatives living in America, including precious money for passage across the Atlantic.[9] The King was the implicitly trusted courier of these funds.

Peats Mhicí was also was a physically large man with a powerful, even dominating, personal presence. His grandfather and predecessor King was also said to be a big man, so this may have been a hereditary trait. No doubt his physique was well toned by virtue of many years of rowing his *naomhóg* across Blasket Sound, first as a strapping youth and then later as postman.[10]

Finally, the fact that his was one of the longest-tenured families on the island and that his paternal grandfather had served as King not long before could have been collateral considerations.

Overall, the evidence suggests that island kingship was, to a large extent, a meritocracy. Despite the informality involved, it was not a designation conferred lightly, and there is ample evidence that Peats Mhicí was highly deserving of the title of King.

The King's Role

Given the lack of a defined 'job description' for the Blasket King, Peats Mhicí was generally free to determine his own role as he saw fit under the circumstances. Among his day-to-day functions as King of the Great Blasket were the following seven general roles:

- **Leader:** the King provided leadership in coordinating island activities, particularly where a major communal effort was to be undertaken, such as in organising transportation to the mainland or in putting together major collaborative fishing expeditions.[11]

- **Postman:** the King travelled across Blasket Sound by *naomhóg* twice weekly, weather permitting, to send and collect the island mail.[12]

- **Intermediary:** the King brought oral and published information from the mainland detailing local, regional, national and world events. He often read newspapers aloud for all to hear. The King also had a command of English, the official language of the government at the time. He often represented the islanders in matters involving government officials and businesses.[13]

- **Transporter:** the King often provided transportation by way of *naomhóg* to islanders and others, including visitors, going into the island from the mainland or the reverse. This role dovetailed with his responsibilities as postman, because his were the only regular trips between the island and the mainland.

- **Host-in-Chief:** the King was a goodwill ambassador, offering semi-official welcomes and farewells to visitors. He also regularly provided accommodation to visitors in his house.

- **Adviser and Counsellor:** the King was a paragon of common sense and the islanders came to rely on him for guidance on a wide range of issues.

- **Arbitrator:** the King was called upon to resolve disputes among islanders and he did so by applying reason and common sense to a particular situation.

Day-to-day examples illustrating the King's performance in these respective roles are provided in Chapter 7.

The King's Character

There are multiple brief descriptions in the literature of Peats Mhicí's stewardship as King. These reviews by islanders, visitors and scholars alike are consistently positive in nature. By all accounts, Peats Mhicí was a man of extraordinarily high character. The following observations illustrate his personality and temperament:

- Writing in the journal *An Claidheamh Soluis* in 1908, scholar and author Donn Mac Milidh (a pseudonym for author Seámas Ó Súilleabháin) gave the following assessment of Peats Mhicí: 'Here is a report on the excellence of his person and his disposition. He is a stalwart, powerful, cleanshaven man, between forty and fifty years old. It does not seem necessary to state here that he is the greatest, bravest and most unblemished man on the island, for the crown does not go by heredity but by making choice of the strongest, most handsome and most intelligent and most well-read person, and also of least blemish and reproach. He is over six feet tall and more that a yard wide across the shoulders. He is a firm, strong man, but lively and trim.'[14]

- In his book *Oidhreacht an Bhlascaoid*, Pádraig Ua Maoileoin, Tomás Ó Criomhthain's grandson, observed of the King: 'The King was a big man, in person and in mind ... and he fills every page with his frame and broadmindedness, as he has the right to do.'[15]

- The King's granddaughter, Máire (Ní Ghuithín) Uí Chiobháin in her book *An tOileán a Bhí (The Island that Was)* wrote that 'The King was a strong, courageous, direct, honest and truthful man. [Robin] Flower would give lectures about the Island in Dublin and he would send whatever money he got back to the King to share out among the Islanders – and the King would do so fairly. God rest his soul.'[16]

- According to Peig Sayers' son Mícheál Ó Guithín, the island poet: 'He was always very soft with us ... He was a hearty man ...'[17]

- Photographer Thomas H. Mason visited the Great Blasket with Robin Flower in the mid-1920s. He later wrote that 'Keane is the principal name on the island' and of Peats Mhicí 'When I was there the *chief man* [italics added] was a fine specimen of manhood ...'[18]

- Nóra Ní Shéaghdha, the island teacher from 1927 to 1934, described the King as 'a smooth-skinned, knowledgeable man who fully deserved the title of King.'[19]

- The King's niece, his brother Muiris' daughter Kate Keane O'Dowd (Cáit Ní Chatháin), wrote in her memoir *The Lone Seagull*: 'My uncle, Peats Mhicí, was the finest man, both in appearance and manner, that ever sat at table: great company and a great singer. He was generous, welcoming and cheerful. There was nothing of the grab-all mentality of the goat about him: a fine cut of a man, well-set and strong.'[20]

From this broad spectrum of primarily contemporary accounts, it is clear that Peats Mhicí Ó Catháin was a quite extraordinary man with an outsized personality who made a significant favourable impression on all who interacted with him. These vivid descriptions seem to make it fairly obvious why he was the likely candidate to be named King of the Great Blasket.

The Last Blasket King: a Profile

The Wealth of Blasket Kings

Great riches hardly accompanied the position of King of the Great Blasket. The first Pádraig Ó Guithín rented the largest amount of land on the island from the Earl of Cork.[21] Thus, he may have enjoyed some measure of personal wealth, particularly in the context of the times, the end of the eighteenth and the beginning of the nineteenth century. Moreover, the wealth of the three known Blasket Kings, as modest as it was, seemed to erode steadily with the passage of time. Tomás Ó Criomhthain tells us:

> I remember when this Patrick Keane – the grandfather of the King we have now – had four or five milch cows. I never saw the other, Guiheen [the first known King] ... I've often heard that he had eight or ten milch cows, a mare and a wooden plough.[22]

So, at the end of the nineteenth century, the wealth of Peaidí Mhártain Ó Catháin, the second King, was less than half that of his predecessor's.[23] As for the third known King, Peats Mhicí owned enough land to support just one cow.[24] He made his living as a fisherman even after being named King,[25] and he supplemented that income with his earnings as postman and from his unpretentious bed-and-breakfast business.

The minimal wealth of the Blasket Kings is obviously inconsistent with the popular concept of a monarchy, but it is consistent with the reality of life on the Great Blasket. In fact, it appears that the wealth of the last King was no greater than that of the average family on the island. This downward trend in wealth among Kings may reflect, in part, the erosion of personal wealth as possessions are divided among descendants as well as an increasingly more challenging economy on the island as time went on.

The Last Blasket King

Tomás Ó Criomhthain and the King

Tomás Ó Criomhthain, the famous islandman, was a very significant figure on the island during his life and times. Based on his books, his letters and the various accounts of his life, he was quite intelligent and a gifted storyteller. Much of his fame, however, was off-island and occurred after his own lifetime as his books, *Island Cross-Talk* and *The Islandman,* became widely read throughout Ireland and beyond.

It is fascinating that Peats Mhicí Ó Catháin and Tomás Ó Criomhthain, two of the giants in the history of the Great Blasket, lived roughly concurrent lives. In today's highly competitive social environment, we might wonder if there was sufficient room on a small island for two such towering figures. But the King and Tomás were lifelong friends, associates and brothers-in law. Apparently they had a mutual respect for each other that began in childhood. As boys, Peats Mhicí and Tomás were drawn to each other. While Peats Mhicí was the oldest of six children, Tomás was the youngest of eight in his family. They were classmates in school and shared many youthful adventures (see Chapter 5) all on or near the island where they spent their entire lives, as neither of them ever travelled beyond West Kerry.

Further, it seems the two men played complementary roles as adults. The King was more of a social and political leader on the island, while Tomás was more the island intellectual and social critic. There were other differences between them as well. Tomás made no secret of the fact that initially he would have preferred not to have married the King's sister, Máire (Ní Chatháin) Uí Chriomhthain. But he quickly came to terms with the situation and went on to fall deeply in love with his spouse (see Chapter 4).

And then, of course, there were politics. Noted author Risteárd Ó Glaisne who visited the island in the late 1940s and early 1950s, writing in in *An Caomhnóir*, the magazine of Fondúireacht an Bhlascaoid, the Blasket Foundation, tells us that:

> the two didn't see eye to eye in politics. It's clear from the different pieces in *Allagar na hInise [Island Cross-Talk]* that the King sided with Redmond [the Irish nationalist member of the British Parliament who achieved the passage of the Irish Home Rule Act – an initiative that was never implemented because the First World War intervened] and his parliamentary party while Tomás and another group's sympathies lay with Sinn Féin.[26]

Matson elaborates on what may have been a little bit of jealousy on Tomás's part and on their conflicting political views on the optimal political strategy for securing a brighter future for Ireland:

> ... the King showed none of Tomás' enthusiasm for the cause of Sinn Féin during the period after the rising when it was crushing the Nationalist party. At the end of the Civil War period, some 'Freestaters' had dinner in his [the King's] house, a situation which Tomás, being more inclined toward the Republican side, would not have endorsed. One suspects that there was also a touch of jealousy; calling him 'Fear na Corónach' [Man with the Crown] as he does, may well have been ironic. Tomás considered himself the outstanding representative of the island people to the world of scholarship and letters; it was at his feet that scholars like Marstrander and Flower sat. Like Mícheál Ó Gaoithín (An File) [The Poet] in the next generation, he had undoubtedly acquired a sense of literary vocation. This was especially so after the publication of *Allagar na hInise* and *An tOileánach [The*

Islandman], though the King's life was by then all but over. Tomás would never have been a popular leader as the King was – in fact he stirred up a certain animosity by some of his claims. Seán Fada [Seán Eoghain Ó Duinnshléibhe] was not the only person to condemn his writings, but he was probably the most vociferous. It would be easy to exaggerate this negative element in Tomás' feeling: after all, the King plays a pivotal part in a great number of the stories he has to tell, and his dominant approach is one of admiration and friendship for this man whose sister, after all, he had married.[27]

Pádraig Ua Maoileoin, Tomás Ó Criomhthain's grandson, writing in *Oidhreacht an Bhlascaoid* even went so far as to say:

Kings are, I suppose, sympathetic to other Kings and their reign. Or at least this King [Peats Mhicí] had certain sympathies with the King of England. Of course, he was no exception at the time; even though the Rising had drastically changed the attitude of the Irish people by the time Ó Criomhthain was writing, which is felt with respect to the majority of the people in the book.[28]

Politics aside, it is clear that Tomás understood the King's leadership role in the island community:

'It was not long,' he said, 'before the King popped his grand radiant head into the house. He was warmly welcomed like the nobles of times past. A chair was put under him, but he did not have time to sit down as he was in a hurry to polish off the task at hand.

The people of the house thought he was about to disclose some sort of secret, but he was not like that, and I had a certain understanding of the King's way of thinking; the likes of him do not tell their business as they pass by the house as a small child might.'[29]

In the second entry in his diary *Island Cross-Talk*, dated 'End of April, 1919,' Tomás shares an episode where the King is the first to hear a rare cuckoo: '"Tadhg [Seán Eoghain Ó Duinnshléibhe]," said she [Seán's wife, Méiní], 'the King heard the cuckoo today. I suppose nobody hears it except a King or a man of high rank like him."' Thus, even in a whimsical conversation, Tomás expresses his clear understanding of the King's special status.[30]

Yet there is some subtlety to their relationship. Ua Maoileoin senses some possible underlying tension: 'He [Tomás] has a very clever way of praising the King; you would hardly realise that he was indeed criticizing him, or so that is how I feel.'[31]

Overall, however, Matson's conclusion seems right on target. There are multiple positive references to the King throughout Tomás's writings. His lifelong respect and affection for Peats Mhicí is clear in Tomás's own words. Tomás was always very proud of the fact that he was the brother-in-law of the King of the island who had been his boyhood friend.[32]

The King's Voice

Virtually all who knew the King made specific mention of his loud and distinctive voice. It was not just that he was loquacious, which he certainly was. Beyond that, he had, by all accounts, a huge booming voice, something quite extraordinary and sure to command attention, even respect. Whether this was natural or a practised voice is impossible to determine. According to Australian scholar Irene Lucchitti, 'It is this authoritative voice that represents the islanders in business on the mainland, and delivers news from the mainland back to the Island; it is this voice that reads aloud the mail that he brings in to the Island along with the newspaper.'[33]

The chorus of comments on the King's voice was led by Tomás Ó Criomhthain who shares the following vignettes:

- I wander on up to the upper end of the village, and the next voice I hear is the King's. Since he is a fine figure of a man, powerful and strong, he had a voice to match directing the cow, the ass and the dog. And since he has the use of two languages, no two commands together were in the same one. You would think the animals understood his English better than his Irish![34]

- When they were all gathered they took to the road, driving about thirty asses [donkeys] in front of them. If one or two had a feeble croak, others could be heard three miles from home. You could not miss the booming voices of the King and Tadhg [Seán Eoghain Ó Duinnshléibhe] however loud the rest.[35]

- The King put his great bull on the nearby island of Beginish to graze. 'The next day, a boat was out fishing, and when it came to the other island, the King's bull saw them and swam out into the sea towards them, and followed the boat through the water. They had to ward him off, and bring him back to shore by hitting him from both sides with their oars until he was back, under control, on the strand.

  They told the King that his bull was acting up, and that there probably would be no sign of him on Beginish the next day. When the King was telling the story to the rest of his household, his voice was loud and threatening. The bull on Beginish heard his master's voice, and he let out a great roar every time he heard his master ... But if it was any other voice he heard roaring or shouting, he wouldn't be interested.'[36]

Others chimed in too:

- According to Méiní (Ní Shé) Uí Dhuinnshléibhe, 'His voice [of her husband Seán Eoghain Ó Duinnshléibhe or Seán 'Fada'] was so powerful, so forceful indeed that Robin Flower likened its trumpet-roar of sound to the battle-horn of the Fianna warriors of Irish legend. Tomás Ó Criomhthain says that when Pats Mhicí Keane and Seán Eoghain were arguing together one could hear them three miles from home.[37]

- The grandson of Tomás Ó Criomhthain, Pádraig Ua Maoileoin, remembered the King as 'a big man with a big voice, bustling, exuberant and powerful'.[38]

- Muiris Ó Súilleabháin said 'The King gave a big, hearty laugh which took an echo out of the cliff, for he was a fine strong man, with a voice without any hoarseness.'[39]

Even beyond his physical voice, the King made a big impression on the islanders with his powerful oratorical skills:

> Some men were standing around the King. He had dug a good piece of ground but his courage had failed him for sowing any seed there. The reason: the change for the worse in the weather. He made a speech, and many had gathered by now.
>
> He declared that he was sixty-five years old himself and he had never seen nor heard of any year like it. There was snow, and rot in the ground. It was no use sowing seed there for, even if it sprouted, it would wilt afterwards and there would be no crop. Moreover – there was strife in the great world and there was no knowing when it would end. It was no use trying to do a stroke when life was in such confusion.

There were some there at the time who had never before heard a speech from the King. They thought he must have heard a voice from Heaven revealing all this to him and they began to shiver with dread, until they found out otherwise.[40]

In summary, Peats Mhicí Ó Catháin was an exceptional human being. His physique, character and pure presence, including his strong voice, combined to give him great stature on the island. As a King, he was clearly more rugged than elegant. He was a man of the people. He did not stand on ceremony. Frankly, there was just too much work to do and he took his various jobs very seriously. He led by example and his diligence was an inspiration to all who knew him.

4. The King's Lineage

The history of the Ó Catháin family on the Great Blasket probably starts with Peats Mhicí Ó Catháin's paternal great-grandfather Mártan Ó Catháin sometime in the late 1700s. This would place the King's family as one of the original permanent families from the mainland that migrated to and settled on the island.[1]

Regrettably, historical information on the Ó Catháin family is scarce, especially in terms of background on Peats Mhicí's grandparents, great-grandparents and further back in time. This reflects the minimal state of public records and the general absence of family history keeping in West Kerry and elsewhere in Ireland before about 1900. This situation was exacerbated by the burning in 1922 of the Public Records Office in Dublin during the Civil War. Generally, the more recent the life of the subject, the more robust the information.

Blasket researcher Leslie Matson has painstakingly assembled whatever information exists in an unpublished compendium of brief life sketches referred to as *Blasket Lives: Biographical Accounts of 125 Blasket People*. Matson's information is taken from Irish census results from 1901 and 1911, Griffith's Valuation survey, baptismal records at St Vincent's Church in Ballyferriter, the archives of the Great Blasket Centre, various Blasket writings and other sources. A draft of this research was completed in 2005. This was an enormous undertaking and now provides an exceptional in-depth insight

The King and a group of Islanders. (L–r): Mícheál (Bofar) Ó Catháin (the King's brother-in law), Mícheál Ó Guithín, Tomás Ó Duinnshelé, Seámas Ó Duinnshelé, Muiris Ó Catháin, Pádraig Ó Catháin (the King) and his daughter Cáit. The other children are unidentified. Photo taken in 1905 by John Millington Synge.

into island life.[2] All Blasket scholars are indebted to Matson for his work.

By borrowing heavily on Matson's research and drawing on other sources wherever possible, a description of the King's family emerges.

The King's Great-grandparents

Seán Ó Criomhthain tells us that Peats Mhicí Ó Catháin's paternal great-grandfather, Mártan Ó Catháin, moved to the Great Blasket Island from Graigue on the mainland, near Ballyferriter and north of Dunquin.[3]

Mártan was married to a woman named Bríd Ferriter and the family relocated to the Great Blasket, probably in the early eighteenth century, with their two sons, Mícheál and Pádraig. A third son, Tomás, was born on the island sometime after the move.[4]

Writing in 1756, County Kerry historian Charles Smith described the community then living on the Great Blasket (*quoted exactly as published*):

> The island called *Innismore*, ie the great island [the Great Blasket Island], is about three miles in length. It hath an high mountain, with some arable ground toward the N.E. end: five or six families reside on it, who pay tithes to a very distant parish called *Ballinvohn*. The inhabitants are strong, lusty and healthy, and, what is very surprising, neither man, woman or child, died on it for the space of forty-five years before I was there, although several persons, who, during that period, came over to the main land, fell sick and died out of the island, almost in sight of their usual abode. Somewhat like this salubrity of the air, is also mentioned of the western isles of *Scotland*. On this island are the ruins of a very ancient church.[5]

Joan and Ray Stagles, who did extensive research on the Great Blasket including a study of its families, wrote that 'it does not seem unreasonable to conclude' that Mártan Ó Catháin's family was one of the 'five or six families' mentioned but not specifically identified by Smith in his epic work.[6]

The King's Grandparents

Mártan Ó Catháin's second son was Pádraig Ó Catháin, known on the Great Blasket as 'Peaidí Mhártain'. He was eventually the island's second King and the paternal grandfather of Peats Mhicí Ó Catháin, the last Blasket King. Thus, the second and third Kings had the same given name, but different patronymic nicknames.

While Peaidí Mhártain's date of birth is unknown, he was probably born in the very early nineteenth century, around the year 1800. This is inferred by Matson, based on the documented baptism of Peaidí Mhártain's first child, Mícheál, in 1827.[7]

Peaidí Mhártain served as King in the mid to late 1800s. He was reputed to be a man of impressive physique and presence, and these characteristics may have contributed to his designation as King. Another possible factor, as indicated earlier, is that he was quite well off by island standards, owning eight or ten 'milch cows'.[8]

Peaidí Mhártain married Máire Mac Chriomhthain from Coumeenole *(Com Dhineoil)* on the mainland, just south of Dunquin, in about 1826. The couple had six children: Mícheál, Mártan, Máire, Cáit, Muiris and Éilís. Their firstborn son Mícheál would eventually be the father of the last Blasket King.[9]

One of the few references to Peaidí Mhártain in the literature comes from Tomás Ó Criomhthain who tells us that his friend Peats Mhicí had once taken a trip to Dingle *(An Daingean)* when he was a boy with his grandfather[10] (in addition to two trips to Dingle he took with his father – see below).

While there is no record of Peaidí Mhártain's death, his grandson Maurice 'Maras Mhuiris' Ó Catháin wrote in *Ar Muir is ar Tír* that Peaidí lived to be over 100, at which time his grandchildren were already grown.[11]

Peats Mhicí said that his grandfather reached the age of 100, which would mean that he died sometime around the year 1900.[12] Note, however, that there is no record of Peaidí Mhártain in the 1901 census.[13] It is generally assumed that his lifetime roughly coincided with the full span of the nineteenth century, a remarkable achievement given the day-to-day challenges of life on the island.

The King's Parents

Mícheál Ó Catháin was born in 1827. Like most islanders, he was a fisherman and for a time partnered with his brother Pádraig and his son, Peats Mhicí, the future King.[14] Unfortunately, little else is known about Mícheál, who was referred to on the island as 'Micí'.

On 27 January 1856, Micí married 21-year-old Eibhlín Ní Dhálaigh from Baile an Ghleanna, Dunquin.[15] The Ó Catháin family home was located at the top of the village, near the so-called *An Dáil* or *Tig na Dála,* the house of Máire (Ní Scannláin) Uí Ceárna and a regular evening gathering place for the islanders. It was also close to *Tobar an Phoncáin*, the Yank's Well, named for Máire's husband, Tomás 'An Poncán' Ó Ceárna, who had emigrated to America in the late 1800s and then returned home to the island. He frequently wore a quite distinctive ten gallon cowboy-type hat that he purchased during his stay in America.[16]

Micí and Eibhlín had five children: Pádraig, the future King (1857), Máire (1859), Cáit or Cáit Mhicí (1860), Eibhlís or Lís (1866) who died very young, Mícheál 'Bofar' (1870), and Muiris or Maras Mhicí (1871).[17]

Writing about her grandfather, Kate Keane O'Dowd tells us that 'Peats, Mícheál and Máire married on the Island. Cáit and Muiris married here in Muiríoch [Murreagh, a seaside village near Ballydavid]. Eibhlís died when she was very young.'[18] She quotes her father Muiris remembering Micí as 'a fine strong man with a big heart and a mighty roar. When he shouted you'd heed him and respond. He had a good generous heart.'[19] She also said that he 'had enough land to keep three or four cows.' His sons each inherited enough land for one cow each.[20]

Peats Mhicí told his best friend Tomás Ó Criomhthain that Micí had taken him on trips to Dingle a couple of times in his youth and that he came back with a supply of sweets.[21] Both these trips must have been very special occasions and an important part of broadening his world view.

In his old age, Micí stayed up to date with current affairs as well as his knowledge of the history of the island, sharing titbits on almost a daily basis with his daughter, the King's sister, Máire (Ní Catháin) Uí Chriomhthain. Leslie Matson describes how Micí passed on information to Máire and others:

> First came old Micí Keane, known as 'Micí Barr a' Bhaile' [Mickey of the Top of the Village] as he lived in the upper village. He was by now badly crippled, but made at least one trip each day to visit his daughter Máire who was married to Tomás Ó Criomhthain. Before returning he would visit Máire Boland and pass on the news of the day to Seán Eoghain [her son]. Micí was the father of the island king Pats Mhicí Keane who, as island postman was the main source of news, since he collected the post from Dunquin twice a week. The news his son brought would be passed on by Micí to his friends. When stop press items were in short supply, Máire and Micí never tired of mulling over the hardships of their early life, savouring in particular memories of their struggles with the landlord's agents.'[22]

No detailed information is available on the deaths of Micí or Eibhlín.

The King's Birth

Pádraig Ó Catháin, the future island King, was born on the Great Blasket in early 1857, and baptised on 17 March of that year. He was the firstborn of Micí and Eibhlín's six children and was known on the island as Peats Mhicí. While there is no documentary evidence of his birth itself, a record of his baptism is maintained at St Vincent's Church in Ballyferriter[23] where island youth were typically baptised.

These christening events typically involved a family pilgrimage to the mainland by *naomhóg* and a walk or ride in a horse-drawn cart along the road to Ballyferriter, usually when the infant was only a couple of days old. It appears from parish records that his godparents were: Guililmo (William) Granville (the King's aunt Máire's husband) and Catharina Daly (probably from the King's mother's family).

Máire (Ní Chatháin) Uí Chriomhthain

Peats Mhicí's sister Máire Ní Chatháin was born in 1859. At the age of nineteen, in 1878, she married none other than Peats Mhicí's best friend, Tomás Ó Criomhthain. Tomás himself chronicles the big event:

> A week from that day we were married – Tomás Crohan [Tomás Ó Criomhthain] and Maura Keane [Máire Ní Chatháin] – in the last week of Shrove [the period before Lent] in the year 1878. There never was a day like it in Ballyferriter. There were four public-houses there, and we spent some time in all of them until it was very late in the day ... We had to leave Ballyferriter at last, just when the fun was at its height, but since the great sea was before us, and there were a lot of us to take across, we had to go.[24]

Actually Tomás was deeply in love with another woman at the time, Cáit Ní Dhálaigh, who lived on the island of Inishvickillane. Tomás's uncle Diarmuid Ó Sé was planning a marriage match for him with Cáit when Tomás's sister Máire got wind of the situation. She intervened and persuaded Tomás that it would be unwise to marry into a family that lived virtually alone on an island that was even more isolated than the Great Blasket.[25]

Instead, Tomás's sister Máire proposed another marriage candidate, the King's younger sister Máire Ní Chatháin, the niece of her own deceased first husband Mártan Ó Catháin, the King's uncle:

> The girl she had such high praise for – and she deserved it – was a sister to the man who is King of the Blasket to-day – thought he hadn't got the title of King in those days [1878] or for long after.[26]

Tomás reluctantly agreed to the new marriage match. He described his feelings as he said goodbye to Cáit Ní Dhálaigh for the last time: 'I wasn't too cheerful, and no wonder, for I was leaving behind me the merriest days I had ever known, and, into the bargain, I was turning my back on the girl I liked best in the whole blessed world right then.'[27] Tomás even had the temerity to sing a song at his wedding to Máire on 5 February 1878 in which a girl laments the unfaithfulness of her lover ('Caisleán Uí Néill'). The abandoned Cáit never married and died of tuberculosis about seven years later.[28]

Although Máire was apparently a very quiet woman, Tomás's love for her quickly grew.[29] He single-handedly built a new house for their family in Bun a Bhaile (the bottom of the village), overlooking the strand. His stonework was very precise, exhibiting painstaking craftsmanship.[30]

In this house Tomás and Máire welcomed twelve children: Seán I (1879), Pádraig (1881), Eibhlín (1883), Tomás (1885), Cáit (1887), Máire I (1890), Dómhnall (1892), Mícheál I (1894), Muiris (1896), Seán II (1898), Mícheál II (1900) and

Máire II (1901).[31] Only six of their children appear to have lived a fairly normal lifespan. Two of them died in infancy (Máire II and Mícheál II), two died from terrible accidents on the island (their firstborn, Seán I, from a fall from a cliff trying to catch a seagull, and Dómhnall in a tragic double drowning with Eibhlín Nic Niocaill (see Chapter 8) and two others died of whooping cough (Máire I and Mícheál I).[32] Indeed, tragedy seemed to stalk the family.

Gradually, Máire's own health and morale began to fail. She died in 1901 at the age of about forty-two after twenty-three years of marriage. Tomás, for all his initial misgivings about the match with Máire, was heartbroken.[33] He wrote: 'when comrades part, the one that remains can but blunder along only too often, and so it was with me ... My low spirits did not leave me soon this time, though I was always struggling to shake them off day by day ... Heaven knows, I had but poor success in it. Something would always be coming across me to wake my trouble again.'[34]

Their son Seán once wrote that he never saw his mother, probably meaning that he had no memory of her. Luckily, he had a father who was always very protective of him and a sister Cáit, eleven years his senior, who must have helped raise both Seán and their brother Muiris.[35]

In the years to follow, three of their children – Tomás, Eibhlín and Muiris – emigrated to America. Their daughter Cáit married Tomás Ó Maoileoin from Coumeenole in 1911. She passed on her father's literary gifts to her son Pádraig Ua Maoileoin, a very successful author with five novels, a memoir and many essays to his credit.[36] But Cáit herself died early while giving birth to her seventh child at the age of thirty-five.[37]

Seán stayed on the island for a time, marrying islander Eibhlís Ní Shúilleabháin, second cousin of author Muiris Ó Súilleabháin, on 6 May 1933, her twenty-second birthday.[38]

Seán affectionately referred to his bride as the 'Queen'.[39] The couple lived in the house Tomás built for Máire and the dedicated Eibhlís cared for him on a daily basis until he passed away, dying peacefully on Sunday morning 7 March 1937 at the age of about eighty-two. He was buried at Baile an Teampaill in Dunquin.[40]

Eibhlís' extensive thirty-year correspondence with Englishman George Chambers, published as *Letters from the Great Blasket*, describes the many facets of the decline of the island as well as her father-in-law Tomás's own personal decline over the years. Chambers, a Londoner, first visited the Great Blasket in the summer of 1931 when Eibhlís was twenty years old and again in 1938 after she had been married for about five years.[41]

Seán and Eibhlís relocated from the island on 14 July 1942 when their daughter Niamh reached school age. The Blasket school closed in December 1941 when the shrinking enrolment was only five 'scholars'.[42] The family moved to Muiríoch near Smerwick Harbour, a distance of only about 16km (10 miles) from the island, but worlds apart.[43] Seán wrote: 'Eibhlís warned me not to come back home without finding some site for a house up there, or it would be the worse for me.'[44] Eibhlís may have been insistent, but Seán was a bit reluctant to leave the island. He once penned the lament: 'I saw with my own eyes on the Western Island [the Great Blasket] the finest life I would ever see.'[45]

A fisherman and construction worker, Seán Ó Criomhthain was recognised as a source of knowledge on the Great Blasket. He was also a successful author. He won a literary prize at the 1968 Oireachtas festival for his memoir, *A Day in Our Life (Lá Dár Saol)*. Like Eibhlís's letters to Chambers, Seán's writing chronicles the decline of the island.[46] He also published a compilation of Blasket lore entitled *Leoithne Aniar (Westerly Breeze)*.

Eibhlís (Ní Shúilleabháin) Uí Chriomhthain with her daughter Niamh in the late 1930s. Photo by George Chambers.

Seán Ó Criomhthain died in 1975 at the age of seventy-seven after being hit by a car while walking near his home. He was predeceased by Eibhlís who died in 1971 at the age of sixty.[47]

Cáit (Ní Chatháin) Uí Conchúir

The King's sister Cáit (Ní Chatháin), known as Cáit Mhicí, moved to Muiríoch upon her marriage to Seán Ó Conchúir in about 1883 at the age of twenty-three.[48]

The couple had seven children: Seán, Mícheál, Nell, Tomás, Máire, Muiris and Peats. All the siblings except Muiris and Peats emigrated to America and settled in Hartford, Connecticut, each marrying spouses born in Ireland. In the aggregate, the Hartford siblings had eighteen children. Máire, who was married to Patrick Landers from Dunquin, was a particularly notable figure in Hartford, providing accommodation and help in finding employment to former Blasket Islanders looking to get established in their new home. Brothers Muiris and Pats 'Downey', were unmarried and lived in Muiríoch throughout their lives.

Cáit's husband Seán died relatively young in a drowning accident on 22 October 1896. Cáit died in 1932 at the age of about seventy-two.[49]

Mícheál 'Bofar' Ó Catháin

Peats Mhicí's brother Mícheál Ó Catháin was born around 1870. He was known on the island as 'Bofar,' a nickname with no particular known meaning, which was not unusual on the island.[50] He was a rugged, industrious man and reputed to be one of the best fishermen on the island.

Bofar married twenty-year-old Máire Ní Dhuinnshléibhe (known as Máire Mháire Eoghain), his next-door neighbour, in 1894. By 1901, their family was living just south of the King in a house inherited from Máire's grandfather Seán Ó Dhuinnshléibhe, the island poet. No trace of this house remains today.[51] Typically, the materials from old houses were recycled in the construction of new homes or additions.

The family later moved to one of the 'new houses' constructed in 1911 by the Congested Districts Board at the top of the village in Slinneán Bán. A family assigned one of these houses had to work on its construction and Bofar's was one of the five that took advantage of the opportunity. The new and larger space in a two-storey semi-detached house was

The King's brother Mícheál 'Bofar' Ó Catháin behind his house *c.*1930. Note the salt stains all islanders had on their clothes from their life on the sea.

also much appreciated because Bofar's family was large and still growing.[52]

In fact, Bofar and his wife had a total of fourteen children. Tragically, only nine lived into adulthood. They were as follows: Tomás (1894, died in infancy of whooping cough), Seán (1896, died aged three from burns), Máire (1898), Eibhlín (1899), Cáit (1901), Muiris (1902, died in infancy), another Muiris (1903), Pádraig (1904), Siobhán or Joan (1905), Eibhlís or Lís (1906), Máiréad or Peig (1908), Mícheál (1909, died aged two from whooping cough), Martín (1910, died aged three from whooping cough), and, finally, Séamus or Séamuisín (1915 who eventually died from meningitis at the age of twenty-one).[53] This is an absolutely dreadful saga indeed.

The King's sister-in-law and Bofar's wife, Máire 'Mháire Eoghain' (Ní Dhuinnshléibhe) Uí Chatháin. Photo by Thomas Mason.

Bofar was quite industrious and made his living fishing, raising sheep and growing vegetables. To supplement their income, he and Máire began to accommodate visitors in their home during the summer months.[54] During his 1924 visit, the Swedish folklore scholar and fluent Irish speaker Carl Wilhelm von Sydow stayed in Bofar's house. He had to share a bed with a visiting schoolmaster from Cork. Fortunately, von Sydow took many photographs, some showing members of Bofar's family and the interior of his house.[55]

Bofar and Máire's home became the venue for many evenings of song and dance, due to their musically inclined brood. They owned a melodeon, which several members of the

Interior of the King's brother-in-law Mícheál 'Bofar' Ó Catháin's 'new' house at the top of the village (*c.*1934). (L–r): the Ó Catháin children Séamuisín Bofar and Peig Bofar, their mother Máire and their father, 'Bofar' himself. Photo by Carl von Sydow.

family could play. Máire was nicknamed 'Máire na nAmhrán' *(Máire of the Songs)* because of her large repertoire of songs.[56]

Leslie Matson puts the family's musical orientation in context:

> In the 1920s there seems to have been a resurgence of musical talent … The melodeon became a popular instrument which was played by Seán Tom Kearney, Cáit Sheásaí Kearney, the children of Mícheál Keane (Buffer) and Mag An Rí who was married to the King's son Seán.[57]

Muiris Ó Catháin described Bofar, his first cousin, as 'his comrade' and gives interesting accounts of lobster-fishing expeditions they made together. They set lobster pots off the Great Blasket or off the islands of Inishvickillane and even Tiaracht, a remarkable 6 or 7 miles away from the Great Blasket. On one occasion they decided to set them in waters off the island of Inis na Bró. The duo built a shelter of stones lined with buckwheat, which they also used as fuel. Their lobster fishing was so successful that they spent eight years working this venture together. But eventually managing his large family forced Bofar to give it up, and Pats Tom Ó Ceárna took his place on the team.[58]

The King's niece Kate Keane O'Dowd remembers Máire and her role as mother to a very large family:

> My auntie Máire, my uncle's [Bofar's] wife was the best woman to make pudding out of a sheep's intestine, and at every other job too. She was a great housekeeper for a woman with a big family. She raised no fool among the lot of them, every one of them better than the other. God bless her and them.[59]

As the 1920s passed, Bofar's family on the island gradually dwindled as their children began to emigrate to America and elsewhere. Eibhlín, Cáit, Muiris, Joan and Éilís settled in Hartford, Connecticut. Pádraig went to work as a garda in Carna, County Galway. Máire married Mícheál Ó Loinsigh in Kilmalkedar (Cill Maoilchéadair) near Muiríoch. Peig married John Cullen from Wexford. Sadly, their youngest child, Séamuisín, died of meningitis at the age of just twenty-one.[60] Shortly thereafter, Bofar and Máire gave up the island life in about 1936 and relocated to Muiríoch, a seaside fishing village on the mainland, the rest of their children having already vacated the family nest.[61]

Mícheál 'Bofar' Ó Catháin died on 11 June 1955 at the age of about eighty-five. His wife Máire Eoghain (Ní

Members of Mícheál 'Bofar' Ó Catháin's family in 1927. Back row (l–r): children Pádraig, Peig and Cáit. Front row (l–r): children Máire and Séamuisín as well as Bofar's wife, Máire (Ní Dhuinnshléibhe) Uí Chatháin. Photo by Carl von Sydow.

Dhuinnshléibhe) Uí Chatháin died in 1957 at about eighty-three years of age.[62]

Muiris Ó Catháin

The King's brother Muiris Ó Catháin, known as Muiris Mhicí, was a fisherman.[63] At the age of twenty-six, he married Siobhán Ní Chonchúir, the daughter of Séamus Ó Conchúir, on 2 March 1897 in Muiríoch. Actually, Muiris and his sister Cáit both married members of the Ó Conchúir family who were cousins.[64] Life was generally better in Muiríoch than on the Great Blasket, but not by much.[65] Muiris and Siobháin had two daughters (Nell and Cáit) and three sons (Mícheál, Muiris and Peats who was the youngest by far), plus other children who did not survive infancy. Muiris Ó Catháin died on 19 December 1953 and his wife Siobháin on 13 June 1955. They were buried in Kilmalkedar.[66]

Their eldest son, Mícheál Ó Catháin, emigrated to America at seventeen on 14 March 1928. He worked as a maintenance man on the New York City subway system, a physically demanding occupation.[67]

Their second son, Muiris Ó Catháin, was a fisherman, remaining in Muiríoch throughout his life.[68] Nicknamed 'Gog', Muiris was widely known as a great singer and won the singing competition at the Oireachtas na Gaeilge in 1945, a nationwide folklore feis or festival held at the Mansion House in Dublin.[69] This was a very prestigious honour indeed and brought great renown to the family.[70]

Their elder daughter, Nell Ní Chatháin, also emigrated to America at an early age, in about 1918. She married an Irishman named Paddy McGeever and they lived in New York City. Nell died of a heart attack at home on St Stephen's Day in 1960.[71]

Their younger daughter, Cáit Ní Chatháin, emigrated to America from Cobh on 22 June 1939 at the age of about twenty-five, after working in West Kerry and in Dublin.[72] Her sister Nell helped her to acclimatise to life in New York. Known in America as Kate Keane O'Dowd, her departure may have been delayed by the stock market crash of 1929 and the subsequent dearth of employment opportunities in America. Like her two siblings who had emigrated earlier, she lived and worked in New York City where she held various housekeeping jobs and was later employed for twenty years at a German bakery in Manhattan.[73] On 2 September 1945, six years after her arrival in America, Cáit married John O'Dowd from Cloghane or 'Below the Hill' over the Conor Pass from Dingle. John worked for the New York, New Haven & Hartford Railroad.[74]

After over thirty-five years in the United States, Cáit and John retired and returned to West Kerry in April 1975, taking up residence in Ballydavid.[75] In the very twilight of her working career she returned to America for several summers, working on Nantucket Island in Massachusetts for a family she had known in her New York City days. Cáit was struck by the vivid contrast between the two islands in her life, by bleak conditions on the Great Blasket with the well-to-do environment on Nantucket.[76]

As she reflected on the span of her life, Cáit wrote a memoir entitled *The Lone Seagull* that discusses her uncle the King and includes stories about visiting the island with her parents as a child. She also describes attending the King's funeral in 1929 with her parents. The family travelled to the church in Dunquin riding in a car for the very first time.[77] Cáit's first job was working for a short time for the King's daughter Cáit (Ní Chatháin) Uí Chathasa at the latter's bed and breakfast in Dunquin.[78]

The youngest son, Peats Ó Catháin, emigrated to Canada, but returned home to Muiríoch after a year. According to his sister Kate, the life of a fisherman did not appeal to Peats. He did not marry and eventually cared for his ageing parents.[79] Peats died on St Stephen's Day in 1978, eighteen years to the day after a heart attack took the life of his sister Nell.[80] He was buried in Ventry, a vigorous row in a *naomhóg* from the island of their father's youth; and she, in America, nearly 3,000 miles away on the other side of the Atlantic Ocean.

5. The King's Youth

The King's Education

Peats Mhicí Ó Catháin completed his formal education at the national school on the Great Blasket. It was a small one-room schoolhouse located in the middle of the village. The students numbered about thirty at the school's peak enrolment in the early twentieth century.

The students were divided into two sections within the single room, younger children on the right and older children on the left. There was a blackboard on the wall facing each group. It was a bit noisy and distracting, but the students seemed to get used to their plain and simple learning environment.[1] There were actually two teachers for a short period of time when enrolment peaked.[2]

Much of what we know about Peats Mhicí's school days comes from a very extensive commentary provided by his best friend as a youth, Tomás Ó Criomhthain, who wrote extensively in *The Islandman* about their schooldays together in the late 1860s and early 1870s. The two boys started their education shortly after the new national school was built on the island. Tomás was about ten years old and Peats Mhicí about eight.[3] This new facility replaced the old Protestant school, the so-called 'Souper's School', with its name referring to the soup these missionaries provided as an inducement to religious practice.

The National School with its shrinking student body in 1930, the year after the King's death. Teacher Máirín Nic Gearailt is on the left. Mike Carney is in the back row, third from the right. MACMONAGLE.COM ARCHIVE

Tomás refers to Peats Mhicí as the 'King' throughout his description of their schooldays together. Of course, Peats Mhicí was not named King until much later in life, when he was in his mid-forties. Tomás's high regard for Peats Mhicí is obvious in the narrative. Their boyhood friendship is confirmed in a scenario where Tomás comes to realise and appreciate Peats Mhicí's feelings for him:

> I had finished examining them all [illustrations that hung on the school wall] when the King came in, and I was delighted to see him. His place was waiting for him and he made his way to the seat beside me, and from the way I saw him thrusting through the others, so as to be next to me, I realized that he was as fond of me as I was of him.[4]

Obviously, Tomás was quite pleased to find that their feelings of friendship for each other were mutual. This would be a lifelong relationship between two of the most important figures on the island during their adulthood.

Their first teacher was Áine Ní Dhonnchú from Dingle who taught on the island for four years.[5] During her tenure, there was a visit from a school inspector. These periodic visits were occasions of great stress for the teachers because their effectiveness was being evaluated and their jobs were on the line. For the students, however, these visits involved exposure to novelties such as the formal attire worn by the inspectors and a phenomenon new to the Blaskets: spectacles.

Tomás describes the visit of a school inspector who wore spectacles at the Great Blasket school:

> 'Holy Mary!' the King said to me in a whisper, 'he's got four eyes!'
>
> 'He has,' said I, 'and a light to match in them.'
>
> 'I've never seen a man like him,' said he.
>
> Whenever he turned his head, there was a glitter in his eyes. At last the whole crowd burst out laughing – all the big ones, and the young ones were screeching for fear. The teacher nearly fainted with shame, and the inspector was beside himself with rage.
>
> 'There'll be murder done,' said the King again under his breath to me. 'I wonder now did anyone ever see another man with four eyes?'
>
> That was the first person wearing spectacles that the children ever saw.
>
> The inspector gave the teacher a good talking-to, in a jargon that neither I nor anyone else in the school understood, and when he'd finished his speech, he seized his bag and went out of the door, and on board the boat that was waiting for him, and never came back to the Blasket again ... The poor mistress fainted as soon

as he'd gone … We had full leave to talk until the teacher recovered.

'We'd better run off home,' said the King to me, 'while she's weak, for she'll surely kill us when she comes to herself.' …

The King was as fascinated as any of the scholars by the sight of four eyes in one man's head, but he never said as the others did – that the man came from hell.[6]

This scenario reveals that Peats Mhicí and Tomás were fairly typical schoolchildren with a penchant for mischievous observation from time to time at the expense of authority figures. Coincidently, both Mícheál Ó Guithín, the island poet, and Robin Flower tell us that the King himself used spectacles to read later in his life.[7]

The end of the school week is usually a delight for schoolchildren the world over as they look forward to a weekend at play. Tomás offers an interesting slant on the theme, indicating how much he valued his time with Peats Mhicí: 'Friday came, and when the day was over and we were getting ready to go home, she told us not to come back till Monday. Most of them were delighted at this announcement, but I wasn't overpleased, for I'd rather have come back, not from any passion for learning, I suppose, but because I liked being with my chum the King.'[8] This is curious because they both lived in a small village on a small island where weekend merriment with each other should have been easy.

Áine Ní Dhonnchú left her teaching post to get married in 1868. Tomás tells us 'the teacher was summoned home at Shrovetide to be married'.[9] Áine's stint on the island was followed by her sister Cáit Ní Dhonnchú who spent a year teaching on the island before she, too, left to marry.[10] In an anecdote that foreshadows the King's role as disseminator of news, Tomás describes how Peats Mhicí let him in on what he perceived as a juicy secret about the teacher leaving the island to get married back in Dingle. Tomás adds a surprising self-assessment of his educational progress:

> The King was in his usual place [in school], and, being big and heavy, must have left his mark on the stool. He was whispering to me about Dingle ... But it was 'sweets' that were at the bottom of his blarney. I knew that well enough, and I should have been a poor friend, too, if I had forgotten him. I handed four to him, and he was very grateful.
>
> We were let out in the middle of the day.
>
> 'Listen,' said the King. 'The mistress [the teacher] will be leaving us soon.'
>
> 'How do you know?' said I.
>
> 'She got a proposal yesterday. She is to be married at once.'
>
> 'What sort of man is he?'
>
> 'A gentleman's coachman somewhere.'
>
> He was right, for she only spent the week with us, and went out on Sunday. The school was shut again ... and I hadn't mastered English or near it.[11]

After Cáit Ní Dhonnchú left, 'the school was closed for a time until a thin lath of a master called Robert Smith came. He wasn't very nice to the rabble of scholars he found. My chum the King didn't like him at all. He had an unfriendly way with him. The King used to pretend to me that he came from Russia.'[12] Obviously, the young Peats Mhicí had a playful mind and was not shy about sharing his teasing thoughts with his friend. Smith lasted only about three months before fleeing for the mainland.

Finally, Muiris Mac Conghail tells us, the pair was taught by 'an old war veteran and his crippled wife'.[13] This was Mícheál Ó hAiniféin, who taught on the island for six years. His wife was Siobhán (Ní Scannláin) Uí hAiniféin from Ceathrú, Dunquin.[14]

This succession of several teachers over a short period of time reflects the fact that the teaching position on the island was regarded as a fairly unattractive assignment. The isolation of the island and the difficult living conditions apparently made it hard to recruit a teacher. Further, island teachers tended to pursue other opportunities elsewhere if and when they presented themselves. The result of these comings and goings of teachers along with the occasional extended sickness of a teacher meant that the operation of the school was often interrupted. Certainly, this kind of repeated disruption did not contribute to the education of the students.

Of course, new teachers always involved a get-acquainted period. Tomás says:

> I nudged Pats Micky, who was sitting by me on the stool. He's the same Pats Micky who has been King over us now for a long while. I asked him in a whisper what was the rigmarole the teacher was talking to the girls round the blackboard.
>
> 'Damned if I know,' says he, 'but I fancy it's a sort of talk nobody will ever understand here.'[15]

Thus, in his own humble fashion, Tomás contrasts the high expectations of this particular teacher with the more practical view of an island scholar.

But the opposite was also true on at least one occasion when the pair took delight in surprising a new teacher with the advanced level of the Great Blasket students. Tomás further described his relationship with the King at the same time:

School again on Monday, you may be sure, and we were all of us at our posts. Sure enough the King found his place next to me. As I was ten years old when I went to school for the first time (1866) I must have been fourteen at that time – that is in the year 1870. The teacher had new little books to distribute. She kept the blackboard going, too, and she was amazed that there was hardly anything she put on the board that one or other of us couldn't explain, so she had to make it harder. The Island children took great delight in this new employ, and, that being so, they had a natural gift for learning. Some of us had the spirit of a King: all of them had the spirit of the sea and the great ocean in them. The breeze blowing from the shore was in their ears every morning of their lives, scouring their brains and driving the dust out of their skulls. Though I had a King in the making to sit by me whom the hammers of a smelting mill couldn't drive from my side – whatever it was that made him take an interest in me – he kept me from going ahead, for he was always glancing restlessly this way and that. That's the chief fault I had to find with him, for he was always distracting me just when I was beginning to make some progress. We got on very well, but we were always glad to see Saturday come to set us free to go romping off wherever we wanted.[16]

Tomás certainly admired his good friend Peats Mhicí and could even perceive a 'regal' distinction between him and their fellow schoolmates:

We spent some time more in school, and the King kept his seat on the stool at my side. He was a fine, easy-going lump of a lad, and so he was always. We were the same age. He'd often point his finger at some boy who was

A justifiably proud Tomás
Ó Criomhthain holding
one of his books in the
mid-1930s, a few years
before his death.

being naughty – screeching out, maybe, or a pair of them
setting about one another with both hands, or a lout
here and there with his nose running. Sights like that
worried the King, and he used to point them out to me.
See how the character that is born in a lad sticks to him
throughout his life. That's how it was with the King when
he was a child. He didn't care for such disgusting, vulgar
sights; but as for the rest of them, it's little enough they
troubled their heads about them.[17]

Matson tells us that 'Tomás, on his own showing, was keener
to learn than Peats, whom he described as loyal but fidgety
and distracting'.[18] Both must have been fairly good students
because in their late teens, after they had 'graduated' from the

island school, Peats Mhicí and Tomás were selected to act as 'monitors', standing in for the teacher who suffered from ill health from February to March 1876.[19]

According to Tomás:

> The school had been closed nearly a year at this time, and it was opened on the Monday. Nobody was absent that day. A new teacher, you know! ...
>
> The King was waiting for me on his stool exact to the minute. He beckoned to me to sit next to him, and I did so. He whispered to me:
>
> 'Hasn't the old chap got a pitted skin?'
>
> 'He's pretty well pocked,' said I. My father had told me that they were the marks of smallpox, but at that time of his life the King didn't know what smallpox was at all ...
>
> This was the last teacher I had, and the King, too, and a lot of others, for he spent a good time in the Island. It was ill health that drove him out at last. He started for Cork, but he died on the way, poor fellow, near Tralee. There was little learning in him that we hadn't picked up before he went ...
>
> As the [new replacement] teacher was in bad health, the fright the inspector gave him made him ill, though the school was open every day. He said that he would be eternally gratefully to me if I would take his place in the school, with the King to help me [both had 'graduated' by this time] ...
>
> The King and I were a couple of teachers for a month, and – keep it dark – we were a pretty poor couple, for, whatever we might have done, the misfortune and the mischief kept us from doing it. There were a lot of sturdy young things in the Blasket school in those days, and they

paid more attention to playing pranks and courting than to making themselves experts in learning. Anyhow we got though the month in this fashion, free of all trouble and care.

Soon after that the teacher died. The school was shut up again and the King and I were together once more, free to follow the chase on hill or sea. If I had a touch of the spoilt child in me still because I was the last of the litter, the King was the same way, because he was the first of the litter. For that reason we were free to do almost anything we liked, good or ill.[20]

Tomás reports that this teacher was already in poor health and that the visit from a school inspector in 1876 put a 'fright' into him. Blasket scholar Tim Enright describes the same series of events: 'Tomás had also learned English, so well that he and the King had been pupil teachers, running the Island school for a month, when the master collapsed after a visit from the inspector! English was the main subject taught in those days.'[21]

Matson says that the school inspectors were keenly interested in the students' progress in English, but that the island students had little interest in the language. This dichotomy clearly raised the teacher's anxiety about the inspector's visits.[22]

It appears that Peats Mhicí and Tomás attended school for about six or seven years – although the school was not open continuously during this period. Upon their 'graduation', they were able to read and write in English to at least some degree. Both spoke fluent Irish, but only Tomás would eventually read and write in his own language.[23] Tomás wrote his famous books, *Island Cross-Talk* and *The Islandman* in Irish and they were later translated into English by others.

The Joys of Youth

In *The Islandman,* Tomás shares with us three interesting stories of his extracurricular activities with his friend Peats Mhicí. Both stories are indicative of the joys of boys growing up on an island and enjoying the wonders of the natural world around them.

The first involves a highly successful boyhood fishing adventure that illustrates their ingenuity in pursuit of a common goal:

> On Monday – since there was no school – the King ran into me pretty early in the morning. He had had his breakfast, too, and I was just beginning mine ... My mother was pressing a hunk of bread and some butter on the King, but he wouldn't take it. Probably he hadn't much appetite left that morning. My mother would never have offered the yellow [corn] bread to him, if he had been called 'King' in those days, but he wasn't.
>
> The King's business with me was to take me fishing from the rocks if we could get a crab for bait ...
>
> Out the door we went to hunt for crabs, but we had no luck at all.
>
> 'There's nothing in these little holes,' said the King. 'We'd better take our clothes off and go under the water in some place where we're likely to get them.'
>
> No sooner said than we were stripped to the pelt and diving under and coming up again both of us. I went into a hole as deep as myself, and when I got my foot into the hole there was a crab there ... I thrust my foot down into the hole again, and what do you think! I fetched him up on one of my big toes. He was a huge male crab, and, usually, if one of those is in a hole, his mate is along with him. I put my foot down again and found the other one ... I had enough bait for the day then.

The King came to me with his clothes all buttoned up.

'Come along,' said he, 'we've got plenty of bait for the day. You have two fine crabs, and so have I.'

I dressed, and off we went along the rocks. The King had to go back to the upper village, for he wanted a line and hooks. But he was with me again at once. We went westwards to Dunleavy's Point, named after the Island poet. Rockfish were biting freely, and every now and again we pulled up a fine fish and put it behind us. At last I was throwing out my line, and if the hook didn't catch in my finger! I'd caught my last fish that day! The King had to cut the twine that bound the hook to the line with his knife. The hook was fixed in my finger with the twine hanging from it. I didn't feel very much pain, as the hook wasn't very far in. We had forty rockfish – twenty apiece. The King carried them all home, and we divided them in our house. The hook was taken out at once ... I suffered a good deal before I was through with it.[24]

The second story is similar to their other adventure together, but this time the best friends' quarry is rabbits:

Off we went, the two of us. He stuffed the ferret down his chest. We had two good dogs, and I carried a spade on my shoulder. We made up the hill at our best pace. When we came near the rabbits, we found a warren. The King pulled out his ferret, tied a string to her and sent her in. Then he stretched a net over each of the holes in the warren. Soon a rabbit rushed out and the net caught him at once ... He picked him out of the net, and set it again as it had been before. That was no sooner done than another rabbit dashed out at another hole. The ferret didn't come back until she'd sent out the last of them to us ... Seven fine rabbits had been hunted out of the hole to us by the ferret and caught in the nets. Off we went to another hunting ground some distance away ...

When the evening was growing late and the sun sinking westwards, the King spoke:

'We'll never be able to carry the rabbits home for hunger,' said he ...

I had a coat with a big pocket inside and a large hunk of bread in the pocket. It wasn't I that put it there, but my mother ... I pulled it out, tore it in two, and gave half to the King. Kings weren't as hard to satisfy in those days as they are to-day. He crunched it down with great satisfaction, and it tasted good to him, for there wasn't enough of it for him. When he'd chewed it all up, he felt himself strong again, and he put the ferret into one hole after another till we had a dozen rabbits apiece when we came home with the stars shining over us.[25]

A third story was in the original draft of *The Islandman*, but was edited from the published version out of concern for the respectability of the book in the eyes of the Irish audience at the time. It involves the two friends, Peats Mhicí and Tomás 'skinny dipping' down by the strand and getting caught in their romp by a group of girls:

When I reached the bottom of this well the King was facing me from the other side and the pair of us naked. When we turned around, what did we find but three big lumps of girls looking straight at us.

The King became embarrassed a lot quicker than I did, and he turned towards the sea with his back to them, trying to hide from them. I remained standing exactly as I was when I entered this world and it occurred to me that there was no reason for me to take fright rather than them.

I hid a certain member of my body with my hands and remained standing firmly without a budge to spite them. Two of them backed off but there were never three women who didn't have a bold one in their number. It was the same here, because there was one big skinny yellow skinned one who didn't back away at all. We weren't far apart and what do you think but she said 'You should have been dry ages ago.'

I replied that there was only one side of me dry yet and that I would have to turn my backside to the sun for another while. 'And since you didn't happen to see anything unusual on this side of me, maybe it would be different if I turned my backside towards you,' I said.

'I would have thought that both sides of you would be dry a long time ago' says she.

'If I had that slippery yellow skin you have it wouldn't take half the time,' says I. It was only then that she moved off toward the others.

The King returned with his clothes on.

'Are you not dressed yet?' says he.

'No. Where's my hurry? Don't I have the sun and its heat,' says I.

'Were you not embarrassed in front of the women and you stark naked?'

'What were they at? They weren't embarrassed and it was them who should have been. And you weren't too brave in front of them. It's a wonder they didn't chase you off to the hill,' I said to him.

The big girl who was giving me the cheek saw a baptism before she ever saw a wedding. And, of course, the signs were on here with her display that day.[26]

Youth of the Great Blasket frolic on the island strand in the 1920s.

This 'boys will be boys' situation seems pretty innocent and even a bit humorous. The closing reference to a pregnancy out of wedlock, however, would have been regarded as scandalous at the time. There seems to have been a concern about how the Great Blasket might be perceived by the outside world if this story were published, and so it was cut from the original manuscript.

Even today, it is easy to relate to these stories of school days and the carefree days of youth. Peats Mhicí and Tomás are best friends growing up, learning lessons that will serve them well throughout their lives. These are intellectual skills, social skills and leadership skills. But to the two best friends at the time, they were just enjoying the exuberance of youth.

It is quite telling that, even as a youth, Peats Mhicí tended to be concerned about perception and respectability. Perhaps he was even a bit shy at the time. Tomás, on the other hand, was the older and bolder of the two and did not hesitate to take the self-assured, even brash approach to a situation. By all accounts, whatever shyness Peats Mhicí may have had as a youth was certainly long gone by the time he reached adulthood.

From these and other childhood experiences there emerged a broadly respected King of the Great Blasket as well as arguably the most important of the several famous island authors. As adults, they both played critically important roles in the island community and in its history.

Competition

Sports were a regular part of life on the Great Blasket. Athletic competition afforded the young males in particular an opportunity to test their skills against their peers in a healthy and spirited environment. Although there is no record of it, Peats Mhicí and Tomás were almost certainly avid participants in these sports and competitors with each other.

The sporting staples on the island were Gaelic football, foot races, high jump, and tug-of-war, with occasional boxing and wrestling matches. These events were held on the relatively flat land on the white strand. The typical competition involved teams from the top of the village versus the bottom of the village with the youth from the middle split up between them. The highlight of the island's sporting year was a football game on the strand on Christmas Day. It was always fiercely competitive.[27]

At a larger regional level, one of the most popular sporting events was the Ventry Regatta, an annual event where boats from various West Kerry communities would compete against each other in a festival-type atmosphere. The four-man crew of a boat typically included highly skilled oarsmen of about twenty years of age, all having great strength and stamina. Working together as a cohesive team with a high level of synchronised movement was critical for success. For the crowd's part, wagering and adult beverages were probably involved.

Muiris Ó Súilleabháin recounts his own first adventurous attendance at the Ventry Regatta in the mid-1920s after that year's event was touted on the island by Peats Mhicí himself (see Chapter 7).

In 1880, a *naomhóg* from the island named the *Beauty* competed in the Ventry Regatta. The sleek new ocean-going vessel, the first of this particular design, was built in Castlegregory, on the north shore of the Dingle Peninsula, over the Conor Pass from Dingle. This type of boat was built for manoeuvrability, as opposed to the larger boats that were previously in use.[28]

To the boundless joy of the islanders, the *Beauty* defeated all comers on that momentous day.[29] This was a huge triumph for the Great Blasket with its very small population. Tomás gives his version of events in *Seanchas ón Oileán Tiar*. He wrote that the islanders were challenged by a group of Ventry men after other entries dropped out. The Ventry men expected an easy win:

> They got themselves ready, like the other naomhógs, and were ready to start the race ... When they got the signal, the naomhóg set out, and in the last course of the race the Island's naomhóg was far ahead of them all. They won very comfortably, and nobody on the beach begrudged them for it because the other naomhóg was far too overconfident and pompous when after they had seen the other boats pull out of the race. When the Blasket's naomhóg came ashore after winning the race, the people ran out into the water around the naomhóg, the men still in it, and picked up the boat ... until it was picked up by a wave.[30]

The four-man crew of the *Beauty* was comprised of the future King, Peats Mhicí Ó Catháin; Peatsaí Ó Guithín, the husband of author Peig Sayers and the father of the last island poet, Mícheál Ó Guithín; Mícheál Mhuiris Ó Catháin, the King's first cousin; and Seán Eoghain Ó Duinnshléibhe.[31] The success of the *Beauty* made this type of *naomhóg* very popular on the Great Blasket and the men of the island learned how to build this type of boat themselves.[32]

After the great victory, Seán Ó Duinnshléibhe, an island poet and probably an ancestor of the crewmember of the same surname, penned a poem entitled '"Bheauty" *Deas an Oileáin*' (Lovely 'Beauty' of the Isle) as a tribute to the winning *naomhóg* and its crew. The following is an excerpt:

> When I saw my '*Beauty*' coming to me on her course from the Awe
> And her crew rowing so smoothly in unity at every draw
> My eyes never left them till I knew they had won the race
> The other boat's crew were out of tune without unity or grace.

> It wasn't on gooseponds our men practised the oar
> Nor on red island by Imlaw's tideless shore
> But on mountainous waves, the wild duck fails to swim
> O arrogance blind, darkened their mind
> To think they could take on the isle, and win.

> You asked me to praise and raise the '*Beauty*' sky high
> I'll prove it to you, I can do it with skill and with pride
> She could double the speed of a pigeon that flees the shotgun's crack
> And to crown it all, in the teeth of a squall her crew she'd land safely back.[33]

Appropriately, the performance of the *Beauty* and her crew was the source of enormous pride on the island and the story was retold for years in regular evening get-togethers at *An Dáil*. The children were required to memorise the Irish version of the poem in school during the 1930s.[34] An island legend was born.

The King's niece, Kate Keane O'Dowd, writing in the late 1970s, recalls the tale of the *Beauty* as being told by her father, the King's brother, Muiris Ó Catháin. Her father had relocated from the island to Muiríoch and married Joan O'Connor (Siobhán Ó Conchúir) in the early twentieth century:

> I often heard my Dad talk about the day the Island crew were up against it in Ventry Harbour ... The crew of the curragh called Beauty ... the pick of the men on the Island ... They carried the day in fine style ... He was very proud ... that his brother Peats Mhicí, his nephew Mícheál, and the other two in the race were all related. They were as fine a crew of men in appearance, in manner and in personality as ever sat on a curragh form, God bless them.[35]

In turn, the four members of the *Beauty*'s crew gained great stature within the island community as a result of their triumph. Certainly, Peats Mhicí Ó Catháin and the other crewmembers were highly regarded as sports heroes of sorts. For Peats Mhicí, his skill with a *naomhóg* may have influenced his later designation as island postman and probably contributed in some indirect way to his eventually being named King of the Great Blasket.

6. The King's Family

A Proposal of Marriage

In the King's time, arranging a marriage in Ireland involved a fairly unstructured matchmaking ritual. Potential marriages would be proposed primarily by relatives, but any other party could do so as well. The prospective couple might or might not know each other. A match could be accepted or rejected by either party, although there was a certain amount of pressure to get married.

Most weddings took place during Shrovetide, the period just before Lent, as weddings were prohibited during Lent itself. There was typically very little time for courting as we think of it in the twenty-first century, since matches were often a last-minute arrangement. According to Mícheál Ó Guithín, Peig Sayers' son, 'People are very fidgety during Shrovetide.'[1] This is certainly understandable.

It was not unusual for a man from the Great Blasket to marry a woman from the mainland. In fact, both Peats Mhicí's Ó Catháin's father and grandfather had themselves married mainland women. Nevertheless, there was some preference for marriages where both parties were islanders.

As time went on, however, women left the island at a faster pace than men, so mainland matches for the remaining men were almost inevitable, if they could be arranged. There was at least some resistance on the part of mainland women to marrying an islander and moving to the island. The prospect of a life of relative isolation on the Great Blasket must have raised some understandable level of apprehension on the part of prospective mainland brides. As a consequence, the percentage of bachelors on the island gradually increased over time.

Leslie Matson tells us:

> As the years passed and life on the island became comparatively harder, the tendency to marry on to the mainland grew more pronounced. The King of the island himself, Pats Mhicí Keane, was married to a Dunquin woman from Carhoo (Ferriter's Quarter), and as early as 1918 his daughter Cáit, the Princess, married John Casey [Seán Cathasa], who lived beside the church [in Dunquin].[2]

Weddings involving residents of the Great Blasket were typically held in St Vincent's Church in Ballyferriter. Celebrations were held afterwards in the local pubs before a journey by *naomhóg* back across Blasket Sound to the island.

Tomás Ó Criomhthain tells us that a 'proposal of marriage' was delivered to Peats Mhicí Ó Catháin when he was about 23 years old.[3] The proposal was on behalf of 21-year-old Eibhlín Ní Ghairbhia of Ceathrú, Dunquin. Peats Mhicí accepted the proposal and they married shortly thereafter on 10 February 1880.[4]

According to Ó Criomhthain, Peats Mhicí's wedding was a wild affair:

> The next Shrovetide ... a marriage proposal came to the King from Dunquin. He hadn't the style of *King* at that time, but, all the same, they were pretty well off. Probably he had plenty of other proposals, for he was a fine man in those days.

There was high feasting at the marriage, you may believe, for there were plenty there to make away with both food and drink. When they were going home, a boat turned bottom upwards in the Blasket creek. Two of the crew were underneath her. When they got them free, they were at their last gasp ...

There were four other marriages in Dunquin the night of the wedding in the King's house, and the people of the parish came near to destroying one another. Little wonder, when you consider how much drink there was and all the scandal which had been talked for years before which now had a chance of venting itself. After the night's medley six of them had to be sent to hospital, and they didn't get off too lightly. One man had been hit with a bottle and another with a stone. One of them got a wipe with the tongs ...[5]

While Peats Mhicí's marriage was a significant social event on the island, it occurred about twenty years or so before he was named King of the Great Blasket.

The King's Children

Peats Mhicí and Eibhlín had six children. In birth order, they were Mícheál (1881), Máire (1882), the first Seán (1884), Cáit (1886), Eibhlín (1888) and, finally, the second Seán (1890). The first Seán and Eibhlín apparently died in infancy[6] (see Chapters 11 and 12 for additional information on the King's surviving children as they moved into adulthood).

Mícheál was known on the island as 'the Crown Prince,' a reference to his status as the King's first-born son.[7] He eventually emigrated to America in at the age of twenty-one in 1902,[8] returned to the island for a time and then emigrated

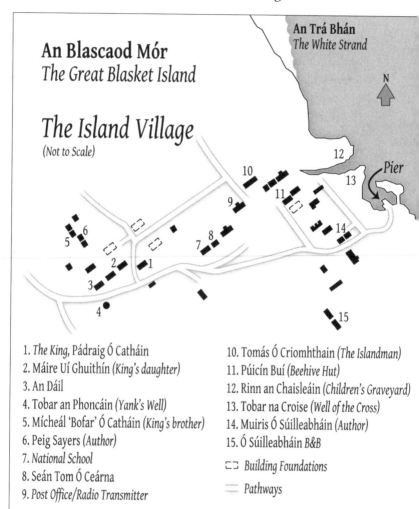

An Blascaod Mór
The Great Blasket Island

An Trá Bhán
The White Strand

The Island Village
(Not to Scale)

N

Pier

1. *The King,* Pádraig Ó Catháin
2. Máire Uí Ghuithín (*King's daughter*)
3. An Dáil
4. Tobar an Phoncáin (*Yank's Well*)
5. Mícheál 'Bofar' Ó Catháin (*King's brother*)
6. Peig Sayers (*Author*)
7. National School
8. Seán Tom Ó Ceárna
9. Post Office/Radio Transmitter
10. Tomás Ó Criomhthain (*The Islandman*)
11. Púicín Buí (*Beehive Hut*)
12. Rinn an Chaisleáin (*Children's Graveyard*)
13. Tobar na Croise (*Well of the Cross*)
14. Muiris Ó Súilleabháin (*Author*)
15. Ó Súilleabháin B&B

⊏⊐ *Building Foundations*

⸗ *Pathways*

Map of the village on the Great Blasket Island.

again in 1905.[9] Mícheál then took up residence in Springfield, Massachusetts, where he became known as Mike 'The Fiddler' Kane. He returned to the island only once more, a brief but memorable visit in 1909 (see Chapter 12).

The King's second child was Máire. Her daughter, also named Máire, tells us that her mother was a bit of an athlete and played hurling on the strand, probably with a home-made stick. As an adult, she hosted many visitors to the island, first in the King's house and later in her own home right next door.[10]

Their first son to be named Seán died in infancy. He was followed by Cáit who as an eighteen-year-old was described as 'bonny' by John Millington Synge and as attractive by others. She was eventually known as 'the Princess', a reference to her status as a daughter of the King. Like her sister Máire, Cáit hosted visitors, first in the King's house and later in her own home in Dunquin after moving to the mainland when she married in 1918.[11]

The second son to be named Seán, known on the island as 'Seán An Rí' (Seán, son of the King), followed two years after the deceased daughter Eibhlín's birth. He was their youngest child and eventually succeeded his father as the island post-man, but not as King.[12] Sadly, the King's wife Eibhlín died in 1890 shortly after Seán's birth. The couple had been married only about ten years at the time. Their oldest child, Mícheál, was nine years old and Máire was just eight. These two oldest children helped to raise the younger Cáit and Seán as well as to manage the family's household.[13]

About ten years later, Peats Mhicí was named King of the Great Blasket. In about 1905, the family began hosting visitors with all members of the Ó Catháin family pitching in to help out (see Chapter 8). As for the King, he remained a widower for the rest of his life.

The 'Palace'

The King's family home, sometimes called 'the palace' or *'Tig an Rí'* was located in the upper village near *An Dáil* and the

(L–r): The houses of the King's daughter Máire (Ní Chatháin) Uí Ghuithín and the King in the early 1930s. The shed to the right of the King's house is for storing fishing gear and salting fish. An addition at the rear was for guests.

Yank's Well. This house (see village map, p. 92, for location) was probably owned by Peats Mhicí's father before it came into his possession, but there is no documentation to this effect.[14]

Even within the small island village, there was some mostly good-natured competition for pre-eminence between the upper (i.e. farthest up the hill) and lower (i.e. closest to the pier) sections of the community:

Pencil sketch of the interior of the King's house by Robin Flower's wife, Ida Streeter Flower. © OXFORD UNIVERSITY PRESS

The village itself was divided into two sections – the lower village and the upper village. There was always a slight edge to the competition between them. They always said that life was nobler in the lower village, and there was some truth in that. Tomás Ó Criomhthain and Muiris Ó Súilleabháin lived there as did Peig Sayers when she married. (In due course, Peig Sayers moved to one of the new houses in the upper village.) Both Island poets, Seán Ó Dhuinnshléibhe and Mícheál Ó Súilleabháin (Muiris Ó Súilleabháin's great-grandfather), lived in the lower village. The best musicians and singers lived there – the Súilleabháin family, the Dálaigh family, and the Catháin family. In these noble pursuits, the lower orders, so to speak, had the upper hand on their neighbours above!

Even so, the upper village had its own distinctiveness. Pádraig Ó Catháin, the King, lived there. When the famous visitors started to arrive they stayed in the upper village – Synge, Marstrander, Flower and many others. 'Where does that leave all your noble ways now' they would say. 'Haven't we got our own poet now, Mícheál, Peig's son?'[15]

Kanigel describes the detailed freehand sketch that Robin Flower's wife, Ida, made of the interior of the King's house:

The pen-and-ink she made of the interior of the king's house suggests all the comforts of home, rudimentary though they were. In the middle, the *croch*, or fireplace crane – the sturdy trusslike structure from which the pots were suspended over the hearth. The settle, a bare wood bench, off to the side. A beam reaching across the breadth of the room, supporting a loft, a kind of rude attic, bearing household gear. All modeled by soft window light.[16]

The King's house was certainly no palace, but it was a cosy, comfortable and practical home that was very similar to the other houses on the Great Blasket.

7. The King's Stewardship

The last King of the Great Blasket was called upon to play many different roles in the course of his 25-year or so 'reign'. Some of his responsibilities were routine and some were quite unconventional for any more typical 'monarch'. As indicated in Chapter 3, the King's role tended to fall into seven general categories: leader, postman, intermediary, transporter, host-in-chief, adviser/counsellor and arbitrator. By all accounts, Peats Mhicí Ó Catháin faithfully discharged all his duties, however minor, with a warm heart and a cheerful attitude. He was a consistent force of reason and stability on the island.

Leader

Decision Making

Despite his recognised stature on the island, the King was not a ruler by any means. Major decisions tended to be made by consensus of the older males after extensive discussion. There was apparently no formal 'council of elders' per se, but the King and a group of male islanders convened from time to time to deliberate on wide range of topics including the pressing issues of the day.[1]

Most probably, such a group would have functioned as a less formal version of the so-called 'Parliament' on St Kilda,

Pádraig Peats Mhicí Ó Catháin, the King of the Great Blasket Island outside his house.

an island off the west coast of Scotland that is similar in many respects to the Great Blasket. On St Kilda, 'the Parliament consisted of all the adult males on the island. There were no set rules, no chairman and the 'members' arrived in their own time. Once assembled the "Parliament" considered the work to be done that day according to each family's abilities and divided up the resources according to their needs. Everything was done for the common good.'[2]

Any decision-making authority even as loosely structured as St Kilda's Parliament was beyond what was perceived as appropriate on the Great Blasket where informality was the rule of the day. Tomás Ó Criomhthain tells us about one of the group of elder's more philosophical conversations on the Great

Blasket and we can expect that the King was an animated participant:

> An outcrop of rock stands a little way from the well and all the grown men who could squeeze in had their backs against it, while they waited for others, who were not ready yet, to join the company. They were arguing fine points of every law under the sun and, although half of them did not know A from B, they aired as much knowledge of the laws as Aristotle.[3]

On a more practical level, the King and the elders probably discussed collaborative work projects, fishing and planting strategies, and the allocation of shared responsibilities. There is no description of the nature of the relationship between the King and the other elders. Consensus was the general approach on governance matters on the Great Blasket and the King was probably no more than first among equals in the midst of such discussions. When it came to interacting with outsiders, however, his position was elevated to that of spokesman representing the islanders' views.

Rent Collection Crisis

One day, the islanders were surprised to see a new and strange object appear across Blasket Sound over on the mainland in Dunquin. Upon investigation, they found that a hut had been set up for a bailiff and three police officers. The islanders had paid no rent to the Earl of Cork in the seven and a half years prior to 1907.[4] At some point during this period, the landlord's agents intended to confiscate any produce either leaving from or destined for the Island as compensation. The islanders gathered to discuss their strategy and the King proposed a plan:

The King spoke, and said quickly that there were other ways to maintain the Island and they didn't have to go to the mainland for a year and a day, because as they knew well, or at least they should, the merchant vessel from Limerick that passed by their jetty once a week was full all sorts of foreign produce, and it belonged to a good strong merchant known as 'the Russian,' and all they had to do was sent him a message and let him know how things were on the Island and he would send them produce on the days he passed by the Island.[5]

The islanders agreed to this approach and they moved forward with confidence in the face of the landlord's efforts to exact compensation. The King's judgment and leadership proved decisive.

Land Ownership and the Reorganisation of the Fields

The year 1907 marked the beginning of a major improvement in the social and economic standing of the islanders. The parish priest in Ballyferriter had written to the British government and requested that the island become the responsibility of the Congested Districts Board, a British government agency.[6] As a result, the island was acquired by the Board from the Earl of Cork for the sum of £500. Subsequently, the ownership of specific parcels of land was transferred to the islanders over time: 'The land was purchased from the landlord by the Congested Districts Board in 1907 and reallocated in the following years "so that every man knows his own plot and has it fenced," as Tomás O'Crohan tells us in *The Islandman*.'[7]

The transition to becoming landowners was a major shift for the island community. Like most Irish tenants, the islanders had a visceral dislike for paying what they regarded as excessive and unfair rent over the years. The island folklore includes an infamous story of the women of the island raining stones down upon a bailiff representing the Earl of Cork who landed at the island pier with the intention of collecting the rent. The bailiff eventually gave up trying because there was not enough rent to be collected for the amount of aggravation involved.[8] After this strained history, the thought that the islanders would become landowners must have been almost inconceivable to them.

In addition to the transfer of ownership, the arable land on the island was reorganised in a ten-year process that also began in 1907. According to Joan and Ray Stagles, 'no family had more than three or four acres capable of cultivation; most had much less.' Under the reorganisation, each family continued to be allocated a combination of fertile and not-so-fertile land.[9] But the periodic rotation of assigned plots of land was eliminated. This change was designed to create more incentives for maximising the productivity of the land, but the idea was received with even more scepticism. Ray Stagles and Sue Redican tell us:

> Until 1907 a medieval type of strip farming operated. Considerable discussion took place before agreement was reached on how the land should be redistributed within the new field boundaries. In the end most households were allocated several fields scattered over the whole area, so giving each family a mixture of higher, rougher pasture and lower more fertile fields.[10]

According to Padraic Keane of County Sligo, a descendant of the first known King and grandnephew of Peats Mhicí, the islanders actually felt that they had worked out a fair and equitable system of sharing the land over the years. This may have been the Blasket version of the rundale system (see Chapter 2).

The arable land on the island varied in quality. Some was very sandy and did not produce good crops in a dry year, while other areas were very productive. This meant each family controlled several plots of land in different places. The Congested District Board planned to consolidate each family farm and to make the assignments permanent, overriding the historic well-thought-out configuration. The possibility of a family being allocated all their land in a sandy area caused considerable debate and concern on the island. This reorganisation focused primarily on land suitable for cultivation and was apart from the rough grazing land which was shared in common. Each family also had grazing rights for a number of cows and sheep.[11]

During Spanish author Plácido Ramón Castro del Rio's visit to the Great Blasket in 1928, the King described the field reorganisation process in one of their many conversations:

> I accompany the King to his land. Next to the village, there is a small triangle of farmed land, split into small plots, all of them more or less of the same dimensions. Years ago, the allocation of the land was irregular. Every farmer had tiny pieces of land in different places and farming was impossible, but the English government managed to convince farmers of the advantages of a more rational distribution. The allocation was done with great difficulty because each farmer was convinced that he was given less land than he had before. But thanks to the services of an old man, of great authority in the island, who did the allocation by himself, this improvement that actually benefited all, was finally done. Here the Islanders cultivate their potatoes, cabbages and oats that, together with fish, bread and tea, form the principal nourishment.[12]

Tomás Ó Criomhthain assisted in the survey of the land that was undertaken by the Congested Districts Board as part of the reorganisation. He recounts the experience in *The Islandman*:

> Before long the officer of the Board came. He put up a tent and spent some time among us measuring and apportioning the land. It was I who held the other end of the chain for him ... The Board improved our holdings so that every man knows his own plot and has it fenced so that he can do his sowing in a part of it whenever he likes ... When the land was all tidily settled by the Board and every man had his own field here and there, trimly fenced, there was nothing to prevent us sowing all we wanted, and we used to do that, and more.[13]

In his book *The Western Island*, Robin Flower wrote:

> You may imagine the process of ingenious and complicated judging by which this metamorphosis was effected ... It is one of the great regrets of my life that this happened at a time when my knowledge of Irish was so rudimentary that I could not follow the arguments that went on round me, turning the conversational surface of the Island, if I may be allowed the term, into the semblance of a sea in a storm ... It was long before the noise of the debate died down, but now I think the old system is almost forgotten, and the conveniences of the new have silenced the echoes of that storm.[14]

When the new plots of land were being marked out some changes in their shape were necessary. When a field was squared from a long narrow strip it caused considerable wariness as it did not appear to the naked eye to include as much land as previously. The island men gathered every night in one of the houses where the discussion went on late into the night regarding the day's activities. The ashes from the fireplace were smoothed out on the hearth in front of the fire and the shapes of the fields drawn with a stick and compared. It took a long time for some people to be convinced that a square or triangular field could be the same size as a long narrow strip of land.[15]

The device used to lay out the new configuration was a 'Gunter's chain' comprised of 100 metal links, measuring 22 yards (20m) long in total. Two people were needed to hold the chain and areas were marked out in triangles, which were then calculated. It is no wonder that the islanders were confused watching this procedure and they were very wary as to the outcome. It was slow work, but many of the Islanders helped out and took turns holding the end of the chain, building credibility for the process.

The Great Blasket was not the only locale that was evolving from the rundale system. Land on the island of Inishkea, County Mayo, for example, was reorganised by the Congested Districts Board in 1906, roughly simultaneously with the process that was undertaken on the Great Blasket.[16]

Two other related improvements were implemented at about the same time. Very rough cart paths were constructed, one upper and one lower, so that the furthest plots of land could be reached without crossing a neighbour's plot, and the plots of land were properly fenced so there was no longer any need to spend time herding the cattle and protecting the crops.

In the final analysis, the favourable reaction of the islanders was palpable. The islanders were relieved of their fear of the much-hated land agents. Seán Ó Criomhthain was quoted as saying 'Bess and Clara [notorious former land agents of the Earl of Cork, Bess Rice and Clara Hussey], the landlord's agents, were under the sod and young Islanders were dancing to music on their own land. That is how the wheels of this world rotate.'[17] Despite initial reservations, it is apparent that the resulting land reconfiguration benefited all the island families in a fair and equitable fashion.

It is intriguing that the literature is without a more detailed reference to such a milestone event as the reorganisation process. According to Dáithí de Mórdha, the chief archivist at the Great Blasket Centre, the heads of all island families were probably directly involved in the negotiations with the Congested Districts Board in this difficult, sensitive and time-consuming process.[18] In a much larger sense, author Tim Enright sees this transfer of the land and the reorganisation of the fields as consistent with the broad yearning for Irish independence:

> The King was ... the intermediary between the Blasket and neighbouring Ireland, with whose struggle for independence he had every sympathy, the Blasket having won its own independence after long years of struggle with bailiffs and landlords.[19]

Given his acknowledged involvement in holding the chain during the surveying process, it is entirely possible that Tomás was the 'old man, of great authority in the island' referred to in the conversation between Peats Mhicí and Castro del Rio (see above).

It is also possible that this could have been the King. Peats Mhicí, as King of the Great Blasket, may have played a central role administrative under the former rundale system by casting lots and carrying out various other functions (see Chapter 2). While there is no documentation to this effect, it would also have been logical for him to have played a key role in the process of reorganising the land in 1907.

Given his stature, Peats Mhicí was almost certainly a vocal participant in these negotiations, having served as King for about five years or so at the time the process began and throughout its duration. At a bare minimum, the King probably acted as the official interpreter between the parties. Further, the foreman for the Congested Districts Board, John Corcoran from County Mayo, stayed in the King's house during his time on the island. More than likely, Peats Mhicí had many discussions with Corcoran about the concerns of the islanders regarding the quality of the varying plots of land and about alternative strategies for resolving differences. Given the positive outcome, Peats Mhicí probably contributed his usual common sense approach for the benefit of all.

Yellow Meal from Government

In *The Islandman*, Tomás Ó Criomhthain gives us an account of a harrowing adventure to retrieve yellow meal (i.e. Indian or corn meal) that was desperately needed on the Great Blasket. The story illustrates Peats Mhicí's dedication to the needs of the islanders:

> That was a hungry year in the Island, and in many other places, too, and a gentlemen set out from the capital of Ireland to find out where the scarcity was, and he came as far as the Blasket. He sent an order for meal and flour to Dingle. We went there to fetch it.
>
> There was an old trawler in the harbour, and she hadn't done a stroke of work for a long while ... The old captain who had command of her was like to be in the same case as his ship ... He wasn't a single day less than eighty ...
>
> She was brought up level with the quay. Soon the last load was aboard her. Then a coastguard came along the

quay and fell to talking with the captain. He asked where was the rest of the ship's crew. The old lad said he didn't need much of a crew – two besides himself.

The King's man [a British coastguard officer] was a strong, vigorous fellow, and he was by way of being angry with him.

'It isn't you we ought to blame,' says he, 'but the people that had anything to do with you, you and your devil's carrion of a ship; and I wouldn't wager half a crown on its chance of making the Island. Have a crew ready by the time I come back, for, if you haven't, I'll take out of her everything that's in her and put it in another boat.'

The reason why the King's man spoke so shortly to him was that he had been intending to go along with him. The white-haired ancient nearly spurted blood from his nose. He turned blue instead of grey ...

'Is there a man of you there from the Island who could raise the sails to the masthead for me and go with me?' says he, with a wild look in his eyes.

Though the Islanders were in sore need of the meal and flour, they were none too ready to answer him ...

The King's man asked our King if he would shirk going aboard the old smack with him and some other good fellow in his company. The King agreed, as was his way when there was need of him – for he was both King and mariner when the call came, as well as being just as handy at planting potatoes and carrying manure for them; many a time has he harnessed his old, grey, bobtailed ass when all else in the place were in their slumbers. He got another man to go with him.

The King came to me before they put out to sea. He showed me a box, and put it in my charge. They went aboard and the man there set them their tasks at once, and before long the old tub was ready to start from the quay. Then off they started ...

The rest of us started off to trudge the way home. We threw out stuff into the cart, and I put in the King's box very carefully, and never took my eyes off it till we reached Dunquin. There were bottles in it, and nobody was to be trusted in their neighbourhood ...

One man from every house in the Island stayed up all night. When the morning light came, the old hulk was to be seen off Slea Head without a stitch of canvas on her ...

But, as the morning went on, she never came an inch nearer. Before long some of the men went down to the creek brink and decided to go out to her with a boat or two ... When they got to the ship, there wasn't a man on board that looked like himself after the night, even the King. It seemed they had spent the night pumping water out of the old trawler, and she needed it still ... They'd had to strike the mainsail for fear the old boat would split and go down under their feet ...

We tied two ropes to her, and, as the tide was with us, before long we'd brought her to her anchorage. There were eight tons of both meal and flour in her, a great help to the Blasket at that time. When we fell to carrying it home, you'd have thought the harbour was an ant-hill, for every man had his bag on his back ...

The King didn't forget to ask after the box he'd entrusted to me when he went on the ship; and when I told him it was waiting for him at home, safe and sound, he was mighty pleased, and forgot all the troubles of the night.[20]

Obviously, the King was determined to return to the Great Blasket with the free meal from the government. And he was successful in his mission. As for the mysterious box of which he was so protective, it seems that it may well have contained several bottles of strong drink.

Lobstering
Island author Muiris Ó Súilleabháin's father told him a story in May 1919 concerning a discovery that occurred about forty years earlier, about 1880. This story illustrates Peats Mhicí's leadership ability and foreshadows his later designation as King:

'Well, Maurice, one day we were going out to Mass – the King, Shaun Fada, and I – and we were rowing at our ease past Beg-inish to the north when my oar caught in a rope. 'Draw it in,' said Shaun, 'to see what is the meaning of it all.' I began drawing it up, and faith, on every fathom of it was a cork. I thought that very strange and before long I felt a big weight on the rope. I was drawing and drawing till I had it up to the gun-whale. What was it but a pot with a big red crayfish inside, though none of us knew what a crayfish was at the time.

"My heart from the devil,' cried Shaun Fada, 'it is the devil himself is in it. Throw it out quickly!'

'Don't throw it out,' said the King, 'but we will take it to the English people for I dare say this is the fish they are hunting for, whatever it may be.'

Well, the trouble now was to get it out of the pot, for whenever I put in my hand to get hold of it would give a leap and make a great clatter inside.

'Your soul to the devil,' shouted Shaun again, 'throw it out, pot and all, for it is the old fellow [the devil] surely that's in it.'

'Don't throw it out,' said the King.

I was playing it, ever and ever, till at last I got it out and now it was crawling backwards and clattering about in the curragh ... It crawled under Shaun's feet ...

'Take it easy,' said the King, 'it won't kill you.'

'Musha, upon my soul, you don't know what it would do with the devilish haste it is in. Don't ye see all the spike and horns on it?'

'Take it easy,' said the King again, 'till we row in to Beg-inish and then we will learn what it is.'

We went in and two of the Englishman were before us on the shingle. They greeted us and we greeted them, one of them with Irish as fine and fluent as our own. 'Where did you get the crayfish?' said he.

'Faith,' said Shaun Fada, 'that's a name we've never heard before, my good sir.'

We told them how we found it and the wonder we were making of the pots, and we spent the day in their company till in the end they told us how to make them and the people of the Island are fishing lobster ever since.[21]

For many years thereafter, the islanders would use home-made traps to harvest lobster and crayfish in the waters around the island, supplementing their conventional fishing business which was in decline. Lobsters were relatively plentiful from March to August and were stored in a large tank located near the pier on the island until they were sold.[22]

The first lobster buyers came from England with boats with saltwater tanks that would store the catch until they sailed home.[23] After the First World War, a Frenchman named Pierre Trehiou became a regular customer. Trehiou paid in cash and also bartered for fishing supplies with the islanders. At the end of the season, he returned to France, selling Blasket lobsters to restaurants in Paris.[24]

Islanders with a lobster pot (an underwater trap) in 1928. Mike Carney's brother Maurice (barefoot) looks on. Photo by Plácido Ramón Castro del Rio.

This story indicates that Peats Mhicí's was a calm voice in the face of uncertainty, functioning as a kind of counterbalance to the fears and superstitions of others. In this particular situation, his steady demeanour seems to have resulted in a new economic opportunity for the islanders.

The Salvage of the *Quebra*

Fortunes on the Great Blasket took a major turn for the better on 23 August 1916 when the British cargo ship *Quebra,* on a voyage from New York to Liverpool, sank after striking Lóchar Rock, just off the island. Three crewmembers died in the incident, but thirty-four survived.[25]

The tribulation of the ship's owners was a boon for the islanders. The wreck set off a mad scramble to salvage whatever cargo could be retrieved from the water and the rocky shoreline.

It was a pure case of 'finder's keeper's'. For people who had very little in terms of material goods, it was a bonanza.

The King immediately realised the benefit for the islanders and was right in the middle of their efforts to scoop up the spilled cargo. Muiris Ó Súilleabháin recalls the excitement of that day. He first got wind of the situation when he was sitting in his place in school:

> ... we heard a clamour outside. I looked out of the window and saw the Púncán [Tomás 'the Yank' Ó Ceárnaigh] and the King going down the Causeway with thole-pins and ropes, three or four hurrying after them, all with the same gear.
>
> 'Your soul to the devil, Tomás, more wreckage!' ...
>
> 'A big ship has gone down in the Sorrowful Cliff.' ...
>
> Great King of Virtues, it was a marvellous sight – tins, barrels of flour, big black boxes, big white boxes, big boxes of bacon, not a living being to be seen nor a curragh on the stays ...
>
> Away we ran leaping for delight ... 'Oh, my heart, a big ship is gone down on the Lóchar Rock and the sea is full of all sorts of riches,' said she [islander Maura Andrew] ...
>
> Before long we saw a curragh rounding the bottom of Well Point, followed by a boat in which were two sailors. We all made for the quay. When they came ashore, the King spoke to them in English ... 'How did the ship happen to go in there last night?'
>
> 'I am the captain and this is the mate, and the man above is a seaman. We left New York with a cargo of all sorts for London. On our journey we got a message that a submarine was on our route before us.'
>
> 'I understand you well,' said the King, shaking his head.
>
> 'What I did then,' said the captain, was to change my

route and turn north-east. Then the mist fell and I didn't know where in the world I was. I was blind out.'

'It's no wonder,' said the King, shaking his head again.

'I turned the ship south-east then and that is how she struck in there. And, would you believe it, half an hour before she struck she grazed on a rock?'

'I believe you well' said the King, 'for you couldn't help striking Tail Rock in the direction you came.'

'It was about three o'clock in the morning. I ordered to crew to take to the boats. We left her safely, three boats in all, but I don't know where the other two are gone.'

'Oh, upon my word, they are alive, for they were seen going up the Bay of Dingle today.'

'That is good,' said the captain...

'Well, well,' said the King, shutting his eyes in pity for them... 'But upon my word,' said he [the captain], glancing around, 'you are here – fine well-favoured people, mannerly, intelligent, generous, and hospitable.'

'Indeed,' said the King, 'we are very thankful to you for the praise. But I promise you, since the war began, it is many a sailor has been saved here from the sea. And as for attending them well, they get what we have. But you must be cold and wet standing there. Come up into the village.'

The sailors spent two or three hours with us. When they had eaten and rested, they said farewell to the people of the Island and departed for the mainland.

From that out there was plenty and abundance in the Island – food of all sorts, clothes from head to heel, every man, women, and child with a watch in their pockets; not a penny leaving home; everything a mouth could ask for coming in with the tide from day to day – all except the sugar which melted as soon as it touched water.'[26]

Leslie Matson relays the events of that joyous day:

> Very soon, the inhabitants of the island, almost to a man,
> were gathered above the spit of Seal's Cove near Shingle
> Strand [north-facing Tráigh Ghearraí or the pebble
> beach] which was covered in wreckage of all kinds. Every
> *naomhóg* on the island was busy collecting the boxes and
> barrels floating in the water.[27]

In the aftermath of the wreck, the captain was cared for on the
island:

> Máire Guiheen [the King's granddaughter], who was a
> child of about seven at the time, remembered hearing
> that the captain soon fell asleep exhausted at the house of
> Maurice Keane (Maras Mhuiris) who was in his middle
> forties at the time and active in salvaging the cargo with
> his crew. His daughter Kate was particularly struck by
> the gold ring on the captain's finger and told her friend
> Máire Guiheen about it.[28]

All the islanders benefited from the wreck, even the little
ones. The King was fortunate enough to retrieve a big chest of
chocolates to the delight of the island children. He passed them
out with a teasing 'Now, my lads ... if you have good teeth!'[29]

Postman

One of Peats Mhicí's most important day-to-day responsibilities was that of Blasket postman. He travelled by *naomhóg*
to the mainland twice weekly on Tuesdays and Fridays, weather
permitting, to send and collect the island mail. This required
substantial physical strength to row a *naomhóg* back and

forth from the island to the mainland, excellent seamanship skills, a detailed knowledge of the physical dangers that lie in Blasket Sound, a high level of personal integrity and consistent dedication to duty.

Interestingly, this role as postman was seen as separate from his role as King, although it certainly enhanced his stature. The postman was not automatically the King and vice versa. Nevertheless, virtually all contemporaries who comment on the King go out of their way to describe the faithful discharge of his duties in connection with the mail:

- **Máire (Ní Ghuithín) Uí Chiobháin – Máire Mhaidhc Leán (The King's Granddaughter):**

  Pádraig Ó Catháin [the King] was the first postman on the Island. He only had to go to Dunquin once a week to get the letters at the start. After five years, he had to go twice a week. Many a time, during the summer, when the sea was quiet and calm, he would go by himself to get the post in Dunquin. Often he would bring visitors coming to the Island back to stay with him, and if he was on his own, he rowed them back himself.

  He was the postman for twenty-five years. When he gave it up, his son Seán took up the job.[30]

- **Seán Ó Criomhthain:**

  The mail-boat went out to Dunquin twice a week on Tuesdays and Fridays and people would go out there with the postman to get messages. On their return the whole village, at least those who were free, would gather at the edge of the pier where the postman always opened his bag and distributed the letters and parcels

Islanders gather around the King on the slipway at *Caladh an Oileáin* as he distributes the mail. Photo by George Thomson.

and everything else. He even sold them stamps. They'd then question him about this and that, and if he had any bad news they didn't like hearing it. I remember well the time of the Easter Rising in Dublin when the islanders had relatives living there. They became very worried on hearing about Dublin being on fire and about the soldiers and the fighting and so on. And then again when France was involved in the Great War the poor fishermen were very upset because there was nobody coming to buy the lobsters from them except the French. I am telling you that what was happening on the mainland worried all that were in their right minds, if indeed they were in their right minds, because they got a hard time of it from the world and from life.[31]

- **Leslie Matson:**

> The King's arrival with the post, weather permitting, on Tuesday and Friday morning were high points in the week for the Blasket islanders. When his *naomhóg* arrived at the *'Niúin'* [the island harbour] and was safely up on its *stáitsí* [rack], he climbed, followed by his retinue, to the top of the cliff, this 'big, heavy man, with the broad, benignant face and the easy authoritative air'. Now he opened up his bag, donned his spectacles (no longer made fun of) and distributed the post to the families or their representatives from the upper or lower village. His loud voice would then retail the gossip from the mainland, or welcome any visitors that he had brought with him.[32]

Intermediary

Living on the Great Blasket was characterised by isolation from the mainland and the world at large. But events off the island had a significant impact on the island itself, particularly in the economic and political spheres. As a natural extension of his postman duties, the King brought back and interpreted news of current events on the mainland and beyond. In turn, he represented the islanders in their dealings with government officials and mainland businesspeople where his rare facility in English was indispensable.

Risteárd Ó Glaisne describes Peats Mhicí's role as follows: 'The King was always the source of knowledge of the happenings of the world. In addition, he was as Charon [a ferryman in Greek mythology] was transporting people over the Styx [a mythical river boundary between death and the afterlife], bringing them across the way with his *naomhóg*.'[33]

The King's arrival with the news was eagerly anticipated:

> When Mickey Ó Catháin, the King, would go to the post
> office on the mainland for mail, everybody would ask
> 'What's the news today, Rí?' when he returned. If there
> was anything going on around the country, the islanders
> wanted to know about it. What were the big issues of the
> day? What was going to be done about them?
>
> The King would bring back old newspapers, whatever
> was left around in the post office. Sometimes they had
> *The Irish Press*, the *Irish Independent*, or *The Kerryman*.
> We would spread the news around the island as soon as it
> arrived. There was a thirst for information. But, of course,
> it was always old news by the time it got to the island.[34]

Leslie Matson provides greater detail on the role of the King as
the island's interface with the world:

> He was ... the only constant source of information about
> the outside world. He had a good command of English,
> (even using it and Irish to shout at animals), and this
> enabled him to read the newspapers and, gathered in the
> evenings mainly in the 'Dáil', as the Poncán's house at the
> top of the village was called, to interpret what he read for
> such of the other islanders as were interested. Although
> for selfish reasons what interested his hearers more than
> anything else was news of wrecks around their coast, on
> which, during wartime, the economy of the island was
> particularly dependent, one must remember that the
> period in which he was 'in office' was an exceptionally
> active period in Irish History. He could report the
> outbreak and the course of the Great War, the Easter
> Rising, the growth of Sinn Féin (about which he was not
> enthusiastic), the Anglo-Irish 'Troubles' with the death

of Cork's two Lord Mayors, and the Civil War which followed. Inevitably, this gave him an unchallenged status.[35]

The Great War (First World War: 1914–1918)

It was the King who brought the news to the Great Blasket of the outbreak of the Great War with the assassination of Archduke Franz Ferdinand of Austria in Sarajevo on 28 June 1914. According to Robin Flower:

> Thus the news of the outer world comes to the Island; from the mainland, from the next parish, which is America, and from England, which spiritually is so much farther away. I remember, in a fatal year, how I stood watching the little sail of the post-boat flitting across the Sound, and went with the children to await its arrival. The King came slowly up the slope with his bag, set it down on the ground, and, turning to me, said with a grave air: 'There is news to-day. They have killed an Archduke in the eastern world.' It meant so little to us then in that remote isolation of the sea; but in a month's time I was back in London, and the familiar fabric of life was torn like a cobweb in the wind for all of us – and, though the revelation came later, for the Island also. In a few years' time their bay was full of anti-submarine craft, and the tide was bringing the wreckage of ships and the quiet forms of the dead to the Island beaches. But this was for the future when I first knew the Island, and these are not the memories which I cherish most willingly.[36]

Within a year, the Great Blasket was to be touched by the Great War in the aftermath of the sinking of RMS *Lusitania* off Kinsale near Cork on 7 May 1915. Muiris Ó Súilleabháin relates this grisly story of the impact on the Great Blasket as the war got under way:

One evening long after that we were all on the quay before the King in the hope of news from the mainland; the girls maybe looking forward to a letter, a man waiting for the tobacco he had sent for and desiring nothing more than to get a morsel of it in his back teeth.

After handing out the letters the King sat down on his heels and pulled out his pipe and tobacco, as was the habit with him.

'Did you hear any rumours out today, Pádrig?' asked Shaun Michael.

'The devil,' replied the King, 'it is my strong opinion we won't live much longer now.'

'Achván,' said Shaun Michael, 'there must be a plague coming so.'

'It is worse than a plague. The two sides of the world are likely to burst against each other at any moment.'

'Bad enough,' said Shaun Fada.

'Arra, man,' interrupted my grandfather, 'why should it be bad?'

'Your soul to the devil, who will buy the fish? Who will buy the pig or the cow? Where will the buyers be found? That's talk in the air, my boy,' said Shaun Fada, spitting ...

A week later we got tidings that England and Germany were hurled against each other. Every time the King went out to Dunquin he came home with a newspaper. The old men would gather in his house every evening to listen to the news, and it is often it came to a rowan-tree battle [from an ancient legend] between them, some siding with the English and others with the Germans ...

One Friday the King had gone to Dunquin for the post and, as I have said already, the whole village, young and old, had to be on the quay to meet him.

'How is England doing, Pádrig?' asked the Púncán [Tomás 'the Yank' Ó Ceárna who had emigrated to America and returned to the island], when the letters had been given out.

'The devil,' said the King, 'it is likely the end of the world is coming, for they are making no stop now and England is going to send out conscription through the whole of Ireland.'

'Bad indeed so, bad indeed so,' said the Púncán, spitting tobacco.

'Ah, that's not the tidings we want,' said another man, 'but did you hear of a ship being sunk in any place since?'

'The devil,' said the King, 'one went down yesterday near Cork Harbour, the *Lusitania*, the finest ship the Americans ever had. They say there were millionaires in plenty on board and isn't it a terrible thing that not a sinner of them came ashore alive. If this breeze lasts from the south tonight, the coast of the Island will be full of drowned men tomorrow.'

No one went to sleep in the Island that night ... As soon as I got up I went south to the Point ... After about half an hour I thought I noticed something far out to sea ...

'On my oath, Liam, it is a human body.' Do you see it standing straight down in the water? ...'

We ran down the quay. It was a terrible sight, the eyes plucked out by the gulls, the face swollen, and the clothes ready to burst with the swelling of the body ... It was arranged to take the body to Dunquin so that the peelers [the police] could take care of it till its people would take it ...

No one had the courage to go near it. But there was one old man called Mick of the Hill [probably the King's father] standing beside us ... He went down on his knees and began to open the coat. When he had the coat and vest open, he put his hand in one of the pockets and, drawing out a small diary, he handed it to the sergeant. When he opened the book the first thing I saw was the drowned man's name written like this:

HENRY ATKINSON
3 Edward Street, London, W.C.
First-class Officer, S.S. Lusitania

They all helped to carry the body to the top of the cliff [up from Dunquin pier]. Then they laid it in the sergeant's motor car and went off with it to Ballyferriter.[37]

Legend has it that one of the deckchairs from the sunken *Lusitania* washed up on the Great Blasket in the aftermath of the tragedy and was years later taken to the mainland by an islander in the evacuation in 1953.

Once the war was under way in earnest, the King kept the islanders abreast of its progress. Mícheál Ó Ghuithín describes the King's role in *A Pity Youth Does Not Last*:

'Have you and news for us today, Pats?' Seán Fada asked him one day. 'How's the war going, or is any side giving in?'

'On my word, Seán, neither side is giving in yet, whatever. There's a paper inside here in the postbag and 'twould put the heart crossways in anyone who reads it. All that's in the world entirely now, Seán, is only slaughtering and battering and no one can say when there will be an end to it.'

'Yerra, leave them to it,' said Seán. 'We're far from them.'

'By my palms, Seán, I'm afraid there's trouble ahead for us such as there never was.'

'You must have good cause for saying it, man.'

'I have, Seán. I have letters here today under seal from Dublin Castle from England's man in Ireland, for the young lads of the Island, to tell them to be making themselves ready to go to the war. And isn't that bad news, man.'

'It isn't good or fit news,' said Seán. 'If only there was a remedy for it.'

There was squabbling there the likes of which no one had ever seen, for no one would take those letters from him, and he had to put them away again in his bag.

Your man went off up the boreen [road] and he wasn't too well pleased with himself, for he had a letter for his own son as well as the next and that was the letter he had no wish to hand over.[38]

The Easter Rising (1916)

In *An Old Woman's Reflections*, Peig Sayers describes the King bringing the news of the Easter Rising of 24 April 1916 to the Great Blasket:

Long years after my coming to the island, there was clamour and confusion, that there was a destroying battle between Irish and Strangers [the British] in Dublin. At first you wouldn't believe a word of it. A big story, a wonderful story it was. The postman brought us the story, may God grant his soul eternal rest! He said that Dublin City was one huge fire and the big guns of the Stranger battering it and the fragrant blood of the Irish being spilled.

'The Irish are awake again,' said he, 'and the people are stirred as I never saw them; and it's danger in my mind that life won't be too peaceful with Yellow John [John Bull].' ...

'I suppose, musha, that in Irish talk there never was but cliff grass compared with this heavy blow that has been struck in the Royal City of Ireland, if it's true.'

'If it's true,' said the King, with sarcasm in his voice. 'As sure as there's grey whiskers on your jawbone the heaviest beating that has ever been beaten in Ireland is going on there. And worse than that there's a warship firing in on the city. They say total destruction is done already there. I heard that the girls of the city were fighting shoulder to shoulder with the lads, my music they!'

''Twas of their ancestors' kind to have the noble royal drop in them,' said Big John Carney, 'but my regret and worry, the enemy is too strong, I fear, and they will be vanquished early! Did you hear was there any stirring being done by the other people of Ireland?'

'I did. They are already preparing themselves for the battle, but 'tis said it's not to Dublin they are inclined to go but that 'tis how they'll be engaging the enemy in battle here and there. But many of the Volunteers are facing for Dublin. It seems they would rather fall in the battle than let the enemy go victorious.'[39]

In his book *A Pity Youth Does Not Last*, Mícheál Ó Ghuithín, Peig Sayers' son and the last Blasket poet, describes the reaction to the news of the Easter Rising. Ó Ghuithín observes that the King was astute enough to read the atmosphere of the times accurately and predict that the fight would be sustained over time and that it would spread throughout Ireland.

> A couple of days later the postman [the King] was out in the mainland and everybody's heart was high that there would be good news.

When he landed back, Seán Fada asked if he had any news.

'On my soul, Seán, I have no good news today, whatever. The Rising that was in Dublin is over since yesterday morning. The leaders – but no chieftains I should say – of the Volunteers are arrested and have been sent over to England. The Army shot the biggest part of them. Patrick Pearse has fallen.'

'Is he dead?'

'He is, Seán, and his brother was executed too and many gentlemen besides. There is terror in the hearts of everyone in the whole country today. The terrible destruction brought on the people in Dublin by the English finished the Rising. But I think myself that the English will pay dearly for it yet, for instead of the Irish losing heart, it only gave them more courage. I never before saw the people so stirred.'

'I suppose, Pats,' said my father, 'that they're no omen of peace for England.'

'They're not, Patsy. The old hatred that was ever there between Ireland and England is as fresh today before the minds of the people as it was hundreds of years ago. Unless I'm greatly mistaken, the fight will soon be on all over Ireland.'

'God save us, I suppose it will,' said my father. 'There set upon it, it seems.' ...

'I'm afraid, Patsy,' said the postman, 'the number of men that fell in Easter Week won't be the last in this country, before there's an end of it.'

With that he went off up the boreen.

The postman was right, for it wasn't long before the fight started throughout the whole of Ireland.[40]

In addition to being a kind of newscaster, the King also offered his interpretation of these and other events, sometimes offering a forecast as to the future direction of external affairs. In the case of the Easter Rising, his sense of the implications of these events was right on target.

Ventry Regatta

Sometimes the information the King brought from the mainland led to young men exploring the world beyond the island. Muiris Ó Súilleabháin tells of the King's announcement of *naomhóg* races in Ventry in the mid-1920s:

> One fine day in the month of August the King was after coming in from Dunquin with the post-bag. It is the custom of the Island for everyone to be on the quay for his coming, young and old, and often he would have enough to do to draw breath with the crowd around him, thrusting in their heads and chattering.
>
> 'I dare say you have no news from the outside?' said Shaun Fada [Seán Eoghain Ó Duinnshléibhe, Méiní's husband and a good friend of the King and Tomás Ó Criomhthain] ...
>
> 'Any man now who has any spirit,' said the King, getting up, 'let him take a curragh south to Ventry next Sunday. There's going to be a great race in it.'
>
> 'They won't go – no fear of it. Did you hear of any curragh to be going in for it?' asked Shaun, turning to the King.
>
> 'Indeed there are – a curragh from the Cooas, one from Ballymore and another from Leitriúch.'
>
> There was now no talk in the village of anything else but the races.[41]

This all led to a day's outing to observe the races with then teenaged Muiris Ó Súilleabháin and his equally young friend Tomás Ó Ceárna experimenting with drink, gambling and other minor misadventures. It was a coming-of-age adventure for the lads.

Transporter

As postman, Peats Mhicí made the only scheduled trips from the island to the mainland and back. Many islanders and visitors took advantages of these services and he emerged as the main means of conveyance. In providing transportation, however, the King actually played a larger role as the first and last contact for his non-islander passengers, offering words of welcome and words of farewell. No examples illustrate the King's larger role in transportation more poignantly than two particular trips he made with Muiris Ó Súilleabháin, which essentially bookended the author's life on the island.

Muiris Ó Súilleabháin Returns to the Great Blasket

Muiris Ó Súilleabháin, the famous Blasket author and the last of five children, was born on the island on 19 February 1904. A year later, his mother died and young Muiris was placed in an orphanage in Dingle where English was spoken exclusively. When he moved back to the island to live at home with his father at the age of seven, Muiris was fluent in English, but now needed to learn Irish from scratch.[42]

Of course, it was the King who provided the necessary transportation over to the island. In *Twenty Years A-Growing*, Ó Súilleabháin reminisces about his first exposure to a *naomhóg* and his trip across Blasket Sound to the place of his birth. It was a voyage that brought some surprises and challenged his stomach:

'Where are we going now?' said I.

It was a week-day, and, as soon as we reached the top of the cliff, the King of the Island came up with his post-bag on his back. He spoke to my father, but not a word could I understand. There were many others round the place and they all with their own talk. I don't know in the world, said I in my own mind, will the day ever come when I will be able to understand them.

The King turned to me. 'Musha, how are you?' said he, stretching out his hand.

I looked at him – a fine, courteous, mannerly, well-favoured man. 'Thank you very much,' said I (in English).

'The devil,' said he. 'I think you have no understanding of the Irish?'

'I have not,' said I.

But he himself had the two languages, fluent and vigorous. 'How does it please you to be going into the Island?' he asked me.

'I do not know,' said I. 'It does not look too nice altogether.'

'Upon my word, Shaun,' said the King, turning to my father, 'it is time for us to be starting in.' And he began to move down ...

When I came in sight of the quay, what did I see but twenty black beetles twice as big as a cow!

'Oh, dad,' said I, 'are those beetles dangerous?'

The King gave a big, hearty laugh which took an echo out of the cliff, for he was a fine strong man, with a voice without any hoarseness.

'Indeed, my boy,' said he, 'it is no bad guess you made, and you are not the first that gave them that name ...'

Then I turned my eyes toward the slip and what did I see but one of the big black beetles walking out toward me. My heart leapt. I caught hold of my aunt's shawl, crying, 'Oh, the beetle!'

'Have no fear,' said she, 'that is a curragh they are carrying down on their backs ...'

The curragh was now afloat, like a cork on the water, as light as an egg-shell. In went my uncle, and the way he set her rocking I thought every moment she would overturn. In went the King, and, faith, I was sure she would go down with the weight that was in the man. I was the last to be put in. The King was seated at his ease on the thwart, his pipe lit. My aunts were in the stern, I at their feet sitting on a tin of sweets.

'Now,' said the King, 'let us move her out in the name of God.'

Soon the curragh was mounting the waves, then down again on the other side, sending bright jets of foam into the air every time she struck the water ...

Then I began to feel my guts going in and out of each other ...

'Lift up your head, my boy,' said the King, 'and take a whiff of the wind' ... I wanted to throw up ...

'Heave it up,' said the King, 'and nothing more will ail you.'

Seven attempts I made, but with no success ... Then up came the burden and I threw it out ...

[Eventually] The curragh stretched up alongside the slip [on the Island]. I got out ...

'Be off!' said the King to the children who were in his way. They scattered in fear.[43]

Thus, the King was directly involved in Muiris's reintroduction to his native island. The memories that Muiris was to accumulate during the following years were eventually the basis for his classic island book *Twenty Years A-Growing*.

Muiris Ó Súilleabháin Joins the Garda Síochána

One of the saddest aspects of the King's role was to provide transportation to islanders who were leaving for what were perceived to be greener pastures on the mainland or in America. Invariable, these departures were preceded by 'An American Wake,' a going-away party named after a real wake for the departed of a different sort (see Chapter 12).

The emigration of Muiris Ó Súilleabháin to enlist in the Garda Síochána, the national police, on 15 March 1927 must have been particularly difficult for the King since he had rowed him to the island when he moved back as a youth sixteen years earlier in 1911. Ó Súilleabháin describes the heart-rending day he left the island, being less than fully forthcoming with the King about his intentions:

> The next morning was fine and soft. It was a Tuesday, the 15th of March 1927. I got myself ready early, for it was the day for the King to go out to bring in the post, so I was in the yard watching out for him for fear he would go unknown to me. There was everything in readiness with me, my mind at rest, my holiday clothes on, and no one knowing my destination but only my own people.
>
> After a while I saw Shaun Fada approaching. He stopped and looked me over from top to toe without speaking a word.
>
> 'I see there is some intention in your head today, son of O'Sullivan,' said he at last.
>
> 'I am for taking the leap.'
>
> 'Whither are you travelling?'

'Yé, where would it be, Shaun, but to spend a week in the town of Dingle. Amn't I tired of this place?'

... At that moment I saw the King coming down the Causeway. 'Faith, Shaun,' said I, 'here is the King going out. It is as well for me to be moving.'

'It is as well for you,' said he, going east.

The King soon came up with me on the top of the quay.

'Are you going out?'

'I am resolved on it.'

'If so,' said he, looking at me, 'it seems to me that you will not be coming back.'

'Ahh, maybe I would spend a week on my wanderings,' said I.

Soon we were on our way out from the pool, my back to the Island of my birth and my face to the mainland ...

I heard a voice behind me: 'Are you there still?'

I looked back and saw the King. 'Faith, I am,' said I, shaking myself. 'There is no great hurry on me.'

'I suppose you will be going to Dingle tonight?'

'I will. Is the road to the north the shortest?'

'Without doubt it is.'

We said good-bye and parted. I set out on my road, and the King on his way up towards Bally-na-Raha.

I was alone now, groping my way to the north and a west mist over the road.[44]

Muiris had also considered emigrating to America, but with George Thomson's encouragement, he decided to enlist in the Gardaí. His training took place in Phoenix Park, Dublin. This was small consolation to the King as the island lost another of its sons.

Adviser and Counsellor

The King sometimes provided advice to islanders on a whole range of matters of a personal nature. In some cases, the advice took the form of an unsolicited admonition which, understandably, drew mixed reactions. In other cases, his intervention was sought after as islanders searched for a way to resolve sensitive interpersonal issues. In both cases, this role as counsellor is beyond what we typically think of as appropriate for a King, but it illustrates Peats Mhicí's stature as a man worthy of the islander's trust and confidence.

Religion

On at least one occasion, the King demonstrated his commitment to Catholicism by not-so-subtly reminding the islanders of their religious obligations. In *Allagar na hInise*, Tomás Ó Criomhthain recounts a scenario on an particular Easter Sunday. The islanders had gathered together and were bragging about the amount of eggs they had eaten and they did not seem to be too worried about going over to Mass.

> 'The King came along with an air of authority,' he says, 'and mingled with the people, but since they did not pay him any attention just like anyone else, he made his presence felt. He got five or six who were previously undecided to go out to Mass [over the Sound to St Gobnet's Church in Dunquin by way of *naomhóg*] – the King manages to arouse religious sentiments because he has the big name.
>
> 'It is a great shame,' says the King, 'that anyone in full health should stay and not go to God's Mass on a soft calm day like today.'
>
> Tomás was not sure that the King's intervention in this situation was appropriate. "I suppose,' says Tomás,

'that he was right in a way, but another scripture says, "Mind your own business and do not bother anyone else. The man who rises himself will be lowered, and the man who lowers himself will be risen."[45]

There is no record of whether Tomás himself heeded the King's admonition on that Easter Sunday, but one can be absolutely certain that he made up his own mind.

Méiní Elopes

In one exceedingly difficult family situation, the King was asked to carry a sensitive message of reconciliation between a contrite mother, Máire Keating O'Shea of Dunquin, and her estranged daughter, Méiní (Ní Shé) Uí Dhuinnshléibhe, by then living on the Great Blasket. This may have occurred in Peats Mhicí's pre-King days, yet he was still referred to in this story as the King.

Méiní was born in 1875 in Chicopee, Massachusetts to parents who had emigrated from Ballykeen, Dunquin to America a year earlier. Her father died in Chicopee when she was just two years old. Two years later, her mother Máire moved back to Dunquin with Méiní and her older sister Junie in tow.[46]

At the age of sixteen, Méiní herself decided to seek a better life in America. She emigrated from Dunquin with two girlfriends and lived in Chicopee and later in Hartford, Connecticut, working in a factory. But three years after her journey across the Atlantic, work-related health issues forced her to return to Dunquin. She received a warm welcome and moved back into the family home.

Since Méiní was now approaching twenty years of age, she and her mother Máire began to consider candidates for a marriage match for her. Máire took the lead and proposed one candidate whose delaying tactics offended Méiní. Then Méiní herself proposed an alternative candidate to her mother who found the man unacceptable. Mother and daughter were at a stalemate.

Shortly thereafter, Seán Eoghain Ó Duinnshléibhe from the Great Blasket told Méiní that he intended to ask her mother for permission to have her hand in marriage. The two knew each other and there was a history of some mild flirting between them. Méiní was very much in favour of the proposed match:

> A blush came to my cheek, the words he spoke gave me such a shock. I thought such a thing would never happen. I admit it was the sweetest sound my ears had ever heard.
> 'On my soul, my bright love, stay away from her!'
> ... I ran into his arms and kissed him and he kissed me.[47]

Méiní warned Seán to 'stay away' from her mother because she knew Máire would never bless the match. Seán was a widower with two children. He was fifteen years older than Méiní and he lived on the island, which Máire regarded as an unsuitable place for her daughter to live.

So the new lovebirds conspired to be married in secret; they decided to elope. The unannounced wedding took place in Ballyferriter the following Saturday, 25 April 1896, with a celebration following in Dingle. Máire found out about her daughter's nuptials about two hours after they were over. As might be expected, she was absolutely furious. Méiní, of course, immediately moved to the island with her new husband. A period of estrangement between mother and daughter ensued.

After the strong-willed Máire had time to reflect on the situation, she thought better of the rift with her daughter and sought a way to reconcile. The future King of the Great Blasket was to be the intermediary:

> Three months after the elopement, Máire sent a message to Méiní by Pats Kane, the island postman and King. She was to come out of the island the following Sunday when the *naomhóga* were coming across for Mass in the Dunquin church at Baile an Teampaill.[48]

One can only imagine the conversation between the King and Méiní as he presented Máire's proposal of a get-together. He was entrusted with a very delicate message from a mother who had recovered from a fit of anger that was not without some justification. The message needed to be delivered with the utmost tact.

Somehow, the King found just the right words. Méiní agreed to visit Máire. The King provided her with transportation to Dunquin by *naomhóg*. And he probably also provided her with some words of wisdom and encouragement. The trip across Blasket Sound to the mainland must have been full of anxious anticipation for the recent bride.

As it turns out, the initial rapprochement at Máire's house went well. Méiní remained at home for a week before returning to her husband on the Great Blasket the following Sunday. It may have been that both women wanted to put the matter behind them:

> When she returned to the island, Méiní brought with her a pet lamb as a wedding present from her mother.
>
> One problem alone remained: Seán Eoghain himself [the new husband] was still not welcome in the house in Ballykeen. After all, he had not asked their blessing before eloping with Méiní, and the runaway marriage had been a blow to their pride. Méiní determined to put matters to rights.[49]

Méiní (Ní Shé) Uí Dhuinnshléibhe, known as the Blasket nurse, in her later years. Photo by Leslie Matson.

A few weeks later, Méiní and Seán were in Dunquin. Méiní visited her parents while Seán visited his friends. Méiní had been wearing Seán's coat as protection against an alleged chill, but she deliberately left it at her mother's home when she returned to the pier to meet Seán. She somehow coaxed a reluctant Seán into retrieving it for her while she waited at the pier.

After a cup of tea with Méiní's mother and her grandparents, Seán struck up a relationship and a family reconciliation was under way. Seán returned to the pier with his 'forgotten' coat and things were trending in the right direction. The family shared a couple of rounds of spirits during Méiní and Seán's next trip to Dunquin and the issue was behind them. Méiní's clever strategy had worked.

Seán Eoghain was a big personality and a real character on the island. He was fun loving, loud, blustery and argumentative with a fiery temperament. Yet he had a gentle side as well, including a flair for poetry. He achieved some island fame as member of the winning crew of the *Beauty* in the legendary Ventry Race[50] (see Chapter 5).

Méiní, of course, went on to become a central figure on the island. Although she had no formal training, she was widely known as 'the Blasket nurse'. She was familiar with folk healing techniques. She learned the art of delivering babies from midwives and local doctors. She became highly skilled and was trusted implicitly by the women of the island. For thirty-six years, Méiní assisted at virtually every Blasket birth.[51] Despite her devoted efforts, infant mortality and the death of the mother in childbirth were quite high.[52]

For his part, the Blasket King was certainly no family counsellor. In this awkward situation, he would never have pretended to be more than a messenger and a means of conveyance. But he played the essential role of catalyst in bringing the family back together again. Again, the King was equal to the delicate task at hand.

Méiní's beloved husband Seán died on the island in March 1932, three years after the King's death. Shortly thereafter, Méiní moved back to Dunquin with the able assistance of the King's son, Seán An Rí.[53] There she continued to work as a midwife for many years, sharing her fascinating life story with all who would listen. She died in 1967 at the age of ninety-one, about thirty-four years after her husband Seán Eoghain's passing.[54] She was a truly remarkable woman in every respect.

Host-in-Chief

Visitors
The last Blasket King played a multidimensional role in facilitating visits to the Great Blasket by the increasing numbers of

'cultural tourists' (see Chapter 8). He provided transportation across Blasket Sound to and from the island via his ever-reliable *naomhóg.* He offered greetings to the visitors on behalf of the islanders and introduced them around the island. He was also a kind of concierge, connecting visitors with various island resources (e.g. introducing a visitor to someone who could help him or her learn the Irish language, arranging guided hikes to the back of the island, etc.). He even maintained a correspondence with some of the visitors for a number of years after their visit, representing and maintaining the link between the island and the outside world.

The King's Bed and Breakfast
Some of the islanders expanded their modest island homes to accommodate the flow of visitors to the Great Blasket. This typically involved constructing a simple one-room addition off the back or on the side of the house. The King was among the first islanders to take advantage of this economic opportunity. Author Mícheál Ó Dubhshláine describes the King's addition:

> There was a felt roof on it, complete with a fireplace and a fine window facing out to the ocean with a view of Dún Chaoin, Mount Eagle and Cruach Mhárthan across the Bealach [Blasket Sound]. His was the first house on the island to keep visitors. The new room doubled up as a classroom for those such as Marstrander and later Robin Flower, who were taught there by the Islandman himself, Tomás Ó Criomhthain.[55]

The King's bed and breakfast was very popular among visitors and did a brisk business in the summer. Tomás Ó Criomhthain wrote to Ida Flower that 'The King and business is well. He is getting any amount of demands from people all around, to keep room for them. This Island will be flocked with people next summer.'[56]

This bed and breakfast operated from around 1905 until his daughter Cáit married and moved to the mainland in 1918, leaving only Seán An Rí and the King living at home (see Chapter 8). A year later, Seán got married and the King's bed and breakfast was effectively out of business. But his daughters Máire and Cáit remained in the hospitality business in their own homes for years to come.

Courting

Leslie Matson tells us of an unusual role that the King played in facilitating the courting process on the island. It was hosting of a different sort indeed. On one occasion, this role put him in conflict with a visiting priest. On this issue, Méiní, the Blasket nurse, sided with the King:

> The trade [in porter or beer] had continued for some time when the power of another law was made clear in the person of a visiting priest from England who was staying in the King's house. Unfortunately there was a nice sheltered little cubbyhole beside the King's house which was used by courting couples after dark on summer evenings, and the priest's bedroom window overlooked this very spot. Méiní approved of the activity going on among those whose nature it was to be so inclined: 'We were all like that,' she said, 'when our years of frolicsomeness and airiness of heart were on us, and it isn't right for priest or brother to be too hard on the natural inclinations of youth.' The priest took a markedly less liberal view, especially when those natural inclinations assumed an alcoholic hue.[57]

Mike Carney remembers the King's cubbyhole very well, but he declines to share any information about his own possible use thereof. He says this is 'classified information'.[58]

Arbitrator

Multiple sources indicate that the King played a quasi-judicial role on the island. In fact, he was probably more of an arbitrator of disagreements that occurred on the island from time to time. According to Mike Carney:

> The islanders seldom got into an argument amongst themselves. For the most part, there were able to get along with each other. If they had a problem, it did not last very long. They had no court on the island. They did not need one. They resolved their own disputes. If need be, the King would settle differences using common sense. Afterwards, they would shake hands and that was the end of it.[59]

A cow feeding on someone else's land or disputes related to the operation of the old rundale system were typical of the matters resolved by the King.[60] While mention is made of the King's role as arbitrator in the Blasket literature, there is no specific documentation of the exercise of this important function.[61]

This role must have been critically important to the islanders and others, because it was one of the few aspects of his service as King that was specifically mentioned in Peats Mhicí's published obituary:

> When any dispute occurred among the Islanders the matter was referred to the 'king' for arbitration and his ruling was never questioned. The Islanders, therefore,

never had recourse to a court of law. The King always gave justice to both parties.[62]

The fact that the islanders entrusted Peats Mhicí with this responsibility is a tribute to his integrity and his ability to exercise sound and impartial judgment in practical matters where there were differing points of view. His wisdom and diplomacy were very much a factor in the day-to-day life on the island.

A Man for all Seasons

It would be fair to say that very few kings of any type played such a wide range of roles that demanded so much of a human being. But Peats Mhicí appears to have been equal to the challenge and managed to endear himself to the islanders at the same time.

In each of his many roles, it appears that the King was focused on getting things done, even at the expense of some minor offence to others. He was a bit impatient, even with friends, seemingly preoccupied with completing whatever work needed to be accomplished. It was not easy for others to live up to his expectations.

Matson tells us that 'Tomás is not an uncritical admirer [of the King], – he even complains that the King dislikes chat when there is work to be done'.[63] On one occasion, an unhappy King visited Tomás looking for his regular workmate who was missing:

> The King calls round to my house on his way back from the field to ask me where Tadhg the Joker [a pseudonym Tomás used for Seán Eoghain Ó Duinnshléibhe] was;

he had been lonesome after him since morning. 'But,' says he, 'he has lost his senses this year where work is concerned. He has been poor company.'

'But he says it is you that have lost yours!' I answered.[64]

In concluding the 'hill-side parliament' of island elders described by Robin Flower, the King again demonstrates his 'nose to the grindstone' attitude:

> A moment later, as though at a signal, all the speakers in this 'parle on a hill' rose up, and the King said meditatively: 'Well, talking never brought the turf home yet'; and, each recovering his ass, they scattered slowly over the wide arc of the rick-dotted hill.[65]

The King certainly did not expect others to wait on him. To the contrary, he was constantly busy tending to his duties as postman along with fishing, planting and caring for guests. In the process, he set a high standard for others. Matson tells us that 'Amid all this activity, he still found the time to rear a bullock or two.'[66]

According to Tomás:

> The King crossed over to the mainland. Whenever he has an important task in hand he takes his time until he has it completed. Then he saunters down the main road in full view so that everyone can see him – everyone, that is, who might have business on the mainland himself. They cannot fail to see him and, since his curragh is conveniently available, he is seldom without a crew for it, which is most convenient for him too. His pay is waiting for him on the table on the mainland, and he does not look askance at it, although there is many a King all over the world who would have a nosebleed at the thought of

earning a day's pay. But if they have no sense, our King here has no remedy for them.[67]

Clearly, Tomás did not hesitate to share his opinion with his lifelong friend, even suggesting that the King might be a bit too enthusiastic about his work. But the underlying message is clear. Peats Mhicí Ó Catháin was a hard-working King in every sense of the term.

Overall, the King was a remarkably well-rounded man with a big personality and natural leadership skills. Dáithí de Mórdha says that 'Pats Mhicí, the last King, was outgoing, chatty, had an opinion on local events, was loyal to the community's best interests, and a character ...'[68]

With his brute strength, his strong communication skills, his sensitivity to complicated situations, his work ethic and his dedication to service, Peats Mhicí earned the title of King of the Great Blasket every single day by his indomitable commitment to his duty as he saw it.

8. Island Visitors and the King

In the early twentieth century, a series of writers, scholars and other prominent people travelled to the Great Blasket for extended holidays. Collectively referred to on the island as the 'visitors', they were generally focused on improving their knowledge of the Irish language and studying the unique folk culture of the island. Essentially, they were 'cultural tourists'.

Visits to the Great Blasket generally occurred during the summer months when the weather was much more favourable and days were considerably longer. A few of the visitors returned several times over a period of as much as ten or eleven years.

The typical island stay involved fairly informal yet rigorous lessons in the Irish language. According to Mike Carney, 'The island was one of the few places where people spoke only Irish and its form of Irish was pure. If you were an Irish scholar, the island was the place to go. It was a kind of an educational holiday in a very beautiful place.'[1] The instructors were all islanders who were, of course, not at all trained as teachers. But they compensated for their lack of credentials by providing a highly effective language and social immersion experience over a period of weeks or sometimes even months.

Island culture was also regarded as worthy of study. Distinctive because of its isolation, the Great Blasket seemed unaffected by the corroding influences of the steadily evolving

The King's house, on the right, is where John Millington Synge and Carl Marstrander stayed, and Robin Flower during his first visit. The King's daughter Máire (Ní Chatháin) Uí Ghuithín's house, on the left, is where Flower stayed on subsequent visits, as well as Kenneth Jackson and other visitors. This photo was taken after the King's death. His son, Seán An Rí, can be seen in front of Máire's house. Photo by Thomas Waddicor

culture on mainland and the increasing exposure to the advantages of life in America. The island was a place that afforded rare and valuable insight into an earlier and far less complex way of life.

The arrival of visitors always created excitement on the Great Blasket:

> It was always a big deal when the visitors arrived. We could see them coming across the Sound in a *naomhóg* and we always gave them a big welcome. When the visitors landed, we would greet them saying '*Fáilte, a dhuine uasal*' [Welcome, honourable sir]. This was a traditional

greeting in them days. The visitors would usually respond with '*Lá breá*' ['fine day']. These were often the only Irish words that they knew. So the islanders started to call the visitors the '*Lá breás*'.

There was no hotel on the island, so the visitors would stay with island families that had extra room. The visitors would pay for their room and board. It was a 'bed and breakfast' type of situation.'[2]

We learn from Seán Ó Criomhthain that the islanders recognised the new financial opportunities afforded by the influx of visitors and responded in kind by providing for the basic hospitality needs of the visitors as best they could:

> The island houses in those days weren't suitable for keeping visitors but those visitors didn't mind as long as they were taken in and given the same food as the islanders themselves ate. Visitors weren't charged thirty shillings a week. The charge was a mere ten shillings a week which was great money at that time. From then on the islanders weren't at all afraid of visitors.[3]

The King's friend, Tomás Ó Criomhthain, emerged as the premier resource for the teaching of Irish on the Great Blasket. Mairéad Nic Craith tells us:

> Tomás' friends were interested in the language and Gaelic culture when they arrived to the Blaskets, and they didn't have any particular interest in Tomás over the other Islanders. His reputation as a writer had not been established at this point and even though scholars such as Flower and Marstrander sought him out from early on, the reason he got to know them was, moreover, due to the fact that the guesthouse belonged to his brother in

law [the King], and they were happy for Tomás to get a few extra pennies ... It was this connection through marriage between himself and the King, as well as their longstanding friendship, that granted Tomás access to the visitors in the 'Palace' [the King's house].[4]

The King provided, in his own home, a new one-bedroom addition that doubled as a classroom where Carl Marstrander and Robin Flower were taught Irish by Ó Criomhthain. This room was known as 'the Norseman's room,' a reference to Marstrander. Nic Craith described this 'classroom' as follows:

> There is a window in this Palace which looks out to the open sea. The man himself has a table that runs across it, and he spreads his books out on it. He has a decorative chair and another chair for anyone he trusts enough at the other end of the table. There is not a saying that cannot be voiced at that table which's meaning and root cannot be seen with your very own eyes out this window, and it is my opinion there isn't a university window in the country that could compare in presenting such a vision before the eyes of the students, it wasn't difficult for anyone who called by to acquire precision and perfection of the language. There is not a colour ever seen by the eye, blue, green, white, purple, red or yellow, that cannot forever be seen from the window of the palace.[5]

Mike Carney tells us: 'We would have long conversations with other visitors in Irish and this would improve their knowledge of the language. And we would listen to the visitors and pick up some English. The learning was a two-way street.'[6]

While the principal focus of these visits was on language and culture, there was always time for fun:

The visitors loved to go hiking and swimming. And they loved the storytelling. They usually carried notebooks and they were constantly writing things down.

On nice days, we would take the visitors back up to the top of the hill to the Fort and the Crow [high points on the island] and show them the whole island. They would give us a shilling or two for our trouble.[7]

One highlight of these visits was always the evening get-togethers involving storytelling, music and dance. Sometimes held indoors in someone's house, and sometimes outdoors down by the pier in the summer when the weather allowed, these events featured displays of island talent, including the great *seanchaithe* or storytellers of the time. Everybody was invited to join in the festivities, visitors included.

Much or our understanding of the last King of the Great Blasket, Peats Mhicí Ó Catháin, and of life on the island in general comes from the writings of the visitors. Fascinated with this tiny kingdom with its very own King, they often described his role in some detail. Many shared nearly identical accounts of their initial arrival on the island including their first encounter with the King. It becomes apparent that this was almost a standard introductory ritual that made a huge and enduring impression on all who made the pilgrimage to the island.

The most important legacy of the visitors was in encouraging three of the islanders to write down their own stories and then helping them to do so. According to Mike Carney, 'This was the basis for all the great literature that came from the island.'[8] The famous island authors Tomás Ó Criomhthain, Muiris Ó Súilleabháin and Peig Sayers were all significantly influenced by the visitors and benefited greatly from their literary mentoring.

The literature of the Great Blasket provides an opportunity to understand the King better as a leader and as an individual

A young Seán
Ó Criomhthain, son
of Tomás and husband
of author Eibhlís Ní
Shúilleabháin, with his
fiddle. Photo by Carl
Von Sydow.

through the writings of the visitors. Unfortunately, not all visitors shared their impressions of the King, but what first-hand accounts we have are rich with recollections of and observations about of the King that are particularly valuable because they were written during the King's lifetime.

John Millington Synge (the Great Blasket Visit: 1905)

The first significant cultural visitor to the Great Blasket was author John Millington Synge. A learned man with bushy hair and a moustache, Synge sought out the rough island lifestyle despite his chronic health issues. Having some basic knowledge of Irish, his visit was primarily cultural in nature and followed his five earlier extended visits to the Aran Islands off Galway.[9]

The first major cultural visitor to the Great Blasket, Irish author John Millington Synge.

In *Hungry for Home*, author Cole Moreton describes Synge's arrival: 'One fine day in August 1905, a *naomhóg* crossed the Blasket Sound carrying a neat young man with a moustache, in a woollen suit. John Millington Synge, a 34-year-old graduate of the Royal Irish Academy, was a friend of the poet William Butler Yeats and had accepted the older man's advice to study what remained of the Irish language and culture in the most distant parts of the country.'[10]

In his book *On an Irish Island*, Robert Kanigel tells us:

He [Synge] stayed in the house of *an rí*, the king, who was no hereditary ruler at all but simply acknowledged for his strength and personal stature, much as tribal chieftains were in times past. His name was Pádraig Ó Catháin – Anglicized it would be Patrick Keane – and he spoke a little English, being among the few on the Island who did.[11]

At that time, the island was not accustomed to receiving guests. Previous visitors to the island had involved landlord agents and bailiffs seeking to collect rent. So the islanders can be excused for a bit of early suspicion of outsiders. But Synge was purely a cultural tourist. He also brought along something very rare on the island: a camera. In fact, Synge took some of the earliest photos of people and life on the island. It is through these photos and others that we are able to observe island life at the very beginning of the twentieth century.

The delight that Synge took in his visit to the Great Blasket is apparent as he recalls his trip across Blasket Sound with the island King, Peats Mhící, who is referred to in this narrative as 'my host'. He also describes his arrival on the island and his first impressions of the King's family:

> I came out to-day, a holiday, to the Great Blasket Island with a schoolmaster and two young men from the village, who were coming for the afternoon only. The day was admirably clear, with a blue sea and sky, and the voyage in the long canoe – I had not been in one for two or three years – gave me indescribable enjoyment. We passed Dunmore Head, and then stood Out [*sic*] nearly due west towards the Great Blasket itself, the height of the mountains round the bay and the sharpness of the rocks making the place singularly different from the sounds about Aran, where I had last travelled in a curragh. As usual, three men were rowing – the man I have come to stay with [the King], his son, and a tall neighbour, all dressed in blue jerseys, homespun trousers and shirts, and talking in Irish only, though my host could speak good English when he chose to. As we came nearer the island, which seemed to rise like a mountain straight out of the sea, we could make out a crowd of people in their holiday

clothes standing or sitting along the brow of the cliff watching our approach, and just beyond them a patch of cottages with roofs of tarred felt. A little later we doubled into a cove among the rocks, where I landed at a boat slip, and then scrambled up a steep zig-zag pathway to the head of the cliff where the people crowded round us and shook hands with the men who had come with me.

This cottage where I am to stay is one of the highest of the group, and as we passed up to it through little paths among the cottages many white, wolfish-looking dogs came out and barked furiously. My host had gone on in front with my bag, and when I reached his threshold he came forward and shook hands with me again, with a finished speech of welcome. His eldest daughter, a young married woman of about twenty, who manages the house, shook hands with me also, and then, without asking if we were hungry, began making us tea in a metal teapot and frying rashers of bacon. She is a small, beautifully-formed woman, with brown hair and eyes – instead of the black hair and blue eyes that are usually found with this type in Ireland – and delicate feet and ankles that are not common in these parts, where the woman's work is so hard. Her sister, who lives in the house also, is a bonny girl of about eighteen, full of humour and spirits.[12]

Synge is referring in this narrative to the King's two daughters. He calls the older Máire 'the little hostess' in his book *In Wicklow and West Kerry* and 'the little queen' in his contemporaneous notes. The younger Cáit is called 'the little princess.'[13] Synge also makes mention of them when recalling his first extended conversation with the King which took place quite late on his first night on the Great Blasket after an evening of music and conversation:

The King's daughter, Máire (Ní Chatháin) Uí Ghuithín, Synge's 'little hostess', beside the fire at her home.

At eleven o'clock the people got up as one man and went away, leaving me with the little hostess – the man of the house [the King] had gone to the mainland with the young men – her husband and sister. I told them I was sleepy, and ready to go to bed; so the little hostess lighted a candle, carried it into the room beyond the kitchen, and stuck it up on the end of the bedpost of one of the beds with a few drops of grease. Then she took off her apron, and fastened it up in the window as a blind, laid another apron on the wet earthen floor for me to stand on, and left me to myself. The room had two beds, running from wall to wall with a small space between them, a chair that the little hostess had brought in, an old hair brush that was propping the window open, and no other article. When I had been in bed for some time, I heard the host's voice in the kitchen, and a moment or two later he came in with a candle in his hand, and made a long apology for having been away the whole of my first evening on the island, holding the candle while he talked very close to my face. I told him I had been well entertained by his family and neighbours, and had hardly missed him. He went away, and half an hour later opened the door again with the iron spoon which serves to lift the latch, and came in, in a suit of white homespuns, and said he must ask me to let him stretch out in the other bed, as there was no place else for him to lie. I told him that he was welcome, and he got into the other bed and lit his pipe. Then we had a long talk about this place and America and the younger generations.[14]

That night, the King tells Synge about the challenges of the fishing business on the island and even voices his concern about what he sees as a disturbing deterioration in the quality of the island's youth, a concern typical among elder statesmen everywhere.

He also sheepishly asks for his new guest's name, a detail that apparently got lost in the shuffle of Synge's arrival on the island:

Then we talked about the chances of the mackerel season. 'If the season is good,' he said, 'we get on well; but it is not certain at all. We do pay four pounds for a net, and sometimes the dogfish will get into it the first day and tear it into pieces as if you'd cut it with a knife. Sometimes the mackerel will die in the net, and then ten men would be hard set to pull them up into the canoe, so that if the wind rises on us we must cut loose, and let down the net to the bottom of the sea. When we get fish here in the night we go to Dunquin and sell them to buyers in the morning; and, believe me, it is a dangerous thing to cross that sound when you have too great a load taken into your canoe. When it is too bad to cross over we do salt the fish ourselves – we must salt them cleanly and put them in clean barrels – and then the first day it is calm buyers will be out after them from the town of Dingle.'

Afterwards he spoke of the people who go away to America, and the younger generations that are growing up now in Ireland.

'The young people is no use,' he said. I am not as good a man as my father was, and my son is growing up worse than I am.' Then he put up his pipe on the end of the bed-post.

'You'll be tired now,' he went on, 'so it's time we were sleeping; and, I humbly beg your pardon, might I ask your name?' I told him.

'Well, good night so,' he said, 'and may you have a good sleep your first night in this island.'

Then he put out the candle and we settled to sleep. In a few minutes I could hear that he was in his dreams ...'[15]

Despite their late night of conversation, the King and Synge were up bright and early the next morning. It was a somewhat surprising wake-up call:

> I awoke in the morning about six o'clock, and not long afterwards the host awoke also, and asked how I did. Then he wanted to know if I ever drank whisky; and when he heard that I did so, he began calling for one of his daughters at the top of his voice. In a few moments the younger girl [Cáit] came in, her eyes closing with sleep, and, at the host's bidding, got the whisky bottle, some water, and a green wine-glass out of the kitchen. She came first to my bedside and gave me a dram, then she did the same for her father and brother, handed us our pipes and tobacco, and went back to the kitchen.[16]

As they discussed their plans for the day, the King played the role of host, going out of his way to protect the safety and even the sensibilities of his house guest:

> There were to be sports at noon in Ballyferriter, and when we had talked for a while I asked the host if he would think well of my going over to see them. 'I would not,' he said 'you'd do better to stay quiet in this place where you are; the men will be all drunk coming back, fighting and kicking in the canoes, and a man the like of you, who aren't used to us, would be frightened. Then, if you went, the people would be taking you into one public-house, and then into another, till you'd maybe get drunk yourself, and that wouldn't be a nice thing for a gentleman. Stay where you are in this island and you'll be safest so.'[17]

Synge took the King's advice and stayed on the island for the day, getting oriented to the village and its people. Eventually, the island men returned from their big excursion across Blasket Sound to Ballyferriter. The King's premonition about the potential rowdiness of the trip to 'the sports' proved accurate:

> ... some one said a niavogue was on its way home from the sports. We went out to the door, but it was too dark to see anything except the lights of a little steamer that was passing up the sound, almost beneath us, on its way to Limerick or Tralee. When it had gone by we could hear a furious drunken uproar coming up from a canoe that was somewhere out in the bay. It sounded as if the men were strangling or murdering each other, and it seemed almost miraculous that they should be able to manage their canoe. The people seemed to think they were in no special danger, and we went in again to the fire and talked about porter and whisky ... A little later some young men came in, in their Sunday clothes, and told us the news of the sports.[18]

It is apparent that Synge was quite captivated with the King's daughter Máire, known on the island as 'Máire Pheats Mhicí' who, at the time, was managing the King's house where Synge was staying. There is even a hint of mild flirting between them. Yet, the then 23-year-old Máire is a recently married woman, having wedded islander Mícheál Ó Guithín just the previous February.

This beautiful young woman was apparently the inspiration for one of the immortal figures of Irish stage history, Pegeen Mike (meaning little Peg, daughter of Mike), the lead female character in Synge's famous and somewhat controversial play, *The Playboy of the Western World*. Synge continues his commentary and goes on to describe her personality as well as her physical appearance:

I showed them some photographs of the Aran Islands and Wicklow, which they looked at with eagerness. The little hostess [Máire] was especially taken with two or three that had babies or children in their foreground; and as she put her hands on my shoulders, and leaned over to look at them, with the confidence that is so usual in these places, I could see that she had her full share of the passion for children which is so powerful in all women who are permanently and profoundly attractive.[19]

Later that day, Synge was caught in the rain during a walk on the island and returned to take shelter at the King's house in a soaking-wet state:

Before I reached the house the cloud had turned to a sharp shower of rain, and as I went in the water was dripping from my hat. 'Oh! dear me,' said the little hostess, when she saw me, 'Ta tu an-rhluc anois' (You are very wet now). She was alone in the house, breathing audibly with a sort of simple self-importance, as she washed her jugs and teacups.[20]

Another day, when the King and Cáit had gone to the mainland, Synge is left alone with Máire. While combing out her hair, she asks him about the letters he has received and succeeds in persuading him to reveal their contents, a process which was interrupted by Cáit's arrival back home.[21] In another instance, Máire helps Synge make the most of a rainy day, when fishing would have been difficult if not impossible. As the islanders pass time mending fishing nets in the King's house, she assists him in taking care of some lapsed personal grooming:

While they were at work [on the nets] the kitchen emptied and filled continually with islanders passing in and out, and discussing the weather and the season. Then they started cutting each other's hair, the man who was being cut sitting with an oilskin round him on a little stool by the door, and some other men came in to sharpen their razor on the host's [the King's] razor-strop, which seems to be the only one on the island. I had not shaved since I arrived so the little hostess asked me after a while if I would like to shave myself before dinner. I told her I would, so she got me some water in the potato-dish and put it on a chair; then her sister got me a little piece of broken looking-glass and put it on a nail near the door, where there was some light. I set to work, and as I stood with my back to the people I could catch a score of eyes in the glass, watching me intently. 'That is a great improvement to you now,' said the host, when I had done; 'and whenever you want a beard, God bless you, you'll have a thick one surely.'[22]

The King invited his visitor to participate in evening story-telling, music and dance. Synge even played a couple of tunes on the fiddle when it was his turn. Synge describes the King getting into the act himself:

After the dance the host, who had come in, sang a long English doggerel about a poor scholar who went to Maynooth [seminary] and had great success in his studies, so that he was praised by the bishop. Then he went home for his holiday, and a young woman who had great riches asked him into her parlour and told him it was no fit life for a fine young man to be a priest, always saying Mass for poor people, and that he would have a right to give up his Latin and get married to herself. He refused her offers and went back to his college. When he was gone she went to the justice in great anger, and swore an oath against him that he had seduced her and left her with child. He was brought back for his trial, and he was to be degraded and hanged, when a man rode up on a horse and said it was himself was the lover of the lady, and the father of her child.[23]

After his sixteen-day holiday on the Great Blasket, it was time for Synge to return to Dublin. The King would provide transportation across Blasket Sound to Dunquin. Máire presented Synge with a modest parting gift: a clean handkerchief. It was a heartfelt farewell indeed:

> I have left the island again. I walked round the cliffs in the morning, and then packed my bag in my room, several girls putting their heads Into [*sic*] the little window while I did so, to say it was a great pity I was not staying on for another week or a fortnight. Then the men went off with my bag in a heavy shower, and I waited a minute or two while the little hostess buttered some bread for my lunch, and tied it up in a clean handkerchief of her own. Then I bid them good-bye, and set off down to the slip with three girls, who came with me to see that I did not go astray among the innumerable paths. It was still raining heavily, so I told them to put my cape, which they were carrying, over their heads. They did so with delight, and ran down the path before me, to the great amusement of the islanders. At the head of the cliff many people were standing about to bid me good-bye and wish me a good voyage.
>
> The wind was in our favour, so the men took in their oars after rowing for about a quarter of a mile and lay down in the bottom of the canoe, while one man ran up the sail, and the host [the King] steered with an oar.

At Dunquin the host hired me a dray, without springs, kissed my hand in farewell, and I was driven away.[24]

Several aspects of Synge's narrative gave rise to some controversy on the island after his account of the visit was published in the journal *The Shanachie* in 1907 and later as a book entitled *In Wicklow and West Kerry*. The first issue was the suggestion that the 'little hostess' might have overdone it on the hospitality, serving up bacon to Synge without being asked. But the islanders felt that 'Hospitality to strangers is one of the highest duties, and criticising their hospitality – however mildly – one of the greatest sins.' In another mild affront, Máire took exception to the passage about using her apron for curtains. She insisted that the house had curtains made in America.[25] Finally, there was Synge's published reference to her feet and ankles, which could have been a bit embarrassing for her.

Taken in context, these perceived slights to Máire were probably unintentional, especially given his comment about her beauty, his flirting with her and a beautiful poem of appreciation he wrote about her.[26] But the most important consideration here may be Synge's apparent choice of Máire as the prototype for the heroine Pegeen Mike. In fact, the most important thing Synge took from his stay on the Great Blasket may have been his vivid impression of the King's family and of his 'little hostess', Máire. Synge could have paid no higher tribute to Máire than to borrow heavily on her life story to create the unforgettable Pegeen Mike.

Kanigel succinctly summarises the case made by multiple literary scholars, including the American scholar and Synge's biographer, David H. Green:

The real Máire and the fictional Pegeen are about the same age. Both tend to their father's affairs, presiding over the place where most of the action takes place. Both do so ably; all their actions suggest competence and lively intelligence; Máire, like Pegeen, is a 'big' figure, no mere drudge supplying a servant's labor in exchange for the ten pence a week Synge paid for room and board. And just as Pegeen showers Christy [the main male character] with attention once she falls under his spell, so Máire does Synge.[27]

It is ironic that such a key figure in Irish literary history was the unfortunate target of unintended slights by Synge. He would have been very disappointed indeed.

Méiní, the Blasket nurse, gives us another not-so-positive perspective on Synge's visit. Her biographer Leslie Matson tells us:

Méiní records how he [Synge] went around making pencil sketches, and his photographs are among the earliest taken on the island. She expresses surprise that Synge stayed so long there, because the villagers, amused by his strange gait, constantly made fun of him. 'If I had been in his shoes,' Méiní comments, 'I wouldn't have stayed one week on the island. He didn't understand the mockery that the islanders were directing at him and they didn't know that he was writing about them.'[28]

This view overlooks the fact that Synge's apparent intent was to portray Blasket life accurately as he saw it. He seemed to convey genuine appreciation for the hospitality he was shown, particularly by the King and Máire. Furthermore, the photos he took indicate a high level of sensitivity to the people of the island.[29]

While it is clear that later sentiment about Synge's visit was somewhat mixed, this reaction gives us a keen insight into the clash of two perspectives: that of the visitor observing a folk lifestyle that had largely disappeared elsewhere, with a fiercely proud community that tolerated no denigration of their way of life, however minor. Despite the controversy, the fact that the islanders went on to welcome other visitors would suggest that any ill feeling in the aftermath of their experience with Synge was quite short-lived.

On the distinctly more positive side, Synge's assessment of conditions on the Great Blasket was 'very different from what had previously been written about the Blaskets by Protestant missionaries, bailiffs and land-agents'.[30] These include Mrs D. P. Thomson in 1843 and Jeremiah Curtin in 1892 who were alarmed by the poverty and lack of education.[31]

The inescapable conclusion is that conditions on the island had noticeably improved over time. As Australian scholar Irene Lucchitti wrote:

> Synge's description of the physical aspects of domestic life on the Island contains no hint of the deprivation that dominated earlier descriptions of Island life. Instead, he portrays a host who, with an unstinting hospitality, offers him all that he has, and meets all of his needs. He shows the community's acceptance of their visitor when they come to the king's house to dance in the kitchen amid swirling dust, in a curious display of gaiety and solemnity combined.[32]

The assertion here that the King provided 'unstinting hospitality' and that community acceptance was evident in the welcoming event in the King's house are particularly telling about the King's approach to the island's first significant visitor.

Kanigel makes the following observations about conditions on the Great Blasket at the time of Synge's visit and of the King himself:

He [Synge] kept a notebook – 'Notes in Ballyferriter and the Great Blasket Island, August, 1905' – but also took pictures. And both tell of a place far better off than others, like Jeremiah Curtin or Mrs. Thomson, had intimated a generation before. The villagers were poor, certainly. But the period right after the turn of the century was a relatively prosperous one and you can see it in Synge's photos. In one, taken in front of the King's house, the sun streams in from high overhead. The men, in sweaters and caps, don't look ragged. They don't look forlorn. The king himself, head amiably cocked, a little welcome smile on his face, a picture of confidence and composure, wears a jaunty flared hat. His daughter Cáit could pass fashion muster even today. She wears a long skirt, perhaps from America, with a cinched waist, decorated with fabric strips at the hem; a belt with a metal buckle that looks like the Celtic pewter you find today in Irish handicraft stores; a string of beads down the front of her long-sleeved blouse, with little flounces at the wrists.[33]

From all accounts of his visit, it is clear that Synge was more of an observer than an active participant in the life of the island. He did not even try to become one of them. For the islanders' part, they were not used to visitors at that time. Perhaps there was some mutual wariness at play. According to Seán Ó Criomhthain:

All this man wanted was to be indoors from the night-sky and get a bite to eat sometime during the day. He told the man of the house [the King] that he was a writer and that writing was his livelihood. He spent a fortnight on the Island and wrote about everything which he witnessed with his own two eyes. Having written about all that was to be seen he went off by sea again.[34]

The King could not have known it at the time, but Synge's visit was the harbinger of things to come. Through his own natural instinct for hospitality, he had unwittingly played a key role in establishing the Great Blasket as a significant cultural tourism destination. Many more visitors would follow over the years and the splendid isolation of the island was about to change.

Regrettably, Synge's life took a turn an unexpected turn for the worse soon after his brief stint on the Great Blasket. This young and already accomplished author and playwright took ill and died just six years later, before he turned forty, a victim of Hodgkin's disease.[35]

Carl Marstrander (the Great Blasket Visit: 1907)

The next historically significant cultural visitor to the Great Blasket, and the first visitor from beyond the British Isles, was Carl Johan Sverdrup Marstrander from Norway. Born in 1883, he was twenty-four years old at the time of his visit, arriving in August 1907. He stayed for about five months, until just before Christmas. Marstrander was a linguist by profession and his specialty was the Irish language. His primary interest in travelling to the Great Blasket was to study the purest form of Irish he could find. Later, Marstrander was a long-time professor at the University of Oslo in Norway.[36]

Marstrander's physical appearance was quite different from the islanders'. Seán Ó Criomhthain tells us: 'He was a strong, hardy and athletic man over six feet in height and had little spare flesh on him but he was as healthy as a salmon.'[37] Blasket legend has it that Marstrander, a pole-vault champion back home in Norway, qualified to represent his country in the 1908 Olympic Games held in London, but gave up his place on Norway's team to pursue his interest in the Great Blasket.[38] According to the legend, one time he jumped right over a house on the island using the mast from a *naomhóg* for a pole.[39] Whether this is true or not is impossible to ascertain, but the story lives on in Blasket folklore. This story may account for at least some small part of the great admiration of the islanders had for the man.

As in the case of Synge, the King acted as host and as overall facilitator of Marstrander's visit. Seán Ó Criomhthain describes Marstrander's arrival on the Great Blasket as follows:

> As soon as he reached Dingle he began to make enquiries and found out that an islander named Ó Catháin lived in the town. Ó Catháin was a relative of our own. He told Marstrander that the living Irish was to the west and that the best place for him to go was west and if he could to go to the Blasket ... so he went to Dunquin where he met with the postman and made arrangements with him to go in. He also got lodgings in the postman's house. That man was the King. They set off and Marstrander was delighted. They reached the Island and Marstrander got out of the nayvogue on to the pier ... He went to the King's house and stayed there. Next day he went around the village and had a look around. He asked the King endless questions and the King sent him to my father who he knew could read and write Irish. He also told Marstrander that if my father couldn't fill the bill there was nothing more he himself could do.[40]

Kanigel shares a story that Robin Flower heard directly from Marstrander himself about the moment of the latter's embarkation on the island and his introduction to the King where he offered a few words in broken Irish:

> What happened next is today firmly enshrined in Blasket lore, not least because Marstrander so delighted in telling it. On his arrival, he was met by a delegation of villagers. The king welcomed him with an old Irish greeting. Marstrander expressed thanks in his best Irish, Ta buiochas agam ort a Rí, [I am grateful to you, King] making 'an honest attempt to get my tongue right for this unusual sound.' He failed, utterly. Um, yes, the king replied with consummate grace, the Norwegian language was quite a nice one.[41]

Obviously, the King was sensitive to Marstrander's sincere effort to make a good first impression. While he was puzzled by Marstrander's words which were so garbled that he mistook them for Norwegian, he was also quick on his feet with a clever response that would avoid embarrassing the visitor in his first moments on the island.

Actually, the Great Blasket was Marstrander's second choice as a venue for his immersion in Irish. Ballyferriter had been his original destination, but he was put off by the more bilingual nature of that community. Too much English was spoken in Ballyferriter for his particular purpose. Writing in *The Islandman,* Tomás Ó Criomhthain describes the situation:

> One Sunday at the beginning of July a canoe from Dunquin brought a gentleman to the Blasket. He was a tall, lean, fair-complexioned, blue-eyed man. He had only a flavouring of Irish on his tongue. He went among the people and observed them, and in the evening, he asked some of them whether he could find a place to stay. They told him he could, and he arranged to lodge in

the King's house, and went back again without saying or doing anything else.

Not much of the Monday had gone when he had all his traps collected. He was asked what was the reason he didn't stay in Ballyferriter parish, and he said there was too much English mixed with their Irish, and that didn't suit him; that his business was to get the fine flower of the speech, and that he has observed that the best Irish was here. He asked the King who was the best man to teach him Irish. The King explained to him that I was the man, for I was able to read it and had fine, correct Irish before I ever read it. He came to me at once and questioned me. He put a book before me, '*Niamh*.' 'You're all right, but have you got English?' says he.

'I haven't got a great deal of English, sir,' says I to him. 'That'll do,' says he.

The first day we came together he gave me the style of 'master'.

This was Carl Marstrander ... He spent five months in the Blasket. One sitting a day we had for half that time... He put another question to me: Was it possible for me to spend two sittings a day with him?[42]

Tomás did not hesitate to emphasise his 'own skills and accomplishments' in his very first meeting with Marstrander. Obviously, he was pleased to be able to play his self-described role as 'master' or teacher.[43]

Marstrander was eager to accomplish as much as possible while he was on the Great Blasket. For the couple of weeks at the end of his sojourn, Marstrander's Irish classes were extended from a single evening session from seven to ten o'clock to include a second tutoring session at around midday.[44]

Norwegian visitor to the Great Blasket, Carl Marstrander (photo taken long after his Blasket visit).

During his extended visit to the Great Blasket, Marstrander stayed with the King in 'the palace.' Seán Ó Criomhthain describes the stay: 'Yes, in the King's house. He [Marstrander] and the King and the King's son Seán, God be good to them, were great friends. He settled in on the Blasket and spent twenty-one weeks there speaking nothing whatsoever but Irish, but I was young then and didn't take any interest in their conversations.'[45]

At first, Marstrander was not altogether pleased with his living accommodation in the King's fairly sparse house. He asked the King to make a window for his windowless room and also reported rivulets of rainwater on the floor and mould accumulating on his clothing.[46] The accommodation was particularly important to Marstrander because he took his

Irish lessons from Tomás in this room. Repairs were in order[47] and the King proceeded to upgrade the facilities accordingly.

In contrast to Synge, who was a bit of a loner during his earlier visit, Marstrander was fully engaged and quite popular on the island:

> Marstrander cut a different figure from the solitary Synge ... He soon came to be known as *An Lochlannach*, 'the Viking', a nick-name that conveyed both the affection and the admiration that the islanders felt for him. Island memory of him long after his departure is evident in a letter the king wrote to Flower in 1911, in which mention is made of an *seomra Lochlannaigh* [the Viking's room] (the King's bedroom) some three or four years after his only visit.[48]

The King's long bilateral correspondence with Marstrander is clearly indicative of their feelings for each other. Tomás maintained a separate correspondence with Marstrander for a similar period of time. These friendships were genuine.

Marstrander was a very perceptive man and managed to put his finger one of the great paradoxes of life on the Great Blasket: 'Their outward lives were miserable, yet perhaps – he simply couldn't say for sure – they were happy. "The wet cliffs out there are their whole world. They have no longing for a richer life led under brighter conditions because they have never known anything better."'[49]

That comfortable equilibrium was soon to change, however, as the islanders, through their interaction with visitors as well as from letters sent back to the island by relatives in America were to be exposed to a much higher quality of life beyond the island. By comparison, life on the island seemed sorely lacking in many ways.

Marstrander's visit to the island was historically significant to the Great Blasket for a number of reasons: first, it involved an acknowledgement that the islanders had something of value to offer. According to Kanigel, 'Marstrander lent them stature. They were fisherman? Yes, but something in how they lived was precious and rare.' Secondly, it brought into focus the islanders' expertise in the Irish language. 'Blasket Irish, they came away half convinced, wasn't just Irish, it was the best Irish, the purest.' And thirdly, it spread the awareness of this authentic Irish community with rich language and culture among a wide community of scholars, and it led to the subsequent visits by more scholars over a period of years. Quoting Bo Almqvist, a Swedish scholar of the Great Blasket in the next century, Kanigel tells us that 'It was Marstrander who started the whole thing ... Without Marstrander ... there would hardly be a Blasket culture, and no Blasket writings.'[50]

Whether the King appreciated the significance of Marstrander's visit is doubtful. Yet he certainly played the pivotal role in welcoming his guest with open arms and creating a positive environment where he could pursue his cultural and linguistic mission.

Marstrander subsequently spent some time in Dublin, teaching at the School of Irish Learning which had been established in 1903 by German scholar Kuno Mayer.[51] But, like Synge, he never visited the Great Blasket again, dying in Oslo at the age of eighty-two on 23 December 1965 after a highly successful academic career.[52]

Eibhlín Nic Niocaill (the Great Blasket Visit: 1909)

Eibhlín Nic Niocaill was a Celtic scholar and a student at the School of Irish Learning in Dublin. Regarded as the girlfriend of the famous Irish patriot and newspaperman Pádraig

Eibhlín Nic Niocaill at her graduation with honours from the Royal University, now University College Dublin.

Pearse, she was also an avid feminist.[53] Nic Niocaill visited the Great Blasket for an extended period in the summer of 1909 at the age of twenty-four.[54] She was very popular on the island and enthusiastically participated in the social life of the community.

Nic Niocaill frequently gave swimming lessons to the island children. This was a huge contribution to the island, because almost no islander knew how to swim.[55] This lack of swimming skill seems incongruous with the islanders' lifestyle. They were constantly surrounded by water, they made their living fishing from unstable *naomhóga* and they frequently crossed the rough waters of Blasket Sound back and forth from Dunquin.

But, according to Gearoíd 'Cheaist' Ó Catháin, 'Most of the fisherman never learned how to swim, as they felt it would be better to drown quickly rather than put up a fight. Also, the sea was viewed as a place of work, not of leisure, as the waters around the Great Blasket were strong and dangerous.'[56]

Mícheál Ó Dubhshláine described Nic Niocaill's arrival on the Great Blasket in July 1909 as follows:

'Eibhlín [Nic Niocaill] was led to the King's house and her luggage followed.

They did succeed in getting lodgings for Eibhlín in Peats Mhicí's (Pádraig Ó Catháin), the King's house ... Peats Mhicí had added an extension to his house for visitors ...

When the rowers had partaken of refreshment and listened to a few tunes on the fiddle, they set out again to row home across the straits. Eibhlín waved them goodbye from the Deck [a lookout point] above the pier where she could watch them until they disappeared out of view.

From the moment Eibhlín set foot on the island, she felt at home, and it didn't take long for her to get to know the people, both young and old. The King's daughter, Cáit an Rí, remembered her many years after at the nightly gatherings in the island homes at the storytelling, the music and the dancing: 'At all the gatherings Eibhlín was the life and soul of the party. She was so light on her feet, a withered leaf would not be crumpled by her.'[57]

She soon got to know ... the King's family, the father, mother and the young ones, Cáit and Seán. They had another son, Maidhc, but he had gone to America a few years previously; and then there was Máire (Synge's 'little hostess' who was the prototype for Pegeen Mike in *The Playboy of the Western World*), who was married to Mícheál Ó Guithín and lived next door. Synge had been attracted to her when he visited in 1905. At that time she had taken care of him in her father's house. Now she had two or three young children, including the baby, Máire, who had been born on the ninth of last June.

Cáit, later known as 'Cáit an Rí', or 'the Princess', became very friendly with Eibhlín ... Cáit an Rí had many happy memories of those days with Eibhlín ...

Small wonder Eibhlín enjoyed this land of magic. She confided to Cáit an Rí, 'As long as I live, I will return here.'[58]

Nic Niocaill obviously did not know it at the time, but she had only a few days to live.

On the morning of Friday, 13 August 1909 (yes, a Friday the thirteenth; and the islanders were very superstitious) Nic Niocaill visited the King's daughter Máire's house to admire her new baby, also named Máire. Nic Niocaill lifted little Máire, commonly called Máire Mhaidhc Léan, from her cradle and cuddled her gently.[59] That must have been an awkward moment for Máire Pheats Mhicí. Earlier that day, Tomás Ó Criomhthain's eighteen-year-old son and her own first cousin, Dómhnall Ó Criomhthain, had apparently disclosed to her his love for Nic Niocaill. But, it was probably just a one-sided dalliance on his part. Nic Niocaill, of course, was already spoken for, and she was six years older than Dómhnall.[60]

That very afternoon, Nic Niocaill was teaching twenty-year-old Cáit Ní Chriomhthain, Tomás Ó Criomhthain's daughter, how to swim off *An Tráigh Bháin*. The King's younger daughter, Cáit An Rí, was with them at the strand too, although she was not feeling well and decided not to swim that day. Nic Niocaill had asked her mother to send a new swimsuit to the island as a gift for Cáit An Rí. The package arrived and was opened with great fanfare. Cáit An Rí so taken with the colourful swimsuit that she said it would be a shame to wear something so nice in the water because it might fade. Nevertheless, since she had decided not to go swimming, she lent the new swimsuit to her first cousin, Cáit Ní Chriomhthain.[61]

The water off the strand was fairly calm that day, but suddenly there was panic as a wave hit Cáit Ní Chriomhthain. She lost her footing and swallowed some water. She grabbed Nic Niocaill and there was much thrashing about. The tide was going out, pulling them out with it. Soon the two were near exhaustion. Cáit An Rí splashed into the water, trying to help. While she got close, she could not reach them to pull them to shore.[62]

While all this was unfolding, Dómhnall Ó Criomhthain, Tomás Ó Criomhthain's son, was working just above the strand. Méiní (Ní Shé) Uí Dhuinnshléibhe, who witnessed the event, said that as soon as Dómhnall saw the situation, he ran as fast as he could to the strand. According to an interview with Nic Niocaill's friend James H. Cousins published in the *Cork Constitution*, Dómhnall prevented his sister Cáit from 'making a noble but fruitless sacrifice of her life'.[63] He dived into the water fully clothed, heavy hobnail boots and all, in a desperate attempt to rescue the two struggling swimmers.[64]

Despite Dómhnall's valiant efforts, both he and Nic Niocaill drowned. Cáit Ní Chriomhthain nearly drowned too, but was pulled to safety in a *naomhóg* by Peats Tom Ó Ceárna 'at her last breath'.[65] Cáit An Rí also survived, but was badly shaken.

Tomás Ó Criomhthain arrived on the scene just after the bodies had been recovered from the water. Upon realising that one of the deceased was his son Dómhnall, he let out an almost inhuman wail of sorrow and horror that could be heard throughout the nearby island village.[66]

After the drownings, Nic Niocaill's body was brought to the King's house where she had been staying. Dómhnall's body was brought home to the Ó Criomhthain home.[67] Two wakes were held on the island that night.[68] Cáit Ní Chriomhthain was brought to the King's daughter Máire Pheats Mhicí's house to recover from her own near-drowning.[69]

When the bodies were transported across Blasket Sound for burial the next day, the sad procession of twenty *naomhóga* in the form of a cross was led by the King's *naomhóg* carrying Nic Niocaill's coffin.[70] The convoy of heartbroken mourners was greeted in Dunquin by a throng of people from all over West Kerry and beyond. Dómhnall was buried in the graveyard in Baile an Teampaill, Dunquin.[71] Nic Niocaill's body was placed in St Gobnet's Church overnight, transported to Dingle and then to Dublin by train where there was a huge funeral followed by burial in Glasnevin cemetery.[72]

Before Nic Niocaill's body was transported to Dublin, Cáit An Rí and Dómhnall's father, Tomás Ó Criomhthain, were taken to meet briefly with Nic Niocaill's parents. It must have been a terrible moment of shared loss and grieving.[73]

For his heroic efforts in saving Cáit Ní Chriomhthain, Peats Tom Ó Ceárna was awarded a bronze medal by the King of England himself on 15 October 1910. He wore it proudly for special occasions throughout his life.[74]

While there is no information about the emotional impact of this horrible series of events on the King, one can imagine that they were substantial. After all, Nic Niocaill was a guest in his home and she was waked there was well. As Nic Niocaill's best friend on the island, Cáit An Rí was distraught. In addition to enduring her own near-death trauma, she was left to live with the grief of her failed attempt at rescuing the beloved visitor. One imagines that it took her and all the King's household quite some time to recover in the aftermath.

At this time of extraordinary stress, however, the King understood his proper role in the proceedings and he played a leading part under very trying circumstances.

Robin Flower (the Great Blasket Visits: 1910–1914 and various years to 1939)

Of all the King's guests, the visitor who would maintain the longest-term relationship with the Great Blasket was Robin Ernest William Flower. Born in Leeds, England, in 1881, and educated at Pembroke College, Oxford, Flower went to work at the British Museum in London in 1906[75] where he was Deputy Curator from 1929 to 1944.[76] His first visit to the Great Blasket was in 1910 when he was twenty-nine years old.[77]

According to Mike Carney:

> The visitor who made the biggest impression on me was Robin Flower. He was a student of Marstrander's and a keeper or curator at the British Museum in London. He came back to the island year after year.
>
> Flower's nickname was 'Little Flower' or '*Bláithín*' … He often brought his wife and his family with him. One time he took a leave of absence from his job and spent a whole year on the island with his family …
>
> Flower used to sit down with the people and smoke a cigarette. He was interested in learning as much as he could about island life. We would talk in Irish and English intermixed. The islanders felt that Flower had earned the right to be called an islander.[78]

Flower was encouraged to go to the Great Blasket by Carl Marstrander who was convinced of the value of the cultural immersion experience. According to Seán Ó Criomhthain*:*

A scholarly young Robin Flower at about the time of his first visit to the Great Blasket in 1910.

After returning from the Island to England he [Carl Marstrander] called to Bláithín at the British Museum and informed him that he had just been in the best schoolroom for learning Irish ... Bláithín himself packed his bags the following year and didn't stop nor stay until he reached the Blasket. He was given a room by the King and his daughter Cáit an Rí, a woman who, the Lord have mercy on the dead, was well able to look after him and give him plenty of Irish. He asked Cáit where Marstrander's teacher [Tomás Ó Criomhthain] lived.

'If you looked out the window,' said Cáit an Rí, 'you could see the top of his chimney below the bank.'

'I must call to him,' he said.[79]

Flower was enthusiastic about the cultural environment he found on the Great Blasket. According to Kanigel:

> Flower had been at the [British] Museum for four years when, in August 1910, age twenty-eight, he arrived in the Blaskets. He wrote, with characteristic lightness, from the house of the king: 'I am safe here in the royal palace, which consists of a fair-sized cabin with an earthen floor and two small rooms built on it to accommodate visitors.' He briefly described the village, the houses 'thrown down anywhere where they can find a bit of reasonably level ground,' the *naomhógs* and their curiously stunted oar-blades. He was finally learning to row them, he wrote, after earlier being unable to synchronize with the man behind him. He was happily boating, bathing, reading. 'I lead the life,' he wrote 'of Tír na nÓg [a mythical Irish land of perpetual youth) here'.[80]

Flower describes his very first arrival on the Great Blasket with the King, Peats Mhicí, rowing the *naomhóg* across Blasket Sound:

> We have come in on the post-boat. The big, heavy man with the broad, benignant face and the easy authoritative air as of the captain of a coasting schooner, who leads the way up the path, carries a bag slung over his shoulder. He is the King of the Island, Pádraig Ó Catháin ... He halts on the broad space at the top of the cliff, unslings and opens his bag, and the children gather excitedly round him while he perches a pair of spectacles on his nose and, taking out the letters one by one, reads the addresses aloud. As each address is read a child puts out an eager hand and runs off with the letter to its destination. When

all the letters are gone, and all the crowd dispersed, we move on up the village.[81]

Marstrander had told Flower of his own earlier arrival on the island and 'the laughably miscued Irish between him and the king ... Two months later, like Synge and Marstrander before him, he was in the home of the island king'.[82] As with Marstrander, Tomás Ó Criomhthain was Flower's teacher or 'master'. On this, Flower's first visit to the Blaskets, the King would have been about fifty-three years old. His daughter Cáit was about twenty-four and would have been managing the King's house at this time, though her older sister Máire, now living with her own family next door, probably helped out occasionally.[83]

The following year, Flower brought his young bride Ida Marie Streeter to stay on the island. It was a homecoming of sorts for the King's guest and he gives a vivid description of Cáit gathering the rambunctious children of the island to get their share of the sweets that the Flowers had brought for them.[84] He also describes his dramatic reunion with Tomás Ó Criomhthain.

> Then we enter the King's kitchen, he sets down his bag, and in formal and eloquent words welcomes us back to the Island. We are happy to be here again, and, as friend following friend comes forward to greet us, it is as though from a long absence we were at last home once more.
>
> In Dingle we have provided ourselves with a large can of mixed sweets, and as the news spreads through the houses, there is an instantaneous mobilization of the infantry. The kitchen fills at a rush with wild-haired children, the whole mass swaying with an odd movement, which is a curious mixture of thrusting

forward and drawing back, of boldness and modesty, of good manners and eagerness. The King's daughter marshals the irregular forces and, one by one, they shuffle forward and retire, each happy with a handful of sweets. The kitchen gradually empties as they run out on to the hill to gloat over their prize. But a sudden feeling comes upon you of a new presence in the room. You look up and see, leaning against the wall almost with the air of a being magically materialized out of nothing, a slight but confident figure. The face takes your attention at once and holds it. This face is dark and thin, and there look out of it two quick and living eyes, the vivid witnesses of a fine and self-sufficing intelligence. He comes toward you, and with a grave and courteous intonation, and a picked and running phrase, bids you welcome. You have indeed come home, for this is Tomás Ó Crithin, the Island poet and storyteller.[85]

Flower became almost a regular fixture on the island, returning year after year with his expanding family:

As we've seen, Flower returned to the island in 1911; then he came again every year through 1914. In 1913, he wrote Kuno Meyer [a German Celtic studies scholar and first Director of the School of Irish learning in Dublin where Marstrander taught for a time] that he'd had a productive time, transcribing island stories for three hours a day, hunting rabbits with the king's son, Seán. In 1914 he was on the island when word reached them that the Austrian archduke had been assassinated, setting off the Great War. It was 1925 before Flower returned, this time with his children, as he would many times more over the rest of his life.[86]

Robin Flower with Tomás Ó Criomhthain outside the latter's house. Photo by Thomas Mason.

After his initial visit, the Flower and his wife stayed with the King's daughter Máire and her family. Even though Máire's house was bigger than the King's, it must have been crowded, especially as the Flowers added more children to their brood. In 1925, for example, Flower with his wife and son Patrick stayed there, while his daughters Barbara, Síle and Jean stayed with the King's brother Mícheál 'Bofar' Ó Catháin on one of the 'new houses' next to Peig Sayers at Slinneán Bán at the top of the village.[87] For a time, Flower's children even attended the Blasket school.[88]

Flower very much enjoyed being part of the spontaneous give-and-take of daily conversation on the Great Blasket. There is no indication that his presence interfered with the free exchange of views. He referred to the following discussion as a 'hill-side parliament' with a group of island elders and 'the King on his throne':

> I had caught up with the company now, and we moved along slowly, losing one of our number every now and then as a man and an ass detached themselves, to climb the slope where their own rick showed upon the side of the hill. When we had gone some way back along the Island we came across upon a little group of men, the King one of them, lying on the grass sunning themselves and smoking, while their asses strayed and grazed about them. 'It's a parliament,' said one of the men with me, 'and the King on his throne in the middle of them.' I sat down among the rest, and the flood of talk, interrupted a moment by my coming, resumed its headlong flow. They had been discussing something I had said the night before about the earlier inhabitants of the Island. One of them turned to me, a little man whose face carries on it always an expression equally divided between a country shrewdness and an intense and puzzled surprise.
>
> 'They tell me, Bláheen,' he said (for that is the name I have on the Island, a diminutive for the Irish word for 'flower'), 'that you said last night that there were men living on the Island a thousand years ago.'
>
> 'There were' I answered, 'and it's a wonder to me how they lived.'
>
> 'And who would they be? I've heard tell that the Danes were in it once.'
>
> 'Yes, I said, 'the Danes were here once, but these were earlier than the Danes, men of religion. [There is then debate about this assertion and some doubt expressed.]
>
> ...

'And why wouldn't you [believe it's true],' broke in another, 'when it's Bláheen that says it, one who has read all the books in the world?'

'Well,' said the sceptic, 'it may be that he has his belly full of books, but it isn't everything that is written in a book, and, what's more, there are a lot of lies to be found in those same books.'

At this, the King took his pipe out of his mouth, spat with severity and spoke.

'Now, aren't you the obstinate man!' he said. 'For it isn't only Bláheen that says it, but every scholar and man of learning that comes to the Island they are in the one tale of it. And it is my opinion that they are right. They were great workers of stone in the old times. Doesn't the proverb say that all things in the world are getting better but only poetry and the craft of stoneworking? And the men that put those houses [clocháin] together without mortar or lime, they had the craft of stoneworking if ever any man had.'

This settled the matter, for a proverb is a final argument not to be controverted.[89]

On another occasion in the King's company, Flower was exposed to the sometimes brutal realities of life on the Great Blasket:

We were sitting in the King's kitchen one night, talking idly about everything and nothing, when the door opened and a man came rather wearily in. At his entrance, a complete silence fell on the company, and the King's son, getting up from the settle, went into the inner room and brought out a number of boxes of rough white deal [wood]. 'Will these do?' he asked. 'They will,'

The construction of the island's slipway in 1910. The foreman, John Corcoran from Mayo, stayed at the King's house. Robin Flower is in the centre, hatless, shoeless and sockless but with a big smile. Tomás Ó Criomhthain is to his right. Photo by Ida Streeter Flower.

said the other, and taking the boxes turned on his heel and was gone without another word. For a few minutes a heavy silence fell over the company, and then one spoke, another answered, and the idle, indifferent talk went on. It was not till the next morning that I understood the meaning of this scene.

The day broke in rain, and after breakfast I sat by the fire reading, while the day's supply of bread was baking in the pot oven. At a sudden exclamation from the King's daughter I rose and glanced out the window. A little procession was coming from the top of the village, and from every house, as it passed, the men, women and children came out to join it. The King's daughter ... said: 'It's the funeral. Will you come?'

A few words told me all. A new-born baby had died, and the father had come to us the night before for wood to make the coffin. He walked now at the head of the procession through the rain, with the little box that he had knocked together from that raw, unhallowed wood under his arm. We too went out and joined the company ...

A man with a spade had dug a shallow grave, and there, among the sobs of the women and the muttered prayers of the whole assembly, the father with a weary gesture laid away his child.[90]

The island had a small cemetery called Rinn an Chaisleáin (Castle Point) where unbaptised babies and shipwreck victims were laid to rest.[91] Deceased island adults were buried in a consecrated cemetery over on the mainland adjacent to St Gobnet's Church.

Whenever possible, Flower would join in with the men of the island on their routine business. He describes going off on a hunting expedition:

An hour later I was finishing my breakfast at the table by the window, on the outer sill of which a hen perched with ruffled feathers, looking in on me through the glass ... and Seán an Rígh, the King's son, came in.

'We are going to Inisicíleáin [Inishvickillane] to hunt rabbits,' he said. 'Will you come with us, Bláheen?'

I had long wanted to explore the Inis, and I left my breakfast and the hen, fetched my coat, and went down to the harbour with Seán.[92]

Flower even pitched in with the islanders on community projects, helping with the construction of the new slipway on the island in 1910. And he had the blisters on his hands to show for it.

During these bonding experiences, sometimes an animated casual conversation took on a literary flavour with the King right in the middle of it:

> On one of my visits after a long interval ... we began to reckon up the deaths that had occurred since my last visit. The talk inevitably took the form of a recitation of the rich store of proverbs that accumulated in a folk civilization on the necessity of death and the consolations of religious faith ... At last, however, a silence fell as they waited, visibly searching their minds for a fresh inspiration. Suddenly, an old woman in the corner leaned forward and said with an air of finality:
>
> 'Cá'il an sneachta bhí comh geal anuirig?' (Where is the snow that was so bright last year?)
>
> I sprang up in excitement and cried out: 'Où sont les neiges d'antan?'
>
> 'Who said that?' asked the King, an expert in this lore.
>
> 'Francois Villon said it,' I replied.
>
> 'And who was he?' he returned. 'Was he a Connaught-man?'
>
> 'No, he lived hundreds of years ago and he said it in French, and it was a proverb of his people.'
>
> 'Well,' broke in Tomás, 'you can't better the proverb. I've always heard that the French are a clever people, and I wouldn't put it past them to have said that before we did.'[93]

The relationships that developed during Flower's visits to the Great Blasket were nourished during his time in London though a two-way correspondence: 'Both the Island King, Pádraig Ó Catháin, and Tomás Ó Criomhthain were writing to Robin Flower in London from 1910, and the many visitors over the years maintained correspondence with the community in both Irish and English.'[94]

Flower was generous and regularly sent gifts of money to the islanders, particularly during difficult times such as during the First World War. Flower trusted the King to decide how to distribute the funds equitably among the islanders, yet another indication of the broad confidence in Peats Mhicí's integrity.

On 29 December 1911, a grateful King wrote a 'thank you' note to Flower expressing appreciation for a cash donation:

> A Chara,
>
> It is time for me to write to you and thank you for the present you sent me from Dingle.
>
> It was a great surprise to me that you thought to do such a thing. May God eternally strengthen your hand and grant you abundance.
>
> That is my prayer for you, and no need to say I am very grateful to you.
>
> I hope you arrived home safe and sound and that you will come to us again next year.
>
> Your friend with great respect for you,
> Pádraig Ó Catháin[95]

It was not long before the King, Tomás and the newly married Flower were in each other's company again. The newly married couple would stay in the King's house. The following is a June letter from the 'man of the house' to Flower heartily welcoming the couple to 'the palace:'

> My flawless friend,
>
> I got your letter on Friday and I have to say I was very happy to hear that you were coming to the Island. You will get the room for yourself and your wife (it's the Norseman's room) and you are most welcome write to me if you will and tell me what day you will be in Dunquin. I will be awaiting you there with my boat to bring you over.

(L–r): Visitors Kenneth Jackson and Robin Flower with the King's daughter Máire (Ní Chatháin) Uí Ghuithín and the King's granddaughter Máire Ní Ghuithín in the Ó Guithín home in the early 1930s.

> Hoping you and your wife are well.
> Your friend,
> Pádraig Ó Catháin[96]

Flower travelled to the Great Blasket again on 23 June 1914 and he gives the following report on his arrival:

> The 'King' appeared soon, and we went down the cliff. The King was along and only had one pair of oars. Oars are scarce now, for everybody is at sea now ... even Tomás has taken to the sea again. We were across in about an hour. Kate and Tomás came down to the slip to meet us. Everybody looks just the same.[97]

Interestingly, Tomás gives Flower a report on the King's execution of his responsibility for distributing funds that the Flower had sent to the island:

'The King has your bill [money] ... he has to go to Dingle to break it. I have no more knowledge of the matter, when I do I will let you know. I'm managing myself and I don't know anyone who is truly starving still. I suppose the King will decide based on that, I don't know ...'

By the end of the week, the King had broken the bill. The money was split between the Island people and Tomás got his own fair share of it ...

'Your old master [teacher] got ten shillings from him, the King is always good to me. I think he gave a crown to some of them, and a pound to others, but his intention was to give more or less the same to every house.'[98]

As for how Flower felt about the islanders and his role there over the years, the following remark by Kanigel is instructive:

At least from 1912 if not before, he was called 'Bláithín' on the island, Irish for 'Little Flower'. Of all the distinctions and honours awarded him over the years, it was noted in a radio talk a few days after his death, this 'honour from the little island kingdom was that which Robin Flower appreciated most of all.'[99]

Both the King and Robin Flower had a major hand in the emergence of the Great Blasket from a cultural and literary point of view: 'Although the Island was well known within Ireland as an important source of Irish language material, it was Flower who put the Island on the literary map and brought its culture to a wider audience.'[100]

Robin Flower died in London at the age of sixty-five on 16 January 1946 in London, just one year before Seánín Ó Ceárna's death on the island set of a chain of events that would eventually lead to the evacuation of the island by the government in 1953. In his later years, Flower's memory faded, yet he never forgot his friends on the Great Blasket. So strong was his affection for their company, that he made their island home his final resting place. At his request, Flower's ashes were brought from London and scattered around the peak at An Dún, his favourite place on the island.[101]

Brian Kelly and Pádraig Ó Siochfhradha

Brian Albert Kelly (Brian Ó Ceallaigh) from Killarney arrived on the Great Blasket at twenty-eight years of age in April 1917, right in the middle of the First World War. To achieve a substantial immersion in island life and greater proficiency in the Irish language, he remained for the rest of the year.[102] He was very popular, having brought sweets for the girls and balls for the boys.[103]

Educated at Trinity College Dublin, Kelly had an intriguing background, including time spent in a German prison very early in the First World War and some involvement with Roger Casement and the Irish revolutionaries.[104] He came with some experience in the Irish language. His Irish tutor back home in Killarney in 1916 was none other than Pádraig Ó Siochfhradha (known as 'The Hawk' or *'An Seabhac'*), a teacher, scholar, author and political leader.[105] An Seabhac had also visited the Great Blasket and was familiar with its rich traditional environment for language and culture.[106]

As was customary, the King took the lead in making introductions for this fascinating new guest: 'It was the King who directed Brian towards Tomás [Ó Criomhthain], and the two became very close to the extent that they were a pair from then on.'[107] Kelly was impressed with Tomás's stories and observations about island life and encouraged him to commit his experiences to writing.[108] 'Brian thought that those lively conversations made a great impression on him, when they would sit in the King's Palace, looking out the window.'[109]

All this involved a critically important transition from the oral storytelling tradition of the island to a new written form of communication. This was no small transformation. The Great Blasket Island would never be the same.

To encourage him, Kelly shared with Tomás translations of Pierre Loti's book, *Pêcheur d'Islande (An Iceland Fisherman)* and Maxim Gorky's *My Childhood* and *In the World*, books on Russian peasants. These examples were intended to show that the stories about simple lives could be the basis for great literature.[110]

Tomás himself was less than enthusiastic about the project. According to his son Seán, 'He was kicking against it. He maintained that he had nothing worth starting with and that he had no idea how to start or finish it.'[111]

Despite his reservations, Tomás reluctantly agreed to get under way. Kelly supplied him with a Waterman's pen, ink and paper.[112] 'Sometimes they set to work in the King's Palace, but of course, they would often set the book aside in favour of chat and company ... Sometimes they would read *Séadhna* [one of the first novels written in Irish] on a rock that they called "*gort na mara*" [the field of the sea].'[113]

Kanigel says that Kelly '... practically dragged it out of him [Tomás]'.[114] The progress was slow and laborious, with extensive correspondence back and forth between the two collaborators over a period of as many as six or seven years.[115]

The eventual results of these labours were extraordinary, but still very rough. They included two handwritten manuscripts in Irish. The first was a journal of everyday events, *Island Cross-Talk*, followed by an autobiography, *The Islandman*.[116] This level of production was a considerable literary achievement for Ó Criomhthain, given his modest education and limited

Pádraig Ó Siochfhradha, known as 'The Hawk' or 'An Seabhac,' political leader, teacher, and literary mentor.

exposure to literature. He learned to read and write in Irish with help from multiple sources, including family members on the mainland. He acquired this skill when he was over forty years old, more than halfway through his life.[117]

After the Ó Criomhthain manuscripts were in some form of completion, Kelly decided to move to the continent, apparently for health reasons. He eventually died from poliomyelitis on 28 December 1936 in Split, Yugoslavia. Coincidentally, Tomás Ó Criomhthain would pass away just two months later.[118]

Before leaving for Europe, Kelly asked Ó Siochfhradha to edit the manuscripts further and arrange for them to be published. Ó Siochfhradha agreed.[119] He had no way of knowing the huge cultural significance of the task that he had taken on.

While Ó Siochfhradha's editing is sometimes controversial among purists who feel that he deviated too much from the original manuscript, it resulted in works that he felt were ready for publication. *Island Cross-Talk* and *The Islandman* were published in 1928 and 1929 respectively.[120]

Now, with the first of the books about the Great Blasket in circulation, the proverbial genie was out of the bottle. With all the attention that ensued, the island was about to undergo a metamorphosis.

While both Kelly and Ó Siochfhradha had a significant impact on the island by virtue of their facilitating the writing and publication of these critically important Blasket books, neither man left behind any observations of the King. Nevertheless it was the King who, again, played the key role of making the essential connections between Kelly and Ó Siochfhradha and soon-to-be published author Tomás Ó Criomhthain.

The fruits of their collective labours survived all of them individually, as the books went on to grow in relevance and readership. *Island Cross-Talk* was translated into English by Tim Enright and published in 1986. Tomás's grandson Pádraig Ua Maoileoin published a new and more complete Irish-language edition in 1997.

The Islandman was translated into English by Robin Flower and published in 1937; a new and more complete edition based on the original manuscript in Irish was edited by Seán Ó Coileáin and published in 2002.

George Thomson (the Great Blasket Visits in 1923–1934)

George Derwent Thomson, known among the islanders by his Irish name Seoirse Mac Tomáis, was born in 1903 in Dulwich, London. When he first visited the Great Blasket in 1923, he was a very bright twenty-year-old student at King's College,

Cambridge.[121] A scholar of the Classics and an avid student of Irish, he took the advice of Robin Flower, whom he had met in London, that he should spend some time on of the Great Blasket.[122]

Thomson arrived on the island on 26 August, the very same day as the first Free State general election in Ireland, a momentous date in Irish history.[123] Of course, he was transported from Dunquin to the Great Blasket by the King, perhaps accompanied by his son Seán. He stayed with the King's daughter, Máire (Ní Catháin) Uí Ghuithín. On his first night on the island, Máire made a particular point of inviting him to come and sit by the fire as if he were one of the family; that welcoming spirit characterised all his relations with the family.[124] Máire's hospitality extended to concern about his sleep. On one occasion there was some danger that the normal shouting and carrying on of Máire's children would wake Thomson up. Máire managed the situation and it is doubtful that Thomson was ever aware of the ruckus.[125]

Thomson was a brilliant student. Amazingly, he is reputed to have achieved fluency in Irish in just six weeks.[126] He became fascinated by life on the island and was particularly interested in what he perceived as parallels with ancient Greek literature.[127] The intrigue was mutual.

Thomson made a very positive impression early in his visit. Mícheál Ghuithín, son of Peig Sayers, wrote on 7 September: 'I am going down to the harbour now along with George, an English boy who is lodging with Mike Leán Guiheen, the King's son-in-law. He is a friendly lad and has a camera, taking pictures with it of the King and everyone around.'[128]

Thomson was quite social and spent plenty of time with the young people of the island, some of it teaching them how to play chess.[129] He especially loved the music and dancing in the evening. He wrote, 'We'd dance all night.'[130]

At some point, Thomson's first visit had to end, which it did on 30 September.[131] The islanders said they would miss him, and he must have felt the same because he returned to the Great Blasket many times over the following eleven or so years. Even between visits, Thomson kept the Great Blasket and his island friends in mind; he was noted for sending annual Christmas presents to the island children.[132]

Unfortunately, there is no specific mention in the literature of the relationship between Thomson and the King. A substantial age difference between the two may have been a factor: the King was sixty-six years old on Thomson's first visit to the Great Blasket, when the young student was just twenty. It is unlikely that they would have had much in common or spent much time together. The King probably provided Thomson's transportation to and from the island, but even that is not certain.

What we do know is that Thomson enjoyed particularly close relationships with at least two young adults on the island: the first was Máire Ní Ceárna (Mary Kearney), born in 1908, with whom he eventually fell in love. Thomson was a Protestant, making marriage impossible in Máire's eyes. He even considered converting to Catholicism, but Máire left the island and went to work as a domestic in Dublin for a time before eventually emigrating to America. In Holyoke, Massachusetts, she entered the Sisters of Providence, ministering to needy children as Sr Mary Clemens, SP.[133] This may have been a case of unrequited love on Thomson's part. The second was Muiris Ó Súilleabháin. Thomson and Ó Súilleabháin were about the same age and one can imagine that they spent quite a bit of time together on the island. Thomson may have been drawn to Ó Súilleabháin because of the latter's command of the English language; he was one of the few islanders with whom he could communicate when he

(L–r): George Thomson with Muiris Ó Súilleabháin in his Garda uniform.

arrived. Thomson would later become Muiris's close friend and literary mentor, urging him to use Ó Criomhthain's *The Islandman* as a model for writing the story of his life up until the point when he left the island.[134] This support blossomed into a major role in the 1933 publication of Ó Súilleabháin's book about growing up on the Great Blasket, *Twenty Years A-Growing*.[135] The depth of their relationship is very much evident from this memoir.

Four years after he first met Thomson, Ó Súilleabháin left the island to join the Garda Síochána. Ó Súilleabháin departed on 15 March 1927 and headed to Dublin where he underwent training in Phoenix Park.[136] He had considered emigrating to America, but chose the Gardaí with Thomson's encouragement. The King was heavy hearted as he transported yet another son of the Great Blasket to a life elsewhere (see Chapter 7).

Circumstances conspired to reunite Thomson and Ó Súilleabháin in Galway for a period in the early 1930s. Thomson taught at University College Galway and Ó Súilleabháin was assigned to a garda post nearby. There, they got together weekly and ultimately refined and finished *Twenty Years A-Growing*.[137]

Thomson's greatest contribution to the Great Blasket was his literary encouragement of Muiris Ó Súilleabháin, propelling him to a fair degree of literary accomplishment which, in turn, helped to crystallise Blasket culture for generations. *Twenty Years A-Growing* is distinctive among the early Blasket works because it was written by a younger person, born in the twentieth century, and it describes an 'optimistic, carefree youth'. Other early Blasket works tended to focus more on the hardships of island life. Also unique is that it is written by an islander who had a broader perspective, having lived in Dingle until he moved to the island at the age of seven and then on to Dublin and Galway as a member of the Gardaí.[138]

When eventually published, *Twenty Years A-Growing* was an immediate success and Ó Súilleabháin resigned his post in the Gardaí to write full-time. Unfortunately, he was unable to sustain his early momentum. His subsequent efforts were not able to achieve commercial viability. He then rejoined the Gardaí and got married. In the meantime, Thomson translated *Twenty Years A-Growing* into English and arranged for it to be published. Again, the book was a success.[139]

Thomson went on to be appointed a professor at Birmingham University in 1937 where he enjoyed a long and productive academic career. Always a Marxist, Thomson joined the Communist Party of Great Britain and served as a member of its Executive Committee.[140] Interestingly, in a nod to his Marxist leanings, he once described the Great Blasket as a 'pre-capitalist society'.[141] His politics mellowed later in life, as he was struck by the excesses of Joseph Stalin in Russia and Mao Tse-tung in China.[142]

Thomson died in 1987, aged eighty-four, with vivid memories of the island right to the end of his life.[143] He had maintained his close relationship with Ó Súilleabháin until the latter's tragic drowning some forty-one years previously on a beach at Salthill, near Galway.[144] Thomson's famous protégé was only fifty years old at the time of his death, and was buried in a seaside graveyard in Connemara.[145]

Thomson's visits occurred during a transitional time in the island's history and he was a first-hand witness to the dramatic changes that were evolving. As Kanigel said 'The mid-to-late 1920s, then, was the last time when the island was still something like what it long had been, before it became something else.'[146] And the 'something else' was not good for the island or its people.

Marie-Louise Sjoestedt-Jonval (the Great Blasket Visits: 1925–1929, 1933 and 1936)

The daughter of a Swedish diplomat stationed in Paris, Marie-Louise Sjoestedt-Jonval was a French academic especially interested in Irish mythology. Her many visits to the Great Blasket were part of her extensive research on the Irish language.[147] First visiting in 1925 when she was twenty-four, Sjoestedt-Jonval would visit a total seven times over eleven years, giving her a broad perspective on the Great Blasket.[148] While on the island, Sjoestedt-Jonval enjoyed the company of the King's family, staying with Máire Ní Ghuithín's, daughter of the King, Peats Mhicí.[149] She would write: 'The people of the island are companionable and joyous, very fond of music and dancing and company ... I am full of roguery – just like themselves.'[150]

Visitor to the Great Blasket from France, Marie-Louise Sjoestedt-Jonval.

Sjoestedt-Jonval became fully involved in the Great Blasket and Dunquin communities. In the foreward to her 1938 book, *An Irish Talk – Kerry*, she acknowledges the contributions of the King's daughter Cáit and her husband Seán Ó Cathasa (John Casey), who were then living in Dunquin, Máire Ní Ghuithín, the King's other daughter and her host when staying on the Great Blasket, Peig Sayers and her son, Mícheál Ghuithín and, of course, Thomas Ó Criomhthain.[151]

At one point, Sjoestedt-Jonval may have been close to staying in Ireland for good; she was reportedly keen to marry a man from Dunquin, the famous adventurer, raconteur and student of the Irish language Seán 'an Chóta' Ó Caomhánaigh (Seán 'the Kilt' Cavanagh, the nickname being a reference to his occasionally wearing a kilt). According to Seán, he dithered; she lost interest and moved on, to his lifelong regret.[152]

Romance aside, the primary focus of Sjoestedt-Jonval's visits remained linguistic. Over time, she noticed that the Irish language was eroding, even on the Great Blasket. English from the mainland and America was having an impact. English words were creeping into everyday use. She tried to counter this disconcerting trend by strongly advocating for the publication of Irish books and, in particular, by supporting the literary work of Tomás Ó Criomhthain.[153]

But there were other concerns looming. On Sjoestedt-Jonval's trip from Paris to the Great Blasket in 1929, she stopped en route to the port of Queenstown (now Cobh) outside Cork. There, she witnessed first-hand the long queue of Irish awaiting embarkation to America and Canada. The number of emigrants exceeded 6 million in the century after 1848. Sjoestedt-Jonval refers to this process, which greatly affected the welfare of community on the Great Blasket, as an 'interminable procession'.[154] Like so many people associated with the Great Blasket, Sjoestedt-Jonval died young. In 1941, death came for her in Paris, invited by her own hand.[155]

Little is written about Sjoestedt-Jonval's interaction with the King. That she admired him and appreciated his role on the island is not in doubt. Upon learning of his passing on her arrival in 1929, midway through her series of visits, she waxed: 'I see him as I often did in winter when, alone in his canoe, rowing with powerful strokes, he took the island's mail to the mainland.' According to Kanigel, 'There is much more like this. She is reliving all that the island means to her.'[156] Obviously, the Great Blasket left an indelible mark on her.

Plácido Ramón Castro del Rio (the Great Blasket Visit: 1928)

Journalist and writer Plácido Ramón Castro del Rio, from the Galician region of Spain, visited the Great Blasket during the

Plácido Ramón Castro del Rio, visitor to the Great Blasket in 1928.

early twentieth century. He was not the first Spaniard to make his way to the Blaskets: the famous Spanish Armada made a disastrous visit in very bad weather in 1588, culminating in the loss of the *Santa Maria de la Rosa (Our Lady of the Rosary)*. The ship apparently hit a rock in Blasket Sound and sank with only a single survivor, the young son of the ship's pilot. There is documentation that the Prince of Asculo, the illegitimate son of the King Philip II of Spain was on board the vessel and drowned in the wreck.[157] A stone monument to those lost in this disaster now stands in Dunquin overlooking Blasket Sound.

Castro del Rio arrived on the Great Blasket on 28 September 1928 at the age of twenty-six, accompanying Robin Flower who had invited him to visit West Kerry. At the time, Peats Mhicí was in the last year of his life. As usual, the King played the role of cordial host. Castro del Rio wrote:

We are tracing a curve in order to avoid the strong currents on the strait; and sailing next to frightening black rocks. After three miles we finally reach our destination, the tiny port of Blasket Island. Between some cliffs there is a ramp that is protected from the South Sea by a small wall. The boats almost have no room to turn into the port. The majority of the island's population is crowded next to the cliff. The arrival of a boat, if it's not the weekly one that delivers the mail, is an important event. When we get to the shore, Doctor Flower is surrounded by a multitude of barefoot boys, girls, sailors and old women that welcome their old friend with happiness. He introduces me to all of them and every one shakes my hand and greets me in Gaelic. Between spread [fishing] nets left to dry and upside-down boats, we walk up the hundred metres that separate the village from the port. We enter, like courtesy demands, the house of the King of the Island. It's a seventy-year-old man, with a shaved whitened face and blue eyes, dressed up like the other Islanders. Besides some aged dignity, there is something about his poise and his way of talking that differentiates him from his neighbours. He tells me to consider the Island like my own house.[158]

As was typically the case, the King wanted to give the new visitor the full 'royal' treatment. In the process, Castro del Rio was exposed to the sceptical nature of at least one islander:

Later on, we visited the principal people of the Island. First we went to meet the King's brother, who lives in one of the only houses which, built by the British government [the Congested Districts Board] years ago, is not single floored. When the house was built, they told the King's brother that it would be bigger than the one he had before but he, after having measured the rooms several times, remained with the firm certainty that he had been cheated. He couldn't neither conceive the idea of a two-storey house, nor understand that it could be bigger than a single floored, even having a smaller floor size. He wasn't convinced that he had been given a bigger house than the older one until it was almost ready.[159]

After a week on the island, it was time for Castro del Rio to depart:

> After courteous goodbyes – the King invites me to come back to the Island and he hopes I will speak Gaelic by then – Tomás [Ó Criomhthain] gives us, as presents, some glass balls. We go down to the port where the King's son Sean is waiting for us on his scow. Once on the light sailcloth scow, I take the oar that is offered to me and row without fatigue to Dunquin. Sean congratulates me and feels impressed that I didn't get tired. I disembark happy to have rowed on a *'naomhóg'* ... and satisfied to have received the congratulations from this rough sailor of the Blasket Island.[160]

Castro del Rio was significant as a visitor because he represented an entirely different culture from any that had explored life on the Great Blasket to that date. Yet his observations are remarkably consistent with the visitors from elsewhere, reinforcing the overall impression being conveyed.

Other Visitors to the Great Blasket

There were many more important visitors to the Great Blasket over the years since Synge started the long line in 1905.

The King's brother Mícheál 'Bofar' Ó Catháin at home in one of the 'new' houses at the top of the village in 1924. Photo by Carl von Sydow.

Unfortunately, not all the visitors during the King's lifetime left behind any in-depth insight on the life of the last Blasket King. Among the other visitors during this period was Carl Wilhelm von Sydow, an ethnologist and folklorist from Lund University in Sweden, who visited the Great Blasket in 1920 and again in 1924. He stayed with Mícheál 'Bofar' Ó Catháin, the King's brother.[161] While von Sydow took several valuable early photos of the island and the King, he too shared no written observations of the King. Other guests of the King included Father Seoirse Mac Clúin (the author of *Réiltíní Óir*), Tomás and Áine Ó Raithile, and Richard and Síle Humphries.[162]

Several important visitors arrived on the Great Blasket after the King's passing 1929, including: George Chambers (1931), Kenneth Hurlstone Jackson (1932) who collected material from Peig Sayers, and much later, Muiris Mac

Back row (l–r): Seán Ó Guithín, the King's grandson, unidentified visitor, Máire Ní Ghuithín (the King's granddaughter), unidentified visitor, Celtic scholar Kenneth Jackson, the King's son Seán An Rí (with mailbag) and the King's daughter Máire (Ní Chatháin) Uí Ghuithín. Front row (l–r): unidentified visitor and Muiris Ó Guithín, the King's grandson. Photo by Thomas Waddicor.

Congail (1952) as well as Ray and Joan Stagles (in 1966, thirteen years after the evacuation). Some of these visitors refer to the King in their writings, relying on secondary sources for information about him.

Visitors and the Last Blasket King

From the contemporaneous stories told by these visitors there emerges a pattern that illustrates the life and times of Peats Mhicí, the last Blasket King. It is remarkable that, while these visitors hail from several different countries and their visits occur over a long period of time, there is a high level of consistency in their stories of the King. This suggests that his authentic personality and character is being revealed in their writings.

Peats Mhicí Ó Catháin was ever the gracious host. He was upstanding and reliable in every respect. He was a fount of information for the island community and their interface with the world beyond the island. He was broadly admired and respected. He exerted subtle yet effective leadership. He was strong and hard working. All of these qualities combined to create an environment on the Great Blasket in which a very special brand of cultural and linguistic tourism could and did flourish. And it all happened spontaneously, without plan or forethought.

The initial cultural visitors were not just casual tourists looking for cultural or linguistic immersion: they were great intellectuals. Assuredly, these visitors sought knowledge and insight, but each one of them came away changed in personal and profound ways. The mystique of the Great Blasket capitvated all of them. As Kanigel wrote:

> George Thomson and the others came from the great intellectual capitals of Europe, looking for something. But what they found, it turned out, meant more to them than what they had come to find ... It is a story of friendship, fellowship, and love across a great cultural divide – between a bare speck of a village and the great world of literature and learning; between peasant fishermen and scholars.[163]

As the pace of cultural tourism grew over the years, however, some downside of the parade of visitors became evident. Seán

Ó Criomhthain pointed out that the visitors could be very demanding of the islanders with little appreciation that the Great Blasket was a living, breathing, functioning community, not a tourist attraction.[164] They would show up on the island clutching their copy of *The Islandman*, looking for some connection with their hero. Some were concerned that the island's resources were 'being depleted by these visitors'.[165]

On balance, however, the interaction with the visitors was generally a very positive experience for the island and the islanders. The visitors enabled three particular island authors to achieve success at a much higher level than would otherwise have been possible. And, of course, they were able to chronicle the unique story of the Great Blasket and share it with the world.

9. The King's Passing

Alas, not even a King escapes the tolling of the years. It appears that Peats Mhicí Ó Catháin aged gracefully and quite energetically. Even in his late sixties, he demonstrated remarkable commitment to maintaining his work routine on the island. Tomás Ó Criomhthain was about two years older than Peats Mhicí and he was quite impressed by his friend's persistence in the face of old age:

> Not a bag of seed potatoes has been sown in this Island yet. Our King here plants an acre of potatoes every year and that acre is sprouting grass still. The King will have to turn it all over himself with a spade, and draw a load of turf every day too. The turf is two and a half miles from home – that is five miles there and back. He is sixty-seven years of age, in full fettle still with no sign of weakening. He is the noble King, with the same regard for high and low, God bless him![1]

Nevertheless, the King made some accommodation to his advancing years. He phased out of hosting visitors in his own home at the age of about sixty-one, shortly after his daughter Cáit got married in 1918 and moved to Dunquin. His faithful son Seán An Rí gradually took over some of the burden of the King's regular responsibilities as postman.[2] And Tomás Ó Criomhthain tells us that, as he became older, Peats Mhicí

Ó Catháin was seldom without a crew to help him with his work.[3]

By 1928, the King must have sensed that his many years of hard work were starting to catch up with him. Plácido Ramón Castro del Rio reports the following nostalgia-laced dialogue between the King and his long-time close friend Robin Flower upon the latter's return to the island for a visit:

> [The King asks] my friend [Robin] Flower about his wife's health with these words: 'If she's sick I wish she gets better soon; if she's feeling good she can't be as good as I wish she is ...' And knowing that Mr. Flower is visiting the Island again during the summer, he exclaims: 'How glad I am to know [that]. I am old and I can live a little more, but now if I live until the end of the summer I could die quietly and satisfied.'[4]

As the King grew older, he saw the world around him changing. Again he opens up to Castro del Rio, this time sharing his strongly held views on a wide variety of topics, including his high regard for the people of the Great Blasket:

> Next morning, when coming out of the house, I see the King slowly walking to his land accompanied by his donkey loaded with two baskets of manure. We talk about matters that are important for the Island. The King complains about the low price of mackerel. He also laments about the piracy of the French fishing boats that are these days on the Island's North Coast fishing lobsters in Irish territorial waters. When the islanders go there one week later they will find nothing. In his clear but weird English, he tells me 'they [the government] catch the French, fine them and seize their nets, but they don't bother a bottle. They get fined and their nets

are taken away *but they do not even give a bottle* ... And after all, they too have to make their living'. Once, the English government told the Islander fishermen that if they find French fish traps in territorial waters they were authorized to seize them. But the Islanders rejected to do so. 'This has something to do with the authorities and has nothing to do with us'. It's admirable the sense of law of these fishermen. The King talks about his subjects with patriarchal tone. 'They are good people. There is no need of police here'. He's not keen on teaching Gaelic. Like all the inhabitants of this village, he primarily thinks about emigration and, for those who go to America, English is mandatory.[5]

It is clear that as a senior citizen, the King became frustrated with the state of affairs on the Great Blasket. He saw multiple factors beyond the control of the islanders that were undermining their way of life. He was concerned about its future, yet at a loss as to how to reverse the relentless trend.

Indeed, the King's views on the English language and emigration are only surprising when removed from their context; the King was speaking from a certain level of resignation on his part about the stormy circumstances of the island, at which point knowledge of English could have been a social lifeboat. As in previous instances, the King proves himself to be a shrewd observer and he accurately anticipates the ultimate consequences of the downward spiral.

In fact, the King's gloomy sentiments call to mind the infamous melancholy words of Tomás Ó Criomhthain: '... for the like of us will never be again' *(ní bheidh ár léithéidí arís ann)*.[6]

Finally, Castro del Rio sums up his own deep feelings on the ageing King himself: 'Despite the fact that his role [as King] is nothing more than a tradition that time didn't manage to forget, and that his subjects are but a hundred sailors, he is truly a well-deserved king. It's on the Blasket Island that I felt, finally, monarchial.'[7]

Clearly, Castro del Rio was a keen observer himself.

On a lighter note, the King apparently put on quite a bit of weight as he got older. Writing to Robin Flower's wife Ida, Tomás Ó Criomhthain took the opportunity to poke some fun at his lifelong friend. Mairéad Nic Craith describes the correspondence:

> This was a laugh for a lot of them, especially his old partner, 'The canoe couldn't carry the King now he is so fat. I told him the other day as he had the name of a King, that he ought to be out helping King George, if he has the name it-self he is short in the drop. I suppose he is slow for going out anyway.' But there was no danger that he would take the teasing too far, as the King was married to his own sister, and it was he who sent Flower in Tomás' direction, as he had done with Marstrander before him. He wished him life and health, 'The King, and his family is well. All the Blaskets.'[8]

Peats Mhicí Ó Catháin, the last King of the Great Blasket, died on 11 June 1929 at seventy-three years of age after a short illness.[9] There is no indication of the specific cause of death and it may be that he simply died of old age. He was predeceased by his wife Eibhlín in 1901; she was only forty-one at her death. He had lived as a widower over the final twenty-eight years of his life and during all of his twenty-five or so years as King.

The King's wake and funeral were huge events on the island. Island wakes were typically all-night affairs with lamenting

women *(mná caointe)* keening, the offering of prayers, the
smoking of clay pipes, the sharing of white bread *(builín)* and
jam and the drinking of porter. We can be certain that the King's
wake was no exception. In closing, there was a procession of
naomhóga as the body of the King crossed Blasket Sound for
the very last time after what must have been literally hundreds
of crossings by the King over the years.

The King's obituary published in *The Kerryman* describes
the event:

KING OF BLASKETS

The death of Mr. Patrick Keane, known all over Ireland
as the King of the Blaskets removes a striking personality
from our midst. He was ill only a short time and passed
away at the ripe age of 73 years. When any dispute
occurred amongst the Islanders the matter was referred
to the 'king' for arbitration and his ruling was never questioned. The Islanders, therefore, never had recourse to a
court of law. The king always gave justice to both parties.

The funeral to the mainland at Dunquin on Tuesday
was an edifying spectacle. The canoe bearing the remains
sailed in front and was followed by all the canoes of the
island and mainland in which all the available inhabitants
mustered. As the canoes sailed toward the mainland there
was no sound save the keening of the chief mourners and
the crooning of the waves.[10]

According to the obituary, the 'chief mourners' at the funeral
were three of the King's four living children, Máire (Ní
Chatháin) Uí Ghuithín, Cáit (Ní Chatháin) Uí Chathasa and
Seán An Rí Ó Catháin. (His son Mícheál was in America.)

Another obituary, published in *The Kerry Champion,* read:

Death Lays His Icy Hand on King

After a brief illness, the King of the Blaskets passed away quietly at his island home on Tuesday the 11th inst. at the age of 73. – R.I.P. On Wednesday the funeral cortege of canoes, the foremost bearing the remains, wended its way slowly across the Sound to Dunquin for internment. The traditional 'Caoin' of the islanders blending with noise of the breakers, was a most fitting death dirge. A huge concourse of people from the surrounding districts and from Dingle awaited the arrival of the funeral at the landing-stage and accompanied it to the family burying ground in Dunquin. The funeral was the largest ever witnessed in that Western promontory. The Islanders all looked sad, for he to whom they always looked for guidance was gone from their midst. The deceased King will be succeeded by his son Sean Keane.[11]

The obituary from *The Kerry Champion* is interesting in several respects, in addition to its somewhat startling headline. Most importantly, it clearly indicates the high esteem in which Peats Mhicí was held throughout West Kerry. It actually never identifies the King specifically by name, only as the King of the Blaskets, as if further identification were unnecessary. And, it indicates that he will be succeeded by his son which is true with respect to the role of postman, but is erroneous with respect to the position of King.

It is also interesting that both obituaries made reference to the sounds of the funeral procession; the resonance of the movement of the waves together with the keening or sorrowful singing against a backdrop of silence. It was a fitting symphony of sorts as the deceased King made his way to his grave.

The Ó Catháin family grave in the cemetery at Baile an Teampaill next to
St Gobnet's Church, Dunquin.

Once in Dunquin, the King of the Great Blasket was buried
with the fanfare due a King in the family cemetery plot in Baile
an Teampaill next to St Gobnet's Church.

Reflecting on the changes on the island after the King's
death and before its evacuation, his niece Kate Keane O'Dowd
made the following observation that vaguely suggests a further
deterioration on the island that coincided with the King's
passing: 'No doubt, but life on the Island has changed much
for many's the year before they vacated it ... But, I swear, 'tis a
different story since 1929. That's the year my uncle Peats Mhicí
died. He was King of the Island. He was a nice easygoing man.
He was always singing and 'twas a joy to listen to him reciting
the Rosary. He was devout. There wouldn't be a boo or a peek
out of ye until he had finished.'[12]

Looking back on the long span of his own experiences on
the Great Blasket over the years, Robert Flower was somewhat

wistful as he penned the preface to his book *The Western Island* on 15 October 1944: 'The King is dead and Tomás [Ó Criomhthain] and the greater part of that lamenting company, and all this that follows is the song we made together of the vanished snows of yesteryear.'[13]

Flower was again borrowing from the old French proverb that he remembered from an island conversation with the King and the island elders that had taken place many years earlier (see Chapter 8). It was a proverb and a sentiment befitting a King.

The passing of the last King marked the passing of an era on the island. The downward spiral was now firmly in place. And, at that point, the end result was probably inevitable. Despite the sterling service of the King, a declining economy and accelerating emigration to America and the mainland would eventually lead to the evacuation of the Great Blasket.

10. The Kingdom Evacuated

Peats Mhicí Ó Catháin was deceased for over twenty-four years when the Irish government evacuated the Great Blasket in 1953. In the intervening years, the King would certainly have sought to avert the abandonment of his beloved kingdom by entreating the government to deal with the underlying communications and transportation issues. But the reality is that he would probably have been unable to secure concrete action by the government to improve the situation substantially. And he would probably not have been surprised by the ultimate outcome.

It was the unexpected death of 24-year-old islander Seán Ó Ceárna very early in 1947 that essentially broke the will of the island community to continue to eke out their meagre existence. Seán, commonly called 'Seánín,' meaning little Seán, to distinguish him from his father of the same name, was Mike Carney's youngest brother. He died on the island on 10 January 1947 from treatable meningitis without either medical or spiritual assistance. It was the catalyst that led to the end of life on the island.[1]

Actually, there were already multiple unmistakable signs that life on the Great Blasket was winding down. The school had closed at Christmas in 1941 for lack of enrolment; there were only five 'scholars' remaining at the time. This was a huge psychological blow with important practical implications.

Island families looking to educate their children were forced to move off the island themselves or send their school-age children to live with relatives while attending school. As Dáithí de Mórdha tells us, 'generations of young people left [the island], leaving the majority of the island's population as either old couples or middle-aged bachelors.'[2] Furthermore, the island's natural supply of turf for fuel began to be depleted and supplies had to be imported from the mainland by *naomhóg*, another logistical and economic challenge.[3]

Women especially found island life unappealing. Those who stayed despite the everyday challenges were extraordinary. The King's niece Kate Keane O'Dowd said: 'Island women were very resourceful and quick on the pick-up; they'd survive where women from the mainland would not. In their case necessity was the mother of invention – living on an island, without money and the weather against you. Having to make do ... They weren't one bit sorry to leave.'[4]

Most island women chose a different way of life when the opportunity presented itself and, as a result, marriages and families on the Great Blasket were on the wane. There were only two weddings involving islanders between 1930 and 1953. As Dáithí de Mórdha says, 'If you take away the young people from a community, you take away the future, and without new children being born, the island was doomed.'[5] Islander Séamus Ó Duinnshléibhe put it bluntly and a bit sardonically: 'The only way to relieve our situation is to send a boatload of women.'[6]

Given the steadily shrinking population, the isolation as well as the lack of reliable communications and transportation between the island and the mainland, maintaining a meaningful community on the Great Blasket was virtually impossible. If the difficult circumstances on the island could combine to take the life of a strapping 24-year-old male, then everybody on the island was vulnerable. Seánín's death was the final straw.

After his brother's death, Mike Carney, then living in Dublin, wrote a letter on 26 January 1947 to Taoiseach Éamon de Valera complaining about the government's inaction on the worsening Blasket conditions. He decried the poor communications and transportation, issues he felt the government should have addressed. And he, reluctantly, suggested the relocation of the islanders as a potential solution, writing 'If the Government thinks that it is not worth spending any money on the Blasket Island, why don't they be given a small piece of land on the mainland? That would please the islanders themselves, because it has been too difficult for them to live on the island for the past few years.'[7]

Carney also lobbied Richard Mulcahy, leader of Fine Gael, the opposition party in the Dáil. Mulcahy had been a general in the Irish army and Minister of Defence. Carney's strategy was to approach both the sitting government and the opposition party simultaneously. Mulcahy was sympathetic to the cause and brought up the matter of the conditions on the Great Blasket in the Dáil on 25 February 1947 and again on 12 March 1947. Regrettably, the Minister of Industry and Commerce as well as the Minister of Posts and Telegraphs, both responding on behalf of the government, were somewhat dismissive of the concern, suggesting that these were short-term problems.[8]

Three months later, the message of desperation to Taoiseach de Valera was reinforced. At 2:30 pm on 22 April 1947, the islanders sent an emotional telegram to Dublin containing just ten simple words that communicated volumes: 'DEVALERA DUBLIN: STORMBOUND DISTRESS – SEND FOOD – NOTHING TO EAT = BLASKETS+.'[9]

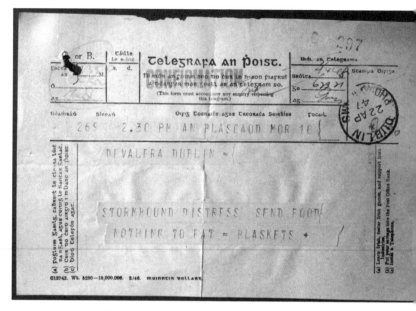

The 1947 telegram desperately pleading for help for the residents of the Great Blasket.

Seán 'Sheáisí' Ó Ceárna, no relation to Mike Carney, who was then the island postman and operator of the radio telephone, probably initiated the telegram for relay though the telegraph in the post office in Dunquin.[10] The next day, 23 April 1947, *The Irish Press* published a story with headline: 'STORMS AND HIGH SEAS ISOLATE BLASKETS.'[11] This drew the public's attention to the plight of the islanders and stepped up pressure on the government. A boat with emergency food and, according to legend, some strong drink, arrived shortly thereafter to alleviate the immediate need.

As a result of these communications and still others, de Valera visited a series of islands around the Irish coast in the summer of 1947. He visited the Great Blasket on Monday, 14 July 1947, arriving on the LÉ *Macha*, named for the ancient Irish goddess of war. The front page of *The Kerryman* proclaimed 'BLASKET ISLANDERS GREET AN TAOISEACH.'[12] Among the islanders that de Valera consulted with on that auspicious occasion was the King's daughter, Máire (Ní Chatháin) Uí Ghuithín. The islanders asked the highly regarded Taoiseach to be resettled on the mainland.

Mike Carney relays the account of de Valera's visit as shared with him by his father, Seán Tom Ó Ceárna, who participated in the event:

> The Taoiseach toured the village and talked with the people in Irish and asked questions about their life on the island. He wanted to understand from them directly what the conditions were and whether they wanted to be moved off the island. There had been no King on the island since the passing of 'Mickey' Ó Catháin. The oldest person on the island, Muiris Ó Catháin [no relation to the King], was the spokesman for the islanders. He told de Valera that they were suffering great hardship and that they wanted to move to the mainland. They talked about the price of fish and the fact that they had no salt to preserve the fish for the winter.
>
> My father told me that he said to de Valera 'Get us some place, sir, where we can walk.' What he meant was, get us away from the island and the ocean and move us over to the mainland.
>
> De Valera left the island without making any commitments, but the islanders felt that they had convinced him to do something about the situation.'[13]

On the other hand, Seán Ó Guithín recalled that de Valera had indicated that 'there were certain people in Dublin who wouldn't be pleased if that [the evacuation] was done.

Taoiseach Éamon de Valera on the Great Blasket talking to the King's daughter, Máire (Ní Chatháin) Uí Ghuithín, Seán Tom Ó Ceárna, Mike Carney's father, and others in 1947. Photo by John Ross.

That is what he said.' According to Seán, these were people who had 'no connection' to the island.[14] Indeed, if anyone expected swift action on the Great Blasket situation by the government, they would be sorely disappointed. Years of study, debate and indecision ensued. An interdepartmental committee was appointed to study the matter. And study it did while conditions on the island continued to deteriorate. The islanders grew disappointed in what they perceived as de Valera's inability to bring the matter to closure.

Then there was a change in the political party running the government in 1948, with de Valera being out of office as Taoiseach for three years as a coalition government took office. This new government had little appetite for dealing with the Blasket issue.

On 17 September 1952, the *Irish Independent* published an article entitled 'ISLANDERS PLEAD FOR NEW LIFE

ON THE MAINLAND'. The story reported that the twenty-eight people still living on the island had once again asked the government to relocate them to the mainland. During storms the previous winter, the islanders had been cut off from all communications with the mainland for a month and their food supplies had run out. For days, they existed on only potatoes and salt.

The *Independent* said that 'to bring their plight before the public', four islanders signed a 'memorial'. This document pointed out that fishing was 'practically gone' and there were 'now only enough able-bodied men to man two boats [i.e. eight men].' The islanders said, 'We are prepared for any migration, anything to leave the island, but we will be satisfied with a house and one acre, or even a house, on the mainland.'

According to the islanders' statement, they had been asking successive governments for many years to house them on the mainland. 'All we received are empty promises ... If people at this stage of civilization and standard of living only realized what hardships of mind and body we endure, we are sure that they would raise their voices and rally to our cause.'

The memorial was signed by four islanders including two of the King's grandsons, Muiris and Seán Ó Guithín, Muiris Maras Mhuiris Ó Catháin (the King's first cousin) and Seán Mharas Mhuiris 'Faeilí' Ó Catháin, a relation of the King (second cousin once removed).[15]

It was only after five long years of investigations, reports, consultation and meetings and that a final decision was made by the government to evacuate the Great Blasket. The plan was to relocate the twenty-two remaining islanders to homes in Dunquin.[16] The evacuation itself, however, was still another year away. The Land Commission acquired property from Dunquin owners who were relocated to better land in Kildare and Meath. Four new homes were constructed and

Four islanders prepare to evacuate the Great Blasket and relocate to Dunquin. Among the belongings they are taking with them are two bags of clothes, an iron bedstead and a pannier. The island post office and poles for the hand-cranked radio telephone can be seen at the rear. (L–r): Maraisín Mharas Mhuiris Ó Catháin (no relation to the King), Peaidí Mhicil Ó Súilleabháin, Muiris Ó Guithín (the King's grandson), and Peaidí Beag Ó Dálaigh.

MACMONAGLE.COM ARCHIVE

two other existing homes were acquired and made available to islanders.[17]

Seán Ó Guithín, the son of the King's daughter Máire, tells us:

> The [new] houses were built [by the government] outside on the mainland in or around 1952 ... Four new houses were built, and some of the islanders got the houses of the two that were transferred up country, Ó Cíomhaín

and Ulick Moran. Seán Ó Catháin got Ulick's house and three islanders were put into Ó Cíomhaín's house ... Then, Seán Ó Catháin was put into Ulick Moran's house. Seán left the island before we did because his son Gearóid had to go to school. We [the King's grandsons Seán and Muiris Ó Guithín] stayed on for a while after. [The family of Seán Cheaist Ó Catháin was the first of the evacuees to move off the island in October 1953] ... As I said my mother left in the month of November as well as Maras Mhuris Ó Catháin and his wife and son Seán.[18]

On the first day of the evacuation, the *Saint Laurence O'Toole*, a fishing boat owned by Michael Brosnan of Dingle, began the evacuation of the Great Blasket. It was bad weather and only six islanders were transported that day from the Great Blasket to Dingle. Most of the remaining islanders were relocated on 23 November 1953.[19] Mike Carney said, 'The islanders were glad to be leaving ... There was no ceremony or speechmaking. Not even a drink. They were just glad to get out of there.'[20]

At the time of the evacuation only three descendants of the King's family were still living on the island: his daughter Máire (Ní Chatháin) Uí Ghuithín and her sons, the King's grandsons, Seán and Muiris Ó Guithín, both lifelong bachelors. All three subsequently moved to Dunquin. With respect to the King's other children, Mícheál had emigrated to America in 1905, Cáit had moved to Dunquin when she married in 1918 and Seán An Rí had passed away in 1934.

The evacuation of the Great Blasket may have been the end of a kingdom, but was certainly not the end of its story. The remaining islanders relocated to Dunquin or other communities in West Kerry. Others had emigrated to America earlier, joining relatives in Springfield and elsewhere. Some of

The evacuation, 17 November 1953. (L–r): Seán 'Sheáisí' Ó Ceárna, Pádraig 'An Fíogach' Mistéal, Seánín Mhicí Ó Súilleabháin, Seán 'Filí' Ó Ceárna, Seán Mhaidhc Léan Ó Guithín (the King's grandson), and Seán 'Faeilí' Ó Catháin (a distant relation to the King) arrive in Dingle.

the former islanders living in Dunquin even kept sheep on the Great Blasket for many years and some continued to fish near the island as well. And a few islanders visited the island during the summer just for old time's sake.

Over time, the old homes on the Great Blasket gradually deteriorated as the forces of nature had their way. The roofs and the whitewash were the first to go, leaving only the remnants of the stone walls standing. The newer and better-built Congested Districts Board houses at the top of the village more effectively withstood the ravages of time and today stand as history's sentinels overlooking the village that was.

The house of the King's daughter, Máire (Ní Chatháin) Uí Ghuithín falling
into ruin after the evacuation.

Anita Fennelly describes her extended visit to the Great
Blasket in the year 2000. The island had been largely abandoned
since 1953. Susan Redican, a weaver from Wales, and a few
other stalwarts lived on the island during the summer. Some
attempts to accommodate visitors were undertaken. 'I had
seen quite a difference since my first school visit to the island.
Peig Sayers's house had become a 22-bed hostel. Next door to
that, the Buffer Keane's house had become the café, while his
old cowshed boasted flush toilets and a rather ripe septic tank.
I dreaded further development of the island, yet it seemed
inevitable.'[21]

Fearing that indiscriminate development would compro-
mise the island, advocates for the Great Blasket banded

Former islanders and mainlanders among the ruins on a visit in 1972. (L–r): Seánín Mhicil Ó Súilleabháin, Willie Devin de Mórdha, Muiris Mhaidhc Léan Ó Guithín (the King's grandson, partially obscured), Seán Pheats Tom Ó Cearnaigh, Seán Mharas Mhuiris Ó Catháin (no relation to the King), and Páidín Ó Catháin (the King's grandson). Photo by Pat Langan

together to urge the government to create a national park on the island. The results of their efforts include the construction of the Great Blasket Centre in Dunquin and the acquisition of most of the Blasket land by the government. The ruins of the old village are now being preserved and basic visitor facilities are being constructed.

In 2015, the ambitious vision of a Great Blasket Island National Park has not yet been achieved, although steady progress is under way, including much-needed physical improvements on the island (see Chapter 13). As a result of these initiatives and in spite of the evacuation, the story of this tiny island kingdom and the memory of its Kings will live on.

11. The King's Descendants in Ireland

As Peats Mhicí Ó Catháin's four surviving children grew up on the Great Blasket (see Chapter 6), they most probably experienced the same temptation to emigrate to the mainland or to America as the island's other young adults. Three of the King's children, Máire, Cáit and Seán, resisted the lure of a life in America and they lived on the island or in Dunquin

The King in front of his house with a donkey ready for collecting turf and his grandson Muiris Léan Ó Guithín, barely visible on the right.

throughout their lives. Only his son Mícheál emigrated to America. And even he had mixed feelings about leaving the island, emigrating twice before finally settling down in Springfield, Massachusetts for good (see Chapter 12).

Author Risteárd Ó Glaisne had a personal relationship with the King's two daughters and four of his grandchildren which developed during his trips to the island and Dunquin in the late 1940s and early 1950s.[1] His personal perspective on the character of the King's descendants that remained in West Kerry was based on his first-hand observations. Ó Glaisne wrote: 'I would say that the royal traits of generosity, gentleness and broadmindedness are inherent in all of them. If the title of King was an honorary title, it came with honour, and it still does.'[2]

Máire (Ní Chatháin) Uí Ghuithín (Máire Pheats Mhicí – 'the little hostess')

In February 1905, at the age of about twenty-three, the King's first daughter, Máire Pheats Mhicí Ní Catháin, married islander Mícheál Mhaidhc Léan Ó Guithín.[3] Before her marriage and continuing for several years thereafter, Máire managed the bed-and-breakfast operation of the King's house. She was 'the little hostess' referred to by John Millington Synge in describing his visit to the island in August of the very year Máire got married (see Chapter 8).[4]

Máire Pheats Mhicí and Maidhc Léan had seven children. In birth order they were: Eibhlín (1906), the first Mícheál (1906), Pádraig (1908), Máire (1909), Seán (1911), a second Mícheál (1913), and finally, seven years later, Muiris (1920). The first Mícheál and the first Pádraig died in infancy.[5]

The family lived in the top of the village, immediately adjacent to the King's house and not far from *An Dáil* and

Máire (Ní Chatháin) Uí Ghuithín darns a sock in the doorway of her home in the late 1930s. Máire's daughter, also named Máire, tends the flowers and her son Seán digs weeds. The King's house is to the right.

the Yank's Well. The location made it convenient for Máire Pheats Mhicí to continue to play a role in managing the King's household even after her marriage. Her own home was somewhat larger than King's, and the extra space would eventually be needed to accommodate Máire's larger family.

Máire Pheats Mhicí held a certain status among the women on the island, perhaps because she was the eldest daughter of the King, and she played a prominent role in life on the Great Blasket. For example, Máire Pheats Mhicí was entrusted with the difficult task of comforting the greatly distressed Cáit Ní Chriomhthain in the aftermath of the drownings of Eibhlín Nic Niocaill and Dómhnall Ó Criomhthain in 1909.[6] Máire was expected to play this important and sensitive role, apparently because of her wisdom and even temperament (see Chapter 8).

The King's daughter Máire Pheats Mhicí (Ní Chatháin) Uí Ghuithín on the island. Máire moved to Dunquin when the island was evacuated in 1953.

Eventually, Máire Pheats Mhicí began hosting visitors in her own house while her younger sister Cáit took responsibility for the visitors staying in the King's house. Máire's business increased when Cáit got married and moved to Dunquin in 1918. At that point, only the King and Seán were living in the King's house and they gradually phased out of the hospitality business. By the mid-1920s, Máire Pheats Mhicí's house was generally recognised as the main accommodation for visitors to the Great Blasket.[7] The family owned a cow which provided milk for her guests as well as for her large family.[8]

The King's niece Kate Keane O'Dowd described visiting Máire Pheats Mhicí as she balanced her obligations to family and visitors: 'Mary Pheats Mhicí [Máire] was the nicest of them all, a gentle elegant woman, slender, neat, as well-groomed as a dove, always generous, welcoming and happy. Many's the night I spent in her house with her family and the well-to-do visitors

The King's daughter Máire Pheats Mhicí (Ní Chatháin) Uí Ghuithín with her sons Muiris (left) and Seán in adulthood and an unidentified boy.

all at the same table. She still didn't give me the cold shoulder and she run off her feet tending to the well-to-do.'[9]

Máire Pheats Mhicí, as well as her younger sister Cáit for that matter, had a reputation as an excellent housekeeper and she took great pride in her work.[10] Her daughter, Máire Mhaidhc Léan (Ní Ghuithín) Uí Chiobháin, described her routine chores and recipes in great detail in her book *Bean an Oileáin (Woman of the Island)*. In addition, Máire Pheats Mhicí was quite knowledgeable about traditional cures for a variety of ailments, including one for the common cold. She was very strict about personal hygiene by the standards of the time.[11]

In 1923, Máire Pheats Mhicí's daughter Eibhlín, her first-born, was moved to the mainland at the age of about seventeen during the advanced stages of a struggle with tuberculosis, probably to be closer to medical attention. She stayed with Máire's married younger sister Cáit (Ní Chatháin) Uí

(L–r): The King's daughter Máire (Ní Chatháin) Uí Ghuithín with author Joan Stagles, 1970s. Stagles urged Máire Mhaidhc Leán (Ní Ghuithín) Uí Chiobháin to write her books on the Great Blasket. Stagles' ashes were scattered on the island westward from *Rinn na gCearalach* near the harbour.

Chathasa in Dunquin. Eibhlín's decline is recounted in the diary of her friend Eibhlín Ní Shúilleabháin, the sister of island author Muiris Ó Súilleabháin. The last island poet, Mícheál Ó Guithín, Peig Sayers' son, was in love with the dying Eibhlín and expressed his deep affection for her in verse. Unfortunately, Eibhlín succumbed to her illness later that year.[12]

Máire Pheats Mhicí's husband, Maidhc Leán Ó Guithín, died in April 1926, just three years after Eibhlín's death. The couple had been married for twenty-one years. At the time, several of Máire's children were still living at home with her. Her son Seán was just fifteen, but he was a strong and capable young man and no doubt a great help. Several photos taken about that time show him bringing home turf that he presumably had harvested himself. Her youngest child, the blond-haired Muiris, was only six.[13] These two lived on the island until the evacuation in 1953 and then moved to Dunquin as did Máire.

The King's grandson and Máire Pheats Mhicí's son, Seán Léan Ó Guithín working on a new *naomhóg* frame.

Mícheál joined the Garda Síochána, serving first in Dublin and later in Galway where he eventually owned a pub.[14] As in the case of the King's own children, this pattern of Máire's children remaining in Ireland contrasts with the widespread emigration of island youth to America.

Through the 1930s and 1940s, Máire Pheats Mhicí's daughter Máire Mhaidhc Léan spent an increasing amount time living with her aunt Cáit (Ní Guithín) Uí Cathasa in Dunquin.[15] The mainland beckoned the younger Máire, but she may have been reluctant to permanently leave her mother on the island living with only her brothers Seán and Muiris.

Máire Mhaidhc Léan also spent some time working at Moibhi College in Glasnevin in Dublin. The college was associated with the Church of Ireland and provided Irish-language instruction for Protestant girls preparing to be teachers. There she performed domestic work for George Annesley Ruth, the principal, and his wife Mary Leeson-Marshall.[16]

In 1947, as she approached her thirty-eighth birthday, Máire Mhaidhc Léan married Labhrás Ó Ciobháin (Larry Kavanagh) from Baile Na Rátha, Dunquin. He was a 'tall man of impressive bearing'.[17] Settling on the mainland, they had two daughters: Caitlín and Máirín.[18]

Máire Pheats Mhicí, however, remained living in her home on the island even as the population dwindled. She became a kind of an elder stateswoman on the Great Blasket. Gearóid 'Cheaist' Ó Catháin, no relation to the King, was the last child brought up on the Great Blasket and was described as 'the loneliest boy in the world' in several newspaper articles that ran around the world from 1948 to 1953.[19] In the early 1950s, when the island was in its last few years of occupancy, one of Gearóid's favourite places to visit was Máire Pheats Mhicí's house. He loved to spend time with Máire as she relived the old days on the island.[20] Nostalgia was one of Marie's strong suits. She enjoyed sharing her memories and Gearóid was an appreciative audience.

In his book, appropriately titled *The Loneliest Boy in the World – The Last Child of the Great Blasket Island*, Gearóid wrote that 'there was a certain refinement about Mary Pheats Mhicí, and indeed about all her family'. Like other observers, he makes mention of her prowess as a cook and a housekeeper. Even as a young boy, he enjoyed becoming acquainted with Máire's many guests, including Scotsman Ian Moffat Pender, called '*Fear an Chóta*', author Risteárd Ó Glaisne originally from Cork and later of Dublin, teacher Críostóir Mac Cárthaigh also from Cork and Father Tom Moriarty from Ballyferriter.[21]

The main evacuation of the Great Blasket took place on 17 November 1953. At that time, only about twenty-two residents remained on the island. Máire Pheats Mhicí was one of them.[22] She was a resolute islander until the bitter end.

Máire's father, the last Blasket King, would have been quite proud of his daughter indeed.

On evacuation day, the weather was so severe that the older people on the island could not make the boat trip on the *Saint Laurence O'Toole* across the rough waters of Blasket Sound. Máire Pheats Mhicí, who was seventy-one at the time, was forced to stay behind in her island home for another few days. She then crossed Blasket Sound and moved in briefly with her daughter Máire (Ní Ghuithín) Uí Ciobháin in Baile an Teampaill, Dunquin. Shortly thereafter she moved in with her sons Seán and Muiris in a new house built by the government in Dunquin.[23]

At that point, the life of the Great Blasket community was pretty much over.

Gearóid Ó Catháin described life for Máire Pheats Mhicí after here relocation to the mainland:

> Mary Pheats Mhicí and her sons Seán Mhaidhc Léan and Maras Mhaidhc Léan owned a small plot of ground around their house [in Dunquin], at the top of the village. The land was flat and much easier to farm than the hilly fields of the Great Blasket. The family kept a cow, sowed oats, grew vegetables and saved hay. Seán Mhaidhc Léan and Maras Mhaidhc Léan continued to fish, mainly for mackerel and lobster, and tended to their sheep on the Great Blasket. They seemed pleased with the move ... Seán Mhaidhc Léan once said ... 'We didn't know how easy life could be until we left. If you wanted to plough on the mainland, you'd use a tractor. The work was far easier than it was on the island ...'
>
> Life for his mother, Mary Pheats Mhicí, was much the same as it had been on the Great Blasket. She still kept tourists, among them the annual guests who had stayed with her on the island. She kept students too.[24]

Seventeen years after her move to the mainland, Máire Pheats Mhicí (Ní Chatháin) Uí Ghuithín died in January 1970 at the age of eighty-seven. She had outlived her husband Mhaidhc Léan by about forty-four years. She is buried beside him and their daughter Eibhlín in the Ó Guithín family plot in Ventry.[25]

Máire's daughter Máire Mhaidhc Léan (Ní Ghuithín) Uí Chiobháin lived in Dunquin for the rest of her life. She became an author, writing two books on the island, *An tOileán a Bhí* and *Bean an Oileáin,* that provide a uniquely female perspective.

In *Bean an Oileáin,* Máire Mhaidhc Léan reminisces about her grandfather the King and recounts some of the many stories he told them:

> After they had crucified and killed our Saviour, the Jews were gathered together over a grand feast. There was a pot on the fire, and a cock cooking in it. The Jews were talking and arguing heatedly about our Saviour. As they were arguing, one of them said that the story was that, 'He would rise again.'
>
> 'He won't,' said another, 'just like the bird down at the bottom of that pot.' No sooner had he uttered those words, the cock rose from the pot, stood up on the edge and cried out twelve times that 'The Virgin's son is saved.'
>
> The Jews were horrified and went to the tomb. The large slab over the tomb had been taken up and our Saviour had been resurrected from the dead. That was the last time they shaked from head to toe with fear, and from then on they believed that Jesus Christ was the Saviour and King of the whole World.
>
> Ever since then, people say that when the cock cries, that is what it is saying, and if you listen properly you will hear that its cry sounds like, 'The Virgin's Son is saved.' That's to say the Saviour has risen from the dead.

People also say since then that the cock has certain powers, for example, if you are out in the middle of the night, there is no need to fear the pookas or the spirits as after the cock has cried.

And a second story:

When Jesus and his mother were walking around on this Earth one afternoon, they came across a certain house. They asked the man of the house could they stay until morning.

'You can and you are welcome – I am sorry for your cause.

Then the man said to his wife, 'We have no meat to give them, I should slaughter the calf for them.' His wife was as generous hearted as he himself. 'Dead,' she said.

He slaughtered the calf, and gave the meat to Jesus and to Blessed Mary. When they left, they bid farewell to the household, thanked them and told them who they were.

The next day, when the man of the house went out to milk the cows, the cow would not give him a drop of her milk, as she was used to having her calf with her.

Then the man of the house began saying to the cow, 'Give, give, my dear, Jesus and Mary came to us last night, and we slaughtered your calf, and give, give, my dear.'

And then the cow gave her milk, more than she ever had before.

Máire Mhaidhc Léan adds: 'When my grandfather was not telling us stories, he would sing to us and he thoroughly enjoyed it. He had a clear gentle voice, and even if you didn't know the song, you would understand it, as he clearly articulated the words as he sang.'[26]

The King's granddaughter, Máire Mhaidhc Leán (Ní Ghuithín) Uí Chiobháin.

In his 1984 article on the King in the *Evening Echo*, Tim Enright described the continuing role that the King's grand-daughter Máire Mhaidhc Léan played in providing Blasket hospitality in Dunquin, carrying on the King's bed-and-breakfast business through to the third generation of the family: 'The King is dead but the traditions of his household live on in Dunquin where Máire holds court today, greeting visitors from many lands, "imparting knowledge" to them with the King's courtesy and, with her husband Labhrás Kavanagh, extending royal hospitality to all.'[27] But no one lasts forever: Máire Mhaidhc Leán (Ní Ghuithín) Uí Chiobháin, died in 1988.

Two of Máire Pheats Mhicí's sons, Seán and Muiris, the King's grandsons, were among the last to leave the Great Blasket in December 1953. Their mother had moved to Dunquin in late November. Seán tells a haunting story of their last lonely Christmas spent on the island when they fashioned a makeshift candle from a few scraps of material they found. On Christmas morning they went down to worship at the image of the Virgin Mary that was left behind in the old abandoned school and they said the rosary together.[28]

After bad weather on Christmas and again on St Stephen's Day, the brothers rowed by *naomhóg* to Dunquin on 27 December 1953. The only family now remaining on the island was the Ó Súilleabháins and they too gave up the island and moved to the mainland on 14 November 1954.[29]

Seán recalled turning the key in the lock of Máire Pheats Mhicí's old house on the island for the very last time:

> I remember it well, closing the door and saying to myself that many was the fine happy day I went in and out that door, going fishing on bright mornings and coming in good and tired in the evenings, and I said to myself that there was an end to all that now … I was lonely leaving right enough, but in another way I wasn't because we had a hard life of it there and I knew what was ahead of me, you see. You have to be sensible about it. If you stayed on for some years the story would only get worse. We'd be getting older and there'd be no place on the mainland for us by then.'[30]

After arriving on the mainland, the pair travelled to Dingle to retrieve the keys to their new house. They then returned to Dunquin, moving into to their home built by the Land Commission in Baile na Rátha at the bottom of the An Clasach road to Ventry. This is the house the brothers shared with their mother Máire Pheats Mhicí. They would remain bachelors, not unlike many of the last remaining islanders.[31]

Seán had a further thought on the whole sad situation: 'There was just one thing, though. I suppose we'd be lonelier after the Island if we were going somewhere out of the sight

The King's grandson Muiris Mhaidhc Léan Ó Guithín at his mainland home in Baile na Rátha, Dunquin in 2005. Remarkably, the dresser at the left was transported to Dunquin from the island athwart a tippy *naomhóg*. Photo by Liam Blake

of it, but there isn't a morning in the year when I get up that I don't go back a few steps behind the house and the first place I look at is the Island.'[32]

Mike Carney fondly recalls that his best friend growing up on the island was Seán's brother Maurice Guiheen (Muiris Ó Guithín). He recalls Maurice's distinctive blonde hair and their boyhood pursuits on the island, which included snaring rabbits and playing football on the strand. Maurice was nicknamed '*creabhar*' or woodcock, a type of fast-moving bird, because he was thought to be very clever.

Interestingly, Carney tells a story about Maurice that is eerily similar to Seán's description of his own daily ritual of viewing the island:

> My friend Maurice Guiheen was one of the last people to move from the island to the mainland. He was involved in the final evacuation of the island in 1953. He was a fisherman all his life. Even way up into his eighties, more than fifty years after he moved off the island, Maurice would get up first thing every morning and go to the

(L–r): The King's grandsons, Seán and Muiris Ó Guithín, with the last traditional lobster pot they made. MACMONAGLE.COM ARCHIVE

gable end of his new house in Dunquin and look out across Blasket Sound toward the island for a good half hour before he started the day. Maurice never lost his love of the place ... a true islander to the end.[33]

Carney notes that both he and Muiris passed the preparatory exam for access to higher education at the end of their island schooling. They both had teaching ambitions, but there were insufficient slots available at the next level, so both were forced to go on to other careers. Carney still harbours a strong sense of lost opportunity for the two bright lads.

In Dunquin, Seán and Muiris made their living in the traditional ways: fishing, lobstering and raising sheep out on the Great Blasket. They were both gifted storytellers who maintained a repertoire of funny sayings for all occasions. They were avid fans of all Kerry sports teams.[34] Seán in particular was reputed to have a graphic memory of all aspects of island life. The two collaborated with Padraig Tyers on a map of the Great Blasket that included several hundred place names on the island painstakingly identified by the brothers.[35]

Seán died on 17 January 1999 at the age of eighty-seven. Muiris followed in 2007, also at the age of eighty-seven.

Seán Ó Guithín was a very perceptive man. One of his most telling comments involved his assessment of the decline of the Great Blasket. He said: 'It was like a ship that requires a certain number of crew members.'[36] And, sadly, this particular ship no longer had sufficient crew.

Cáit (Ní Chatháin) Uí Chathasa (Cáit Pheats Mhicí – Cáit An Rí – 'the Princess' – Kate Casey)

In 1905, John Millington Synge, described the King's second daughter Cáit Ní Chatháin as 'a bonny girl of about eighteen, full of humour and spirit'.[37] She must have been an outgoing and energetic young woman. At that time, Cáit was helping her older sister, Máire Pheats Mhicí, to host the guests staying in the King's house. It was Cáit, commonly called Cáit An Rí or 'the Princess' who famously brought Synge and the King their 'dram of whiskey' early on Synge's first morning on the island.[38] During Robin Flower's visits, Cáit organised the island children to receive their share of the sweets he had brought for them.[39]

Cáit the Princess was a strikingly beautiful woman and her good looks are said to have persisted into her final years. Referring to Cáit, Robin Flower once wrote to his colleagues back at the British Museum: 'Remember me to everybody and tell them I am working hard, learning Irish from the prettiest girl on the island.'[40] She also possessed substantial physical strength. As a young woman, she would row a *naomhóg* alone from the island to Dunquin and back when necessary, a truly remarkable feat.[41]

The King's daughter Cáit (Ní Chatháin) Uí Chathasa, 'the Princess' with her first cousin Dómhnall Ó Criomhthain who died in a futile effort to save Eibhlín Nic Niocaill from drowning just off *An Tráigh Bháin*.

Unfortunately, one of the few insights we have into Cáit's youth involves the infamous island tragedy, the drownings of her friend Eibhlín Nic Niocaill and her first cousin Dómhnall Ó Criomhthain (see Chapter 8). Cáit brought Nic Niocaill's attention to the fact that another first cousin, Cáit Ní Criomhthain, was struggling in the water, leading to the ill-fated rescue attempt.[42] Cáit tried to help the struggling pair and nearly drowned herself in the process. The next day, the heartbroken Cáit met briefly with Nic Niocaill's grieving parents before her body was transported to Dublin.[43]

In February 1918, at the age of about twenty-four, Cáit married John Casey, a handsome man who lived in Baile an

The King's daughter Cáit (Ní Chatháin) Uí Chathasa ('the Princess') by the fire at her Dunquin home in her later years.

Teampaill, Dunquin. He was nicknamed '*Bánach*', a reference to his distinctive white hair.[44] The new couple lived with Cáit's parents-in-law for a time. They eventually moved into their own two-storey house located nearby in Baile an Teampaill across the road from the church.

The couple had no children of their own, but Cáit's niece, Máire Pheats Mhicí's daughter Máire Mhaidhc Léan, sometimes known as '*Clúirín*', came over from the Great Blasket to stay with her during holidays, eventually moving in with her permanently. The two women were very close and Máire Mhaidhc Léan would eventually inherit Cáit's home. Máire Pheats Mhicí's other daughter, Eibhlín, also came from the island to stay with Cáit and John in 1923. As indicated earlier, Eibhlín was in the final stages of tuberculosis and died the same year at the age of seventeen.[45]

Cáit's house was also a frequent stopping place for the islanders when they were visiting the mainland. Her house was

Three generations of the King's family. (L–r): the King's great-grandaughter, young Caitlín Ní Chiobháin, her father Labhrás Ó Ciobháin, her mother and the King's granddaughter Máire (Ní Ghuithín) Uí Chiobháin and the King's daughter, and Caitlín's grand-aunt, Cáit (Ní Chatháin) Uí Chathasa in Dunquin.

located near St Gobnet's Church and this made it a convenient stopping-off point when islanders rowed to Dunquin for Mass on Sundays. This was especially important if the weather turned foul which was not uncommon.

Visitors also made the habit of staying with Cáit on their way to and from the island: Robin and Ida Flower were her guests on many occasions,[46] as were French scholar Marie-Louise Sjoestedt-Jonval, Pádraig Ó Siochfhradha (*An Seabhac*)[47] and Plácido Ramón Castro del Rio.[48] Typically these visitors were seeking to learn Irish or to share in her wide-ranging knowledge of Blasket history and folklore.

Cáit's reputation for hospitality was well deserved. She had learned her trade back on the island, managing the King's house under the watchful eye of her sister Máire Pheats Mhicí. Both Cáit and Máire were noted for their cooking skills, using traditional methods. Cáit kept geese, and maintained that roasted rabbits, chickens, geese and turkeys were at their best when cooked with bacon. While her sister Máire Pheats Mhicí was still living on the island, Cáit would thoughtfully send over fresh blackberries each year.[49]

Typical of an islander, Cáit was also fond of telling stories. One of her many stories, *Beo agus Marbh (The Living and the Dead)*, was included in Robin Flower's anthology of Blasket stories, *Measgra ón Oileán Tiar (Collection from the West Island)*, that was published in *Béaloideas,* the journal of the Folklore of Ireland Society in 1957. This story tells of a man who woke up in the middle of the night confused and he set off for the market. Along the way he had a frightening encounter with a spirit who told him: 'It is time for the Living to be asleep and for the Dead to roam.' The man was terrified and never went out before dawn again.[50]

Cáit's husband John died at the end of 1952. Thereafter, Cáit focused her affections on her niece Máire Mhaidhc Léan's baby daughter Caitlín to whom Cáit was almost a grandmother. Caitlín's real grandmother, Cáit's elder sister Máire Pheats Mhicí, lived close by after relocating from the Great Blasket. Cáit was devoted to her family, but remained ever the innkeeper. Even in her later years, Cáit enjoyed having company, and her warm hospitable personality attracted many curious visitors. Blasket researcher Leslie Matson first visited the Princess in 1955. In 1963, Patrick Flower, son of Robin Flower, and his family stayed with her. It was a happy reminder of old times, since his father had stayed with Cáit and her father, the King, on his first visit to the island fifty-three years before, and on subsequent visits to the island before Cáit's marriage.[51]

Michael Lillis, writing in his essay *Riddled with Light* published in the *Dublin Review of Books* in 2013, described the moving experience of being enlightened by an elderly Cáit the Princess as a young man:

> As a schoolboy, nearly fifty years ago, I spent a magical month in Dún Chaoin in the portentously (if somewhat ungrammatically) named Teach a' Phrinceiss. The Princess's father had been Pádraig Ó Catháin, the last King of the Great Blasket Island. His daughter Cáit, when I knew her in 1962, was an elderly widow living alone with her cat in a two-room house fifty yards from the local church ... She quietly radiated kindness and (for a seventeen-year-old Dubliner) the enthralling dignity of her acknowledged princely status. She was a fund of lore, and not only about the Blaskets; she knew the folktales, poetry and song of all West Kerry. The locals revered her but feared her a little: she had the gentle clarity of penetration into the motivation of both young and old of a Miss Marple of Uíbh Rathach. She was believed to have supernatural powers; the sunlit morning I left her house to walk the mountain path, Mám Clasach, to catch a bus from Dingle to Dublin, she told me, with sadness but without a hint of ostentation, that she had sensed that a particular woman who lived on the other side of the peninsula had died unexpectedly during the night. I learned when I arrived in Ventry that she was right. When you were a schoolboy and when by chance you encountered a much older woman or man who glowed with that intelligence, geniality and authentic goodness, you half-consciously expected that life would, as you were only then beginning to explore its richness, throw up many similar people of great or even greater worth. In fact I never met anyone like her.
>
> She it was who made me the gift of one of the most valuable resources of my life when she introduced me

to the genius of Aogán Ó Rathaille [a poet] and to his masterpiece 'Gile na Gile'. I was only beginning to drink: at about midnight most nights I would come in from Kruger Kavanagh's pub (not an admirable milieu in the unspoken but unmistakable estimation of my hostess) in the slightly tipsy state induced by the two pints of stout my modest means at most permitted. She would be sitting in her wooden armchair by her turf fire with hot cocoa and thick slices of buttered griddle cake ready for her ravenous student. I would pull up a three-legged stool and we would begin. Songs, stories, riddles, all the lore of the Island (never Na h-Oileáin) and how and through whom it had become famous around the learned world. She was not at all embarrassed by my furious note-taking; as I dimly recall she would occasionally pause to help my efforts. One night she took down Canon Dineen's incomparable Irish Texts Society edition of Ó Rathaille and began to read. This for her was book-learning ... which she recited or sang inexhaustibly, leaning back with her eyes tightly closed. [52]

Cáit (Ní Chatháin) Uí Chathasa, the Princess, died on 23 February 1974 at the age of about eighty-seven, outliving her husband John by twenty-two years. She also outlived her older sister Máire Pheats Mhicí, who died in 1970 also at the age of about eighty-seven, by about four years. She was laid to rest in Ventry.[53]

Seán Ó Catháin (Seán An Rí – Seán Pheats Mhicí – John Keane)

Seán Ó Catháin, commonly called by the patronymic Seán An Rí,[54] was the King's youngest child. Baptised on 16 April 1890, his was the King's second son named Seán, the first having died in infancy in 1884. Seán never assumed the title of King, but he took after his father in many ways, such as joining in the reception of visitors and serving as island postman.

When John Millington Synge first came to the Great Blasket in 1905, he was transported across Blasket Sound from Dunquin in a *naomhóg* rowed by the King who was assisted by his son Seán, then just fifteen years old, and another unnamed islander.[55] Two years later, according to Seán Ó Criomhthain, the King and Seán were said to be 'great friends' with visitor Carl Marstrander during his stay on the Great Blasket in August 1907.[56]

According to Patrick Flower, Seán An Rí was 'a big strong man'. In addition to helping the King collect and deliver the mail, he grew potatoes and other vegetables and also raised sheep. He had a reputation for being fearless climbing on the island cliffs, a quality which enabled him both to rescue sheep trapped on ledges and to collect birds' eggs, which gave variety to the family diet. He also cut turf in the bogs on the island hills. This was heavy work even with the help of a donkey.[57] Not unlike his father the King, Seán somehow managed to balance it all. When unable to fish during bad weather, Seán always found nets to be repaired with his father the King and his brother-in-law Mhaidhc Léan. Synge describes them mending nets, as well as cutting each other's hair (see Chapter 8).[58]

One day, Seán invited Robin Flower to come with him on a trip to Inishvickillane. Since he had always wanted to visit that remote island, Flower jumped at the opportunity. He tells us how Seán was involved in the exciting venture of seal hunting, especially in caves, and landing young boys on Inis na Bró so that they could hunt rabbits with their dogs.[59]

As he was a member of a prominent family in a small circle, it is not surprising there was some interest in his personal life. Only about a year after his sister Cáit's wedding, Seán An Rí

The son of the last King of the Great Blasket, Seán An Rí Ó Catháin.

married Máiréad Ní Chiobháin from Bailintslea, Ventry in January 1919.[60] Just before Seán's wedding, word spread on the island that a marriage match was in the offing. As usual, there was curiosity about the identity of the prospective bride. Méiní (Ní Shé) Uí Dhuinnshléibhe was among the very first to inquire. Her husband Seán Eoghain, blunt as always, scolded her for her inquisitiveness, and also took exception to the prospect of the King's son marrying a woman from off the island.[61] This was often a sensitive subject, although there was a long history of islanders marrying off-island, including Seán An Rí's own father, the third King himself, and even the second King, Seán's great-grandfather.

Méiní later tells of needing to wake up her son Séamus because the King was looking for him to go to Ventry in a *naomhóg* to attend Seán's wedding. He may have been involved in a bit too much celebration the previous evening.[62]

Seán An Rí's wife Máiréad was known as 'Mag An Rí' on the island because she was the King's daughter-in-law.[63] The couple

The King outside his house with family members. Back row (l–r): the King, his son Seán An Rí, Seán's wife Mairéad and a visitor. Front row (l–r): Seán's children (the King's grandchildren), Seán, Pádraig, and an unidentified child.

lived in the King's house[64] along with their seven children. Their first child, Mary (1920), was followed by Pádraig (1921), Seán (1923), Eibhlín (1926), Cáit (1927), Máiréad (1932) and Nóirín (1933).[65]

Tomás Ó Criomhthain tells us that on Good Friday in March 1921 he went to gather 'strand fare' with a handkerchief and a spade when the tide went out. Collecting this type of 'shore food' on the strand was a Good Friday tradition on the island. It was a fasting day and islanders customarily did not eat meat or eggs, drink milk or take snacks outside regular meals. Instead, they would prepare a special meal consisting of types of edible seaweed (dilisk), limpets *(báirnigh)*, periwinkles *(giordáin)* and barnacles *(giúrainn)*.

On his way to the strand that day, Tomás had a brief encounter with Seán An Rí: 'I hurried off from the field and

The King's son, Seán An Rí, the island postman, with his wife Mairéad and one of their daughters. Photo by Thomas Waddicor.

faced for the shore. Who should meet me but the Crown Prince of the Blasket keeping up the tradition along with everyone else.'[66] By this date, the King's firstborn son Mícheál, who was earlier known as the Crown Prince *(Flaith an Bhlascaoid)*, had been living in America for almost twenty years, so it would seem that Tomás used the term 'Crown Prince' in this context to refer to Seán. It seemed to please Tomás that members of the King's family set a good example in keeping up the island's customs.

Sometime before the King died in 1929, Seán An Rí took over his duties as postman. Nóra Ní Shéaghdha, a teacher on the island from 1927 to 1934, remembered Seán An Rí at the island pier, distributing letters and parcels. This new job gave him a modest regular income, supplemented by transporting visitors to the island, and bringing the island teachers to and from the mainland on many weekends.[67]

Nóra tells us that she came to know Seán well and greatly respected the way he filled his father's shoes as a convoy: 'At first I used to return home [from the island] every weekend, every Friday afternoon, travelling out by nayvogue with the postman, Seán an Rí, the blessing of God on his soul. He was indeed a helpful man and many is the time he brought me in and out.'[68] His trustworthiness behind the oars also prompted praise from his niece Máire Mhaidhc Léan (Ní Ghuithín) Uí Chiobháin who wrote of her uncle: 'He was a strong spiritly man, and a man who had put many waves of the sea past him. Seán knew how manage a *naomhóg* through the sea as well as any navy captain.'[69]

Leslie Matson tells us of Méiní's reliance on Seán An Rí when it was time for her to move back to the mainland:

> When Méiní decided to bring to an end her island stay of thirty-six years she prepared to move to her mother's house in Ballykeen the few belongings that could be said to belong to her. The obvious person to assist her was the Seán Keane we have mentioned. He had taken over as island postman from his father, the late King, and was continuing the twice weekly journeys, when weather permitted, to collect the post on the mainland. On the occasion of Méiní's exodus he was assisted by Seán Pheats Tom Ó Ceárnaigh, then a boy of nineteen, who told me that he particularly remembers Méiní bringing across her own mattress.[70]

Nóra gives a vivid description of a particularly rough crossing with Cáit 'Lís' Ní Shúilleabháin during which Seán An Rí bolsters the passengers' morale by reminding them that the Blasket oarsmen are descendants of those who were alive in

The King's son, Seán An Rí, the postman at the time, arrives on the island in a *naomhóg* with the mail. Photo by George Chambers.

Seán Ó Dhuinnshléibhe's time and whom that island poet had praised in the poem '"Bheauty" *Deas an Oileáin*'. He would calm their fears by praising his boat repeatedly, saying '*Táir slán beo, a bháidín*' ('Come back safe, little boat').[71]

Patrick Flower described another terrible journey across Blasket Sound navigated by Seán An Rí. The young Patrick was huddled in the bottom of the *naomhóg* with his mother and sister, feeling very ill during the 5km (3-mile) trip to the island, a journey that took as many hours in such wretched conditions. One of the rowers broke his oar during the trip, but Seán, as 'captain', brought them safely home to the island.[72]

Seán and his father the King escorted George Thomson back and forth across the Blasket Sound many times after his first arrival in 1923. Muiris Ó Súilleabháin tells how reluctant Thomson was to leave the island on one particular occasion, so much so that Seán An Rí displayed his impatience with his

The King's house with his cow and members of his family, *c.*1928. The adults in front of the house are (l–r): a visitor and Mairéad (Ní Chiobháin) Uí Chatháin, the King's daughter-in law. The children are (l–r): the King's grandchildren, Máire Pheats Mhicí's daughters Eibhlín and Máire. Note the fishing shed to the right.

dallying passenger and insisted that it was time to get going, saying, 'Bestir yourself, George.'[73]

As hardy as they were, the King and his son were not immortal. When island teacher Nóra Ní Shéaghdha first went to the island fresh out of teacher training in 1927, the King had just two more years to live.[74] Her weekly trips back to the mainland continued until March 1934, when she left her teaching post to get married.[75]

Shockingly, just two and a half months later, Seán An Rí Ó Catháin would be dead at the age of forty-four. He died of an apparent infection after only about fifteen years of marriage.[76]

His obituary in *The Irish Press* said that his death 'at a comparatively early age has removed a great personality from one of the outposts of Gaelic Ireland ... His kindness and hospitality endeared him to the islanders and the visitors that met him … Seán an Rí was a man of Aran in appearance and a tower of strength.'[77]

Islander Eibhlís (Ní Shúilleabháin) Uí Chriomhthain, the author of *Letters from the Great Blasket*, shared the news of Seán An Rí's passing with English visitor George Chambers with whom she corresponded for over thirty years:

> I have a very bad news for you this time which is that all the Islanders are mourning after our dear postman, John Keane (King) R.I.P. which died suddenly last Tuesday night. A very small pimple came on his neck, back, and he scratched it, it blood-poisoned him in two or three days' time and so the weather was awful hot, he used get up every day. He was in Dunquin Friday last for the post and it was on him that day and he was dead Tuesday night. Oh Mr Chambers we couldn't get over it! … None of us expected his death as it was a very very great blow to all us Islanders. Everyone liked him, oh everyone. Many the parcels and letters – good letters – he brought to us. May God rest his soul, Amen.
>
> He left a widow with a family of seven, five girls [and] two boys, the eldest a girl of fifteen, the youngest a baby girl of eight months. Wasn't it a pity. And a very good man at sea, he had great courage at sea and very seldom missed a post day out. Never again a better postman we will see. How we missed him today or yesterday Friday when there is no postman. Next week they say, his sister's son will get it [the postman's job] until his own son is at age to leave school. He had the priest and doctor the very same evening he died. His father – 'The King' we used to call him – died five years ago. What will she do and the small children isn't it very hard on her. She is not a native

here at all she came in to him married. He was only forty-nine years.[78]

Seán An Rí was buried in the family plot in the old graveyard in Baile an Teampaill, where his father the King had been laid to rest just five years before.[79] His widow Mairéad struggled to manage their large brood of children and the intense demands of Blasket living. A brother or an uncle came from Ventry to help her out, staying with her on the island until the family moved to the mainland a couple of years after Seán's death.[80] This relocation was in the best interest of Seán's surviving family, but it removed yet more youths from the interdependent island community.

In November 1936, Eibhlís Ní Shúilleabháin appears to describe this move in another letter to George Chambers. She laments the decline in the population living on the Great Blasket, saying that after Christmas a widow with seven children would be leaving the island. This was probably Seán's widow, Mairéad, with her two sons and five daughters.[81]

The relocation of Seán An Rí's family may have rescued them from untenable conditions, but that does not mean it was voluntary or welcome. In 1984, his daughter Mairéad wrote that they were forced 'to abandon "The King's House," Great Blasket Island, in 1937, due to the tragic death in 1934 of our father Seán A' Rí'.[82] We do not sense any eagerness to leave the island, a sentiment that would heighten among the last of the islanders leading up to the evacuation.

As for Seán and Mairéad's children:[83] Mary died in 1941 at twenty-one; Pádraig, known as Peaidí, lived with his family in Ballyferriter and died, aged ninety, in 2012;[84] Seán lived in London, England, dying in 1987 at sixty-four; Eibhlín married Jack Ferriter of Baile Uachtarach, Ballyferriter, lived in England and retired to Baile Loiscithe, passing away in 2008 at the age

Seán Ó Criomhthain – the son of Tomás Ó Criomhthain – and his wife Eibhlís (Ní Shúilleabháin) Uí Chriomhthain. Photo by George Chambers.

of eighty-two; Cáit was reared by her maternal grandparents in Ventry and married Jerh Dowling from Lixnaw, North Kerry, living in Tralee and dying in 1999 at seventy-two; Mairéad lived in Chicago in the United States for fourteen years and then married Thomas Costelloe from Ballybunion, living in Kent, England, and retiring to Ballyferriter where she still lives; Nóirín lived in Ballyferriter and now resides in the Dingle Community Hospital.

It is interesting to note that three of these siblings lived in England for a major portion of their adult lives, and that two of those returned to live in West Kerry in retirement. Their Irish roots were still very much a force in their lives. Their mother, Seán's widow Mairéad, died on 17 November 1983.[85] She was a heroic woman who raised all seven children alone with very little help after her husband's untimely death.

The King's grandson and Seán An Rí's son Peaidí 'an Oileáin' Ó Catháin, born on the island in 1921, in his house in the Colony, Ballyferriter, *c.* 2009. Photo by Ned Fitzgerald.

Seán 'Sheáisí' Ó Ceárna became the island postman after Seán An Rí's death, in addition to his duties operating the often out-of-service hand-cranked radio telephone. Almost twenty years later, on the day of the evacuation in 1953 he was terminated from his job because 'his services were no longer needed'. According to *The Kerryman*, he moved to the mainland, living with his sister Hannah O'Sullivan in Dingle.[86]

Seán An Rí demonstrated many of his father's best qualities. He was physically strong, brave in the face of danger and dedicated in the discharge of his duties. He was widely admired. It is possible that, if he had lived longer, Seán might have eventually been named King of the Great Blasket himself. Under the circumstances, however, we will never know.

12. The King's Descendants in America

Mícheál Ó Catháin (Mike 'The Fiddler' Kane)

On St Valentine's Day 1881, Peats Mhicí Ó Catháin, the last Blasket King, gained a second title of great importance, that of 'father'.[1] The first of the King's children, his son Mícheál Ó Catháin, was born on the Great Blasket during what was then the coldest Irish winter on record.[2] The lad was nicknamed the 'Crown Prince', a reference to his station as the King's firstborn son.[3] Yet Mícheál would eventually grow up to be an emigrant to America rather than an heir to his father's regal title on the island.

By the time native Blasket writers began describing life on the island, Mícheál was fully grown, and when the visitor writers began to stay in his childhood home in about 1905, he had already moved on to America. Hence, few mentions are made of Mícheál's youth in the Blasket literature. The first is found in Tomás Ó Criomhthain's very sad account of the death of his own son Seán at the age of about eight. The two boys were out for a day's adventure together on 6 July 1887:

> At the time when young birds come and are beginning to mature, the lads used to go after them. My eldest boy [Seán] and the King's son [Mícheál] planned to go to a place where they were likely to get a young gull – for one of those would often live among the chickens in a house for a year and more.

The two went together after the nests to bring a pair or so of the birds home with them. They were in a bad place, and, as my boy was laying hold of the young gull, it flew up and he fell down the cliff, out on the sea, God save the hearers! He remained afloat on the surface for a long time until a canoe going after lobsters came up and took him aboard.

... We had only one comfort – there was no wound or blemish anywhere on his body, though it was a steep fall from the cliff. We must endure it and be content! It was a great solace to me that he could be brought ashore and not left to the mercy of the sea.[4]

As the islanders knew only too well, this tragedy was in the very nature of a life so rugged. But evidently such a life did not entirely suit young Mícheál. Whether he became worn down from the hardships, or whether the promise of America simply called to him as it had already to so many of the local youth, the King's oldest son was sufficiently motivated to leave his island for good – or at least, to attempt such an adventure.

In 1902, as the story goes,[5] 21-year-old Mícheál and his good friend, fellow islander Seán Tom Ó Ceárna, sailed together across the Atlantic toward Springfield, Massachusetts, allegedly by way of Boston. Upon their admission to the United States, each man 'Americanised' his name, following the Blasket convention of taking the father's first name as a middle name. Hence, Mícheál Ó Catháin became Michael Patrick Keane, with his surname later shortened to Kane.[6]

At that time, no sponsor was required for European emi-grants seeking admission to America,[7] so relocating across the Atlantic was relatively easy. Had there been such a requirement, however, an islander would not have gone wanting for Blasket contacts in Springfield. For decades, this city in western

Massachusetts, located about 100 miles (160km) west of Boston, had been the usual destination for emigrants from the Great Blasket. In fact, there were so many Blasket transplants, Mike Carney tells us, that when he was growing up on the island, he had more relatives in Springfield than in Ireland.[8]

Researching this pattern in the 1980s, Blasket scholar Tom Biuso interviewed an elderly man in Holyoke, just north of Springfield, who claimed that the first Blasket islander to emigrate to the area was a man named Guiheen and that he worked for one of the railroads back in the 1850s.[9] With a single islander established in Springfield, others came in growing numbers over the years. 'We all followed one another,' says Carney, 'like wild geese.'[10] It made most sense for new arrivals to seek out relations and friends who had already established housing, employment, and social connections. This tendency sent most islanders to Springfield, and some to nearby Chicopee, Holyoke, and to Hartford, Connecticut, located about 25 miles (40km) to the south.

In each case, the emigration process for islanders was the same: tickets for passage to America were purchased at Galvin's Travel Agency on John Street in Dingle for a fare of only £5.[11] On the night before departure, there would be an 'American Wake' – a big going-away party – with everyone on the island involved. There would be singing and dancing as well as plenty of porter. Tears would be shed by those departing and by those left behind, whose anguish over local conditions was steadily mounting.

The next morning there would be one last trip to the mainland by *naomhóg* followed by a hike up and over *An Clasach* on the road to Dingle, a distance of about 10 miles (16km). During a brief pause at the crest of the hill, those taking their leave would gaze back lovingly on the Great Blasket rising from the Atlantic Ocean, many for the very last time. Then there was

Mike 'The Fiddler' Kane in his Springfield police uniform in the 1940s.

a train ride to Cork followed by a long queue boarding a ship in the harbour at Queenstown (the modern-day port of Cobh). This line was the 'interminable procession' described by Marie-Louise Sjoestedt-Jonval.[12] The often tearful embarkation would be followed by an ocean journey of about five days to New York or Boston, where passengers would be screened for symptoms of contagious disease, mental derangement and criminality.[13]

Most of the emigrants were young. From 1880s to 1950s, it seemed that Ireland's greatest export was its youth – so too for the Great Blasket Island.[14] After getting acclimatised in America, the islanders often sent money back home for other family members to follow. And the Irish emigration parade marched on and on.

Though getting to America was relatively straightforward, adapting to a new life was no easy task for many, including Michael Kane. At the turn of the century, Springfield would have seemed like another planet compared to the rural island he had called home: a booming industrial cityscape teeming with crowds, factory smoke and fumes, and the noise of electric trams as well as what were then cutting-edge factories such as Hendee Manufacturing Company,[15] and the Springfield Armory, which produced the majority of the United States' military firearms for every American war until its closure in 1968.[16] Far from the sea and estranged even from the Connecticut River, residents were boxed in by train tracks going off in all directions.

The 'come-overs', as they were called, typically settled in Springfield's so-called 'Hungry Hill' neighbourhood, an area populated almost entirely by emigrants from southwestern Ireland. This enclave offered enough good company to engage the attention of Michael, or Mike as he was known – for a while, if not forever.

Family members and countrymen – including no fewer than two dozen former Blasket Islanders – provided as warm a welcome to Hungry Hill as Mike could have wanted. There he found something of a colony and a second home to emigrants from the Great Blasket. Mike Carney tells us about life in this vibrant Irish community:

> It was on the top of a hill, about a mile up from Main Street … Lots of Irish people lived in Hungry Hill … In fact, it was mostly Irish at one time … They were good working-class people. Everybody knew everybody.
>
> Hungry Hill was a nice clean place to live. It had tree-lined streets and mostly two family homes with porches

at the front and neat lawns. There were stores on the main streets. Everything was neat and well kept ...

Hungry Hill reminded me of the Island. People were always helping one another. People would help other people to get jobs and babysit for each other. It was close-knit.[17]

It is assumed that Mike Kane boarded not far from Seán Tom, who stayed first with his brother Michael on Everett Street on the north side of the neighbourhood.[18] Seán Tom worked for the Boston & Albany Railroad, but how Mike made ends meet during this period is something of a mystery, as he does not appear in the local directory until 1906. The likely explanation is that he boarded with one or several families who shared his Blasket roots while working 'off the books' at odd jobs for cash.

At some point during Mike's 'lost years', homesickness overtook him as well as his friend Seán Tom. The duo decided to pay another boat fare and return to Ireland.[19] There are no accounts of the reception of the King's wandering son and his friend back on the island, nor of what made the Crown Prince subsequently decide to return to America.

And so, on 25 March 1905,[20] the same year that John Millington Synge stayed with the King during the author's trip to the Great Blasket (see Chapter 8), Mike and Seán Tom sailed away from Ireland once again aboard a steamship, the SS *Celtic,* which was noted for its steadiness in bad weather.[21] They docked in New York on 2 April and made their way back to Springfield, where Mike took up residence as a boarder at 61 Franklin Street, one of some dozen confirmed addresses he would have just west of Hungry Hill over the ensuing years.

By the following year, Mike had moved to nearby 754 Liberty Street and begun working for the sprawling New York, New Haven & Hartford Railroad (known as 'the New Haven'), where he laboured until 1908 in an unspecified capacity, probably shovelling coal or perhaps as an unskilled handler in the freight house located by the edge of the Connecticut River.

It was almost certainly one of the New Haven trains that brought Mike's future bride, Mary A. Foley, up to Springfield from her Hartford home, where they would rekindle their acquaintance from a seemingly previous life. Mary had also been born and brought up in Ireland; prior to emigration in 1904[22] she had lived in her grandmother's house in Fahan, Ventry, where islanders sometimes stayed when stranded on the mainland during rough seas. She herself had visited the Great Blasket, but she did not like to go out to the island because she always got tar on her clothes from the waterproofing in the *naomhóg*.[23]

Mary was a beautiful, outgoing girl who drew many admirers with her auburn-red hair and spirited laugh. So it is certain that Mike possessed a special charm for having wooed her. Mutual nostalgia may have played a role in their bonding, or perhaps it was the time Mary claimed she spent teaching him English (whether back in Ireland or in America, we do not know).[24]

Though the details of their reunion and courtship are uncertain, on 26 January 1910 they formalised their relationship. Michael and Mary were wed at Sacred Heart Church by the locally beloved Reverend Thomas Smyth, himself an emigrant from Ireland.[25] The couple listed themselves on the marriage registry as neighbours on Butler Street. She listed her occupation as a 'homemaker' and he as a 'mill operator' in reference to the job he had begun two years earlier as foreman at Springfield Breweries, where the glass bottles bore the likeness of the Statue of Liberty.[26]

Mary became pregnant soon after the wedding and would go on to bear ten children in total. All survived childhood

Three generations of the King's American descendants. Back row (l–r): Eileen Kane Anderson, Ronnie Bencevenni (oldest grandchild of Mike 'The Fiddler'), Mary Foley Kane (the King's daughter-in-law), John Patrick Kane, and Mike 'The Fiddler' Kane (the King's son). Front row (l–r): Joseph Roland Kane, Dorothy Kane Caramazza, Kathryn Kane Bencevenni and Theresa Kane Byrne.

save one. The eldest, baptised John Patrick but widely known as John Francis,[27] later recalled that the couple got their start in a small downtown apartment, although there is no record of it. Mike moved so frequently, however, that it is quite possible they had such a residence before any census or annual city directory could take note of it. If true, it would be the only place apart from Ireland where Mike would ever live that was more than a few blocks from Sacred Heart Church on Chestnut Street.

In any case, 1910 was Mike's time to plant roots finally for the American branch of the King's family, the Kanes. Though only a year prior he had sailed back to visit the Great Blasket one last time (see p. 267), now he and Mary settled into a house at 68 Butler Street, where they welcomed their first seven children over the course of the next thirteen years.

In the summer of 1911, the couple became naturalised as American citizens, with two of Mike's fellow brewery workers signing off as witnesses.[28] The following year, their second child and first daughter, Helen Elizabeth, was born but, sadly, she died at the early age of six. Her older brother John struggled to remember the circumstances: 'I was only a little kid myself – and she died when she was in the first grade of school. I just remember they said she died of diphtheria, but whether she did or not, I'm not sure. Closed coffin and all that. They used to have wakes in the house then, and they put up a sign because diphtheria was highly contagious.'[29]

By this time, Mary had given birth to three other children: James 'Jim' (1914), Michael 'Mike' (1916) and Mary (1918). The year after little Helen's death, the family welcomed another girl, Kathryn Patricia (1920), the same year that Mike began a six-year stint working at Fisk Tire Company in nearby Chicopee. Agnes Dorothy 'Dotty' (1922)[30] was the last child to arrive before the brood moved from their cramped quarters on Butler Street to Linden Street, although it was not long before they would relocate yet again. This end of Linden Street was technically church property, and the Kane residence had the unfortunate situation of standing exactly where new stairs were needed to access the new Sacred Heart School, then under construction. Their home was eventually demolished, as was their much later residence at 14 Everett Street, this second demolition to make way for the construction of a new highway.[31]

The neighbourhood was seeing other changes, including the composition of its population. Once a devoted Irish haven in 1920, Hungry Hill and environs now boasted a growing ethnic mix. To the west and south of Chestnut Street, most families were of Jewish, Greek or Syrian descent, and with them new churches popped up around the iconic Catholic landmarks.

Sacred Heart Church in Springfield, Massachusetts, the spiritual home of the Kane family.

Still, there was plenty of Irish camaraderie to be enjoyed, and the Kanes did their part by hosting boarders and new arrivals from Ireland such as Mary's cousins (Pat and Maura Foley, who each married Blasket descendants) and another Mike Kane – bringing the total of Mike Kanes in one house to three.[32]

The family upheld this welcoming role throughout their continuous moves to homes of varying sizes and descriptions. In 1930, after a brief stay on Montmorenci Street and at two different houses on Chestnut Street, the family crammed into a small, two-level cottage at 79 Charles Street,[33] behind a former lumberyard. Luckily for them and their intermittent guests, in 1933 a neighbouring family of well-off restaurateurs allowed the Kanes to occupy their much bigger property, just a few houses up the block at number 67 Charles Street, so that it would not remain vacant in their absence. This move allowed the children to enjoy their first taste of relative privacy, as well as the luxury of the owners' extensive private library. They would reside there for the remainder of the decade, until settling into the last and best-known Kane family home at 155 Carew Street.

'The flavour of the house was very chaotic, mainly because there was tons of people,' recalled Kathryn's son Ronnie Bencevenni, who lived with the family as a child. In a 2013 interview, he described the dynamic household: 'They had nine living children who were filtering in and out of there at all times. The girls, most of which were not married at that point, always had boyfriends and so forth, not to mention the Irish relatives that were filtering through and also Irish acquaintances. So it was never lonely. There were always people there; it was a fun house.'[34]

The youngest son and last living sibling, Joseph 'Joe' Roland (1925), agreed. 'I had a very good home life. You could do what you wanted, because they couldn't watch us all the time!' He did, however, admit to some downside: 'I had five sisters, and once you let one in [to the bathroom], you could not get in. If a boy got in, well now they let me in, but otherwise the girls ran the bathroom.' This was a problem Joe solved as soon as he was able by joining the local Young Men's Christian Association (YMCA), where he would go to shower in peace before enjoying a date with his eventual wife, Gloria.[35]

Making it in America

Industrious Mike did everything he could to provide for the burgeoning household, despite having the equivalent of only a fourth-grade education gained back on the Great Blasket.[36] His work history is a jumble of short-term, part-time and overlapping jobs – many capitalising on his status as a special police officer and a licensed second class 'stationary' fireman, such as operating boilers for the Springfield School Department as well as for the Jefferson and Phillips theatres and later at Wico Electric[37] – but the constant in Mike's career was the income he generated as a musician.

While Mike never could read music, he had excellent memory for words and tunes. A natural and talented performer, he and his partner, accordionist Pat Sullivan, enjoyed successful careers as Irish entertainers in Springfield.[38] Mike 'The Fiddler' became the main attraction for downtown social events at places like Ireland 32, Tara Hall, the Eire Club or the John Boyle O'Reilly Club, where widespread nostalgia for Ireland created a huge demand for familiar tunes.[39]

Eventually, Mike started a small band as well as a successful vaudeville act.[40] They played Irish music for *céilithe* (Irish social gatherings), and other events at several venues throughout the Springfield area.[41] The proprietor of a local Irish venue appointed Mike as its 'full-time musician with no responsibilities whatsoever except to play there three nights a week'. The hall became so popular that it proved too small. A larger facility was acquired and Mike was given a small ownership share in the new venture, which proved quite profitable.[42]

Mike was a fine dancer too, as 'it was always said that a musician who can't dance can't be a good musician'.[43] When it came to entertaining, Mike did it all. He was a musician, a dancer and a promoter – sometimes he even acted as security for the event! With his status as special police officer, Mike was qualified to be in charge of keeping the peace at so-called 'block parties', where he and his band would have city permission to turn a street into a temporary concert space. 'All the people would be out there doing dances, and kids running around like myself at that time,' Joe remembers. His father would be there in uniform, hopping back and forth between surveying the crowd and entertaining it.

Writing home to describe his success in America, Mike told of being able to play his fiddle in one room while people in many rooms in many homes could simultaneously hear his music coming out of a special box that they owned. This surprising assertion was the source of great consternation on the Great Blasket. Mike's father, the King, said that surely his son 'had drink taken when he wrote the letter if they expected him to believe that he could play the fiddle in one place and that it could be heard in another place far from home'. But what Mike was describing was an early radio broadcast of his own fiddling, something that was beyond the comprehension of the islanders at the time.[44]

Combining this income with other janitorial work, Mike apparently did well enough that it caused something of a run-in with the local representatives of the Irish Republican Army. As Joe explains, 'We lived on Charles Street and there was a knock at the door in the night around 12 o'clock. Three men were there when my father opened the door and they started punching him and hitting him. My older brothers ran down the stairs and chased them away. When I asked later what that was all about, they did say that they were IRA people, and they wanted more money from my dad, thinking that he had more money than he was willing to give them.'[45]

In reality, money was scarce and the large family always struggled with creative ways to make ends meet. By managing apartments and bartering his handyman skills, Mike sometimes scored rent-free housing for the family, which partly explains their many relocations. But he could not have made things work without the diligence and extraordinary energy of his partner Mary. 'There couldn't have been a better mother,' their daughter Mary recalls. 'It seemed she was running all the time.

Mary Foley Kane, the King's daughter-in law and wife of Mike 'The Fiddler' in Springfield in 1943.

You'd have to run to keep up with her. She was downtown every single day looking for bargains ... We'd rush to her [when she came home], and say, "What did you buy?" And it was always yesterday's, what was left over, one of this, one of that, two of this.'[46]

Mary the elder was a revered cook and baker, a very neat housekeeper, and the family disciplinarian – a title Joe claims she earned from wielding her high-heeled shoes. She was everything except a patient teacher, opting not to instruct her daughters on any of her many domestic skills except sewing. 'We were too slow, that's what she always said,' laughed Mary the younger. No, their matriarch preferred to run the household according to her own high standard, doing everything from the ironing of clothes to the administering of weekly baths. 'My mother would have to heat the water downstairs on the stove, carry it up in buckets and fill the tub, and two or three people would take a bath in it,' Joe recounted with admiration.

Somehow, in addition to the raising of nine children and the maintenance of a revolving-door household, Mary also found the time when necessary to cover for her husband when he could not make it to work. Mike's weakness for the drink was as infamous in the family as his fiddling skills were lauded, and he often took comfort in both simultaneously. According to John, his father would go long stretches without drinking, but when he did start up – usually at the behest of businessmen whom he entertained – it would cause periods of family disruption. During these times, Mary was said to have stepped up and pitched a few shovels of coal into whatever furnace needed it so that Mike would not lose his job.

Always helping out was her consistently reliable eldest son John, who, one might say, fell somewhere between the boundaries of parent and child. Under the circumstances, John did not enjoy the leisurely childhood of his youngest siblings; he started delivering the newspaper, the *Springfield Union*,[47] at a young age to help support the family, and later worked for years as a cashier at Dooley Hardware after school and on Saturdays. Though he barely had time for his studies, much less a social life, John would even summon the energy to spend nights helping his father manage the dance halls by settling the payroll for the other musicians. Every penny he earned, he turned over to his mother. 'By his siblings he was perceived as Superman, Batman, and everyone else all rolled into one. He was definitely the leader of the regiment,' recalls Ronnie, John's nephew and godson. John's first ever holiday, to Nantasket Beach on the Atlantic coast just south of Boston, would have to wait until after he had grown up and left the house.

Family Relations

When John Kane moved out of the family home it was to marry another Blasket descendant, a sweet girl named Helena P. 'Lena' Carney. Joe remembers the excitement as his brother and new sister-in-law filled their house at 89 Wait Street with all new furniture, a rarity in those days. Unfortunately, the happy couple's marital oath was fulfilled prematurely: Lena passed away on 29 January 1941, only about three years after their wedding, from haemorrhaging related to an ectopic pregnancy. John, her parents and a priest were at her side for the moment of her parting, after which she was buried in Saint Michael's Cemetery. Devastated, the widowed John moved back into his parents' house to be consoled by his siblings.[48]

'The family was very tight,' Ronnie observed. 'Uncle Mike and Uncle John were very, very close. But the whole family was close.' They would have to be, sharing one bathroom between them all and living space so lacking that at times some of them had to sleep on the kitchen floor. Indeed, the two brothers shared a particular friendship. Youngest brother Joe remembers the two tinkering with junk cars in the back yard without any particular end goal. They simply enjoyed each other's company. And, they 'were up there on the prankster list' according to nephew Ronnie. This friendship deepened during the brothers' shared wartime service.

After Lena's death, John enrolled in the US Navy and was assigned to the Seabees, an engineering and construction division. At a time when his unit was clearly understaffed, John requested the transfer of his brother Mike, who had been drafted. Because John had enrolled in the military with the name 'Keane' and Mike with the name of 'Kane', they succeeded at skirting the Navy rule against brothers serving together in a single unit.[49]

The nearly two-decade spread among siblings created intimate connections but also stymied others. To wit, the youngest, Eileen Shirley (1927),[50] was not even born when John first moved out of the house, and his sister Theresa (1924) did not have much of an advantage. Each had a role to play in the family dynamic, roles that would become more pronounced as they grew into adulthood. John saw his sisters take after their mother in different ways: Dotty always wanting to feed everyone, Mary attending all the family events, Kathryn as the sociable beauty. Their brother Mike grew into a hard-working proprietor of several local watering holes and liquor stores, which he operated with a work ethic that would make a parent proud. Ronnie recalls that others in the family even worked together at the major auto parts manufacturer of the period, American Bosch, down on Springfield's Main Street.

As for Mike 'The Fiddler' himself, his standing in the family is a matter of whom you ask; opinions varied not just by generation but also by birth order. His wife was reported to be impatient with Mike's drinking, and their older children acknowledge the stress it brought upon them all. Joe, however, describes his father as good and simple man: 'He liked smoking his pipe, and he wasn't much of a talker, but he took me to the Houdini show and fishing down along the Connecticut River with just a throw line. I thought that was great.' Joe goes on to unknowingly reveal a commonality between his father and the King: 'He liked using big words. He'd read the newspaper an awful lot.'[51]

Ronnie, being the oldest of the grandchildren and a resident at 155 Carew Street until Mike passed away when he was about five, also cherishes memories of a more tender, more attentive Mike: 'He knew everybody. We did all these things together; I was always on fire trucks. We'd go down to the railroad station and I had no idea how he knew these people but he knew all the conductors. So we did just about everything together. And when we weren't going somewhere, he'd tell me stories. I'd say, "Popeye, tell me a story" … And he'd then expound upon a story predominantly about Ireland with leprechauns and fairies and trolls.'[52]

Life after Mike 'The Fiddler'

Most of Mike's grandchildren would never have the opportunity to form an opinion of him. On 17 October 1949, after nearly fifty years in Springfield, Mike 'The Fiddler' Kane succumbed to his long struggle with cancer. 'I remember going to the hospital to see him, and he did have an awful lot of paraphernalia on and I didn't know what it all was,' Joe shared in reference to a trip to donate blood at his mother's request. 'He was in there probably a week or two then passed away.' The family had a wake at O'Donnell's funeral home on Chestnut Street, and then the Crown Prince of the Great Blasket was buried at Saint Michael's Cemetery in Springfield.[53]

After Mike's death, his son John became the official patriarch of the Kane family by virtue of his strong character and leadership, unconsciously growing into the by-then abandoned role of 'An Rí,' at least as far as the Kane family was concerned. His sister Mary remembers: 'We went by him. He decided everything that happened. We'd go by him, he was like a father.'[54]

By this time, John had his own new life. He had rebounded from his first wife Lena's death and married Catherine Veronica O'Connor in 1946. But he never left the rest of his large family

The oldest son of Mike 'The Fiddler,' John P. Kane, with his granddaughter
Eliza Catherine Kane born in 1981 and co-author of this book.

behind. John and Katie settled in the nearby Forest Park
neighbourhood to raise their four children on his salary as
head custodian at Springfield's city hall.

Though they never got the chance to hear their grandfather
Mike's stories of Ireland, John's children inherited his own
version of their bi-national background. The oldest, Joanne
(known affectionately as Kandy), recalls her first realisation of
having Irish heritage: '[We spent] every Saturday going to the
John Boyle O'Reilly Club for Irish step dancing and smelling
what turned out to be beer and cigarettes. We did this for
several years, and it was not until I was older that I figured out
what that smell was.'[55] All four of them spent some if not all
of their school years under the strict instruction of the Sisters
of the Holy Name at Sacred Heart High School or the Sisters

of St Joseph at Cathedral High School. The oldest son, John 'Jack' Anthony, Sr seemed to seek out aspects of Blasket life amid the suburbs, mainly in the more than 700-acre 'Forest Park,' where he once even encountered a drowning tragedy.

Jack was only six years old when he and a few neighbourhood boys from Orlando Street happened upon a gruesome scene one Saturday afternoon. They spotted floating in a pond the body of a local young woman who had gone missing that morning during a period of depression. Her death, ruled a suicide, assured that even in landlocked Springfield, the young Blasket descendant would have a healthy awareness of water's fatal power.[56]

While Mike had immersed his family in the Blasket traditions of music, dance and Catholicism, one important aspect of his island upbringing was not passed down: the Irish language. Like many immigrants, Mike wanted his children to succeed in America as Americans, and to surpass the prejudice that many Irish endured at that time. To this end, English became the first and only language of his offspring. 'If they did not want you to understand what they were talking about,' Joe remembers of his parents and their fellow emigrant friends, '*then*, of course, they spoke Gaelic.'

Nevertheless, substantial elements of their Irish heritage were transmitted over the years thanks to Mike's widow. Mary embodied the essence of the family right until the end. On weekends her children took turns having her for dinner, until she eventually lived with son Mike full-time. Her birthday was the annual cause for reunion more than any other holiday, featuring parties in large rented venues, complete with open bars, buffets and a capella ballads.[57] Mary, or 'Nana' as she was known by then, helped raise the grandchildren while their parents were working, and was in turn adored by every generation. They unanimously praised her for effortlessly passing on Irish traditions, from filling their stomachs with home-made soda bread to specially importing woollen jumpers to keep the young ones warm.[58]

As much as Mary Foley Kane embodied the quintessential Irish grandmother, when she died in the winter of 1982 at ninety-six years of age, she was happy to be in Westfield, Massachusetts,[59] about 20 miles (30km) west of Springfield, rather than the country of her birth. Her sons John and Mike had once tried to convince her to accompany them and their wives on a trip to Ireland, but she had no interest. Joe put her argument succinctly: 'She did not care for the damp weather; she said it was so much nicer to go to bed at night with dry sheets and clothing.' It was in such comfort that she passed, survived by eight of her ten children (her son Jim having died in 1961), twenty-four grandchildren, many great-grandchildren, who, like her, would always be, at least in spirit, a little bit from both sides of the sea. Mary was memorialised at the Toomey-O'Brien funeral home in West Springfield and laid to rest in Saint Michael's Cemetery.[60]

Between the two of them, Mike 'The Fiddler' and Mary the younger left quite a substantial legacy for the American family of Ó Catháins/Keanes/Kanes that would follow them. Whatever his shortcomings, the two things that everyone loved about Mike were the two things that people loved about the island of his birth: the first being his music, the other, his stories. 'He was a great storyteller,' Mary replies when asked what she remembered most fondly about her late father. 'Oh tell us a story, Pa!' we'd say. Oh, he always had a story. I can't remember what the stories were about, but he always had a story about Ireland.' Today, no one can recall the specifics of his stories, only that they were fantastic and plentiful. The one vivid tale that does survive among his many descendants, however, is fittingly enough, about Mike 'The Fiddler' himself.

The Famous Kane Fiddle

On a trip to Dingle as a young man, well before his emigration to Springfield, Mike 'The Fiddler', then named Mícheál Ó Catháin, came into the ownership of a violin, or a fiddle as it was commonly called, and brought it home to the Great Blasket. This particular instrument is thought to be the first genuine fiddle owned by an islander.[61] According to Seán Ó Criomhthain, there was actually some deception involved in the transaction. Mícheál, who had very little money, allegedly misled the seller's wife, insisting that he had already paid for the fiddle earlier that day and he was simply picking it up. It was an inauspicious beginning to Mícheál's long musical career.[62]

Fiddles had long been an important part of the island's musical culture. Visitors often brought a fiddle to evenings of song and dance. In fact, they were so well received and appreciated that a few clever islanders even fashioned home-made fiddles from '*reac*' wood that washed up on the island's shore using fishing-net cord for strings.[63] The islanders sometimes called the fiddle a 'sliver' because they thought it resembled a sliver, a device used in spinning yarn. The instrument became so popular that soon there was a sliver in virtually every house on the island where there was a young girl or boy.[64] Mícheál's sisters Máire (Ní Chatháin) Uí Guithín and Cáit (Ní Chatháin) Uí Cathasa were known to say that their brother would 'play it away non-stop every night after returning from fishing.'[65] He seemed to have a natural aptitude for music and it did not take him long to learn to play his new instrument and to 'knock traditional music out of it'.[66] The islanders said 'It was enough for him to hear a tune once or twice to recall and play it. It is often he used to rise in the middle of the night to play a tune which was coming between him and his night's sleep.'[67] Throughout his youth, Mícheál had heard tales of life in the new world in Springfield, the 'second island', from listening to the reading of letters sent back home from those who had made the move across the Atlantic. Mícheál, enticed by the promise of a bright future and perhaps seeking a wider audience for his acknowledged musical talent, decided to seek his fortune in America at the age of about twenty-one – making him the only of the King's children to emigrate to America.

Mícheál first set off for Springfield, Massachusetts in 1902.[68] He would often play his fiddle out on his front porch on Carew Street, one of Springfield's main thoroughfares, and enthusiastically carved out lovely Irish airs, both invented and traditional, to accompany set dances. Passers-by often stopped and listened. They loved the lively music, even though they mostly did not understand any of the Irish lyrics in his extensive repertoire of Irish songs. Over time, he became widely known in Springfield as Mike 'The Fiddler'.[69]

Word quickly spread through the Irish community in Springfield that 'a top-class musician' had arrived from the Great Blasket and could play every reel, jig and hornpipe that was ever played back home. Thereafter, Mike played his fiddle at Irish events all over the city. The many Irish emigrants longed to hear traditional Irish music again as a way of staying connected with their Irish heritage.[70] As a talented performer, Mike was in great demand.

In the summer of 1909, Mike 'The Fiddler' wrote home advising that he had decided to pay a visit to the Great Blasket. He longed to see his family, to be sure, but one imagines that he also wanted to tout his performing success in America. Naturally, Mike would be bringing a fiddle with him, intending to regale the folks at home with his musical talents in the typical evening get-togethers on the island.[71]

Mike arrived in West Kerry one evening on the train from Tralee to Dingle. On his way to the island, he stopped at a pub on Goat Street. The owner was one Martin Keane (Mártan Ó Catháin), a relative originally from the Great Blasket himself. Islanders would often stop in at Martin's establishment when on a visit to Dingle and, if necessary, they would stay overnight upstairs in a kind of boarding house that he operated.

Mike ordered a drink and asked "'Any news?" Martin replied, "There's no news. Everything is quiet since the two were drowned on the island."[72] This information was shocking to Mike. He had heard nothing of the drowning of Eibhlín Nic Niocaill and Dómhnall Ó Criomhthain (see Chapter 8). He was abruptly taken aback. Martin had mistakenly assumed that Mike was aware of the tragedy, as it was certainly regarded as a huge calamity in West Kerry and was at the time a big story all over Ireland, in large measure because of Eibhlín's fame as the girlfriend of Pádraig Pearse.

Martin then relayed the terrible story, including the fact that Mike's own sister, Cáit An Rí (Ní Chatháin) Uí Cathasa, had witnessed the entire event and had nearly drowned herself.[73] This sudden and dreadful revelation gave Mike 'a great shock'; the deceased Dómhnall was his first cousin and he had known the younger man very well.

When the conversation ended, Mike handed his fiddle case over to Martin Keane and said:

> "'Would you ever keep this for me until I return to Dingle on my way back to the States in a couple of weeks?" asked Maidhc [Mike].
>
> "Leave it here and I'll put it in a safe place and you can have it on your way back. But why won't you take it with you now?"

"I would prefer to leave it here rather than take it over to the island. According to what you have just told me, the island is no place for music any more."[74]

And thus Mike left Dingle for his visit to the island without his beloved fiddle.

After spending time with his family as planned, Mike returned to Springfield without stopping by Martin Keane's pub to retrieve his fiddle.[75] Unfortunately, we will never know why Mike did not feel it was right to bring his instrument back to America with him. Perhaps he was leaving something dear to him behind in Ireland as a tribute to his deceased cousin Dómhnall.

Back in Springfield, Mike continued his successful career as an entertainer on a new fiddle, which would, according to his daughter Mary, meet its demise when he eventually sat on it by mistake. Meanwhile, back in Dingle, Martin Keane's grandson, T.P. Ó Conchúir began using Mike's original fiddle sometime in the 1950s, taking lessons from Sister Kevin Potts in the nearby Presentation Convent. One day, the poor lad accidently fell as he ran home down the hill from the Convent to the Post Office after a lesson and he broke the fiddle in the process.[76] In fact, he put his foot right through it and that was the end of the fiddle lessons.[77] T.P.'s mother, Bede Keane, put the broken fiddle aside in an upstairs room in their home over the pub. Eventually, Bede passed away and her other son, Gearóid, inherited the pub. Over time, the business evolved into the Goat Street Café. The broken fiddle was found in its dusty case upstairs by the new owners and was put on display in the cafe.[78]

Around 2005, about a century after Mike 'The Fiddler' moved to Springfield for good, a gifted young fiddler from Belfast then living in Dingle, Mark Mac Riocaird (Mark Crickard), noticed the fiddle on the wall of the Goat Street

Café as an ornament and had an intuition that it might have a story to tell. The instrument was broken, but it was marked with the words 'Manufactured in the U.S.' When Mark expressed an interest in the fiddle, the café's then owner gave it to him as a gift, saying: 'Take it, I don't need it.' Mark commissioned some basic repairs so that the instrument was playable again. He then gave it to his brother in Killarney for safe keeping.[79]

In 2006, Edna Uí Chinnéide, a former teacher and a long-time Blasket advocate, heard about the fiddle through her daughter Dairena who mentioned this 'special' violin.[80] Edna then met with Mark in Dingle and they discussed the intriguing story of the fiddle and its old Blasket connections. She and Mark agreed that the fiddle should be purchased by Fondúireacht an Bhlascaoid, a non-profit organisation dedicated to advancing the heritage of the Blaskets, and undergo a much more extensive refurbishing. They also agreed that the fiddle would be displayed at the Great Blasket Centre and played in live musical performances for all to enjoy as a living Blasket artefact.[81]

In Springfield nearly a decade earlier, John P. Kane, eldest son of the Mike 'The Fiddler' and the grandson of the King, had passed away, and memorial contributions from his family and friends were directed to the Fondúireacht.[82] John's surviving family substantially augmented the initial John P. Kane memorial contributions so that the Fondúireacht could move forward with the acquisition and full restoration of their grandfather's mysterious fiddle. Connor Russell of Kilbride, County Wicklow, a master violin maker, was commissioned to undertake a highly skilled professional restoration in 2007.[83]

Thus Peats Mhicí Ó Catháin, the last Blasket King, along with Mike 'The Fiddler' Kane and their descendants participated in preserving the fiddle for generations to come. The

Four grandchildren of Mike 'The Fiddler' Kane, great-grandchildren of the King, in 2007 with the famous fiddle from the island and Springfield. (L–r): Jack Kane, Joanne Kane Jacob, Mary Kane and Larry Kane.

result of this transatlantic collaboration is an American-made, French-style fiddle of the early twentieth century constructed from maple, spruce and rosewood with an ebony fingerboard – a very special antique violin in perfect working condition. In addition to being on display at the Great Blasket Centre, one of the top tourist attractions in County Kerry, the fiddle has also been played during the school year by a specially selected music student enrolled in Coláiste Íde, a girls' boarding school near Dingle.[84]

It is fascinating that two of the best-known stories of the Great Blasket, the drownings of Eibhlín Nic Niocaill and Dómhnall Ó Criomhthain and the wanderings of the famous fiddle, are intertwined. It is a striking reminder of how events in a small, isolated community are always interconnected and how they can grow in importance over time in the folklore of a community. They are also valuable in providing an insight at a very human level into the life of a community and its people.

In many ways it is the tale of the fiddle that brought together the Kanes of today. And this classic fiddle legend subsequently gained a sequel that brought itself full circle. Mike 'The Fiddler' Kane never explained the disappearance of his first instrument to anyone; in fact, he almost never told his children about the Blaskets at all. It was primarily the second-generation Americans, the King's great-grandchildren who, less burdened by efforts at survival than their Depression-era parents, fostered a curiosity about their heritage and renewed relations between the Springfield Kanes and the Blasket Ó Catháins. In fact, John's four children decided to use their modest inheritance after his December 1997 death to travel to Ireland together, sans spouses or children, for the bonding experience of a lifetime.

Ten years later they were even able to return to Ireland to visit the Great Blasket Centre, this time with their spouses and children in tow, to attend the presentation of the refurbished fiddle. That night, the late John's oldest son Jack made a speech wherein he recounted the tale of his first trip to Ireland in 1996 with his wife and eldest daughter: 'My father and his sister Mary had given me some names of relatives in the Dingle area ... Our first morning in Dingle we spent driving Slea Head and stopping at Kruger's pub to see if we could get out to the Great Blasket Island. The answer was that it was too late in the season, but by chance, the only patron in the pub at that time was Muiris Ó Guithín, my father's first cousin.'[85] It was the barkeeper who deduced their relationship, serving as a translator between the English-speaking Americans and the Irish-speaking senior. Both parties were surprised to have stumbled on such a close relation, quite by chance. So much so, that the Kanes even wondered if they were tourists falling for a local prank!

Muiris suggested they all go over to his nearby house – which the government had provided when he and other islanders were evacuated from the island – to meet 'Seán,' whom Jack presumed would be a bilingual son. In actuality, Seán was Muiris' older brother. The communication barrier remained intact, but it proved to be only a minor nuisance. After parking his rental car dead in the middle of a three-way intersection, as per Muiris's pantomimed instructions, Jack and the ladies entered a tiny cottage, painted pink on the interior, where cats sat by the fireplace warming themselves. The brothers enthusiastically poured heights of whiskey and produced photos of mutual family, including Jack's parents from their 1970 visit. 'That was the start of a connection and love for family in Ireland that I never anticipated,' Jack affirmed.[86]

Like ripples spreading outward, so the story of the Kane fiddle continued to grow. After Jack shared his recollection of these events at the Great Blasket Centre celebration, his son, John A. Kane Jr, in turn, wrote up an account of the proceedings and published it on the Internet on his personal blog, along with some background about the King, 'An Rí'. Years later, John Jr received an improbable email from a perfect stranger, a Dennis 'DK' Kane who tentatively proposed that they might be related. Dennis had found John Jr's blog post while searching the Internet for information about his ancestor also known as 'An Rí'. After some back and forth, the two young men confirmed that their fathers were first cousins and grandsons of Mike 'The Fiddler' Kane.[87] Furthermore, John Jr had the peculiar feeling that Dennis was already familiar – because Dennis's demeanour and surfing lifestyle so greatly resembled that of mutual cousin, fellow Mike 'The Fiddler' great-grandson Lawrence Andrew 'Andy' Jacob.

This surprising discovery occurred in autumn 2012, a most opportune time as it turned out. The Great Blasket Centre was then organising a calendar of events to take part in connection with The Gathering, an international campaign organised by Fáilte Ireland that encouraged those with Irish heritage to reunite in Ireland in 2013. John Jr proposed that Dennis and Andy, who lived on opposite coasts of the US, take The Gathering as an opportunity to meet and explore the land of their shared heritage – or better put, the *water* of their shared heritage. As the co-founder of Vermont-based independent media production company Butter Flavored Films, John Jr and business partner Mark Covino decided to document the meeting and subsequent adventures of these two American surfers in the rough seas of their fishermen forefathers.

The two then launched a successful fund-raising campaign, generating enough money to fly the pair to Ireland with a small professional crew for the documentation of a film titled *The Crest*. As the project grew, more cousins got involved, making it a true family affair. With the help of Kathleen O'Shea of Ventry, a niece of Seán and Muiris Ó Guithín, they were able to connect with descendants of the Ó Catháin family in Ireland.[88] Twenty-one descendants of the King and his son Mike 'The Fiddler' plus six spouses thereof participated in 'The Blasket and West Kerry Gathering' that May, exploring their roots and researching the details of their genealogy.

The week was a great success by any standard. Dennis and Andy made it out to the Great Blasket and ran from *An Tráigh Bháin* into its salty waves, where they surfed on boards built by one and painted by the other. This feat caught the attention of Irish news outlets such as *Nuacht TG4*[89] and *The*

Irish Times. 'Andy and DK have made connections all over the Dingle peninsula it seems, loving the hospitality, the occasion of The Gathering, the freedom that they are living,' *The Irish Times* wrote.[90] 'They spent most of the previous night locked into an unnamed pub in Dingle town, grabbing three hours' sleep before our meeting in the Great Blasket Centre at Dún Chaoin.'[91]

The most valued witnesses, however, were fellow participants in The Gathering, specifically Mike Carney and Ann Flower, daughter of the famous Blasket visitor Robin Flower. They were both on the island with their own family members at the time of Andy and Dennis's triumphant surf, making it a reunion of three prominent branches of the Blasket family. Mike loved the surprising sight of people once again enjoying the cold waters of his youth. 'It's great. It's unbelievable!' he later exclaimed, 'Number one to see them swimming there, and there wasn't a seal in sight.'[92] They all had the occasion to meet up later and trade stories when a group of ten Ó Catháin descendants plus three spouses gathered with Carneys, Flowers and others for a gourmet dinner of mutton pies at John Benny Moriarty's Pub in Dingle, a fitting venue as the pub's namesake proprietor is married to Edna Uí Chinnéide's daughter Éilís.

When word reached Mark Mac Riocaird that night that the family of the King was in town, Mark promptly appeared at John Benny's together with the famous Kane fiddle. To the delight of all in attendance, especially the King's descendants, he coaxed sweet airs out of the historic instrument until the early hours of the morning, the very fiddle that had once been owned by the Kanes' ancestor, Mike 'The Fiddler' Kane.

This historic Blasket fiddle, now restored to its original beauty, is a continuing performing link with the Kanes' forebears as well as with a way of life on the Great Blasket that has now passed into history. It has also become an instrument

Fiddler Mark Mac Riocaird plays the fiddle that once belonged to Mike 'The Fiddler' Kane at John Benny Moriarty's Pub in Dingle in 2013 with ten of the King's descendants and the Ó Cinnéide, Flower and Carney families in attendance. Photo by Jack Kane.

of reunion more than Mike 'The Fiddler' Kane could ever have foreseen. Not only did it possess the power to bring the Irish in Springfield together on sidewalks and in dance halls alike, it also ultimately summoned his future grandchildren and even great-grandchildren for a once-in-a-lifetime memorial. 'A number of us from Ireland and the USA gathered together in Dingle with many of us meeting for the first time. We had a magnificent event at the Dingle Skellig Hotel with a dinner overlooking Dingle Bay, cousins meeting cousins, and Padraic Keane of Sligo showing us his huge genealogical chart of the descendants of An Rí,' Jack remembers. 'It was a wonderful evening that none of us will ever forget.'

The bonds forged during that trip appear to be the kind that last, even into future generations. At the time of this writing, John Kane Jr is leading Andy and Dennis along with his film crew back to Ireland for their second joint trip, where they hope to surf again the finicky waters between the Blaskets and the mainland, waters that have taken lives but also forged a legacy in which the lads take part. And this time, they will be making the trip with a new addition in tow: Andrew AnRi 'Drew' Jacob – Andy's firstborn son. Drew's second name was chosen in the style of the Blasket tradition, as a tribute to his forebear: his great-great-great-grandfather, Peats Mhicí Ó Catháin, An Rí, the last Blasket King.

13. The King's Legacy

Peats Mhicí Ó Catháin, the last King of the Great Blasket, was certainly a larger-than-life individual. While there were certainly other very distinguished residents on the island during his lifetime, including the famous author trio of Tomás Ó Criomhthain, Muiris Ó Súilleabháin and Peig Sayers, Peats Mhicí was clearly the leading personality on the island itself during his 25-year or so 'reign' as King.

What do we know about Peats Mhicí, the King? He was a tall clean-shaven man with broad shoulders and a very loud and forceful voice. He was physically strong and energetic to a fault, with a huge capacity for hard work. He was fluent in English and Irish. He was a steady source of information about the world beyond the island and put breaking news in context for the islanders by interjecting his broad general knowledge about national and world affairs. He was an opinionated and outspoken political leader. He represented the islanders in their dealings with the government. He was a fisherman and postman, and managed a bed-and-breakfast business in his home. He was hospitable by nature, greeting visitors, making connections for them with island resources and maintaining an extensive correspondence with many of them after their departure. He was passionate about Irish culture and loved traditional song and dance. He was a forthright man of great integrity. He was both a long-time widower and a dedicated family man.

The King's house in ruins in 2014 (lower right) with the strand visible at the rear. The ruins to the left are the house of the King's daughter, Máire (Ní Chatháin) Uí Ghuithín. See pp. 94, 145 and 231 to compare this view with earlier photos.

And, in addition to all these things, he played the challenging role of King of the Great Blasket, at least as he saw it, to the absolute hilt.

Peats Mhicí had the good fortune to serve as King during a brief period of relatively good economic times on the Great Blasket, particularly before the First World War.[1] During this period, the islanders became property owners and their very limited growing fields were reorganised in a more efficient fashion for the benefit of all island families. These land reforms were especially important to the islanders and addressed long-festering economic and social issues. Fishing was fairly good as mackerel was in abundance and prices were good. The Congested Districts Board offered employment opportunities for island residents in connection with public works projects on the island (the construction of a new pier, new roads and the east-facing 'new houses' at the top of the village).[2] These public works jobs were a godsend, providing a much-needed infusion of cash for island families.

However, these favourable economic conditions proved to be short-lived and were ultimately insufficient to surmount the external forces that conspired to undermine the island's economy. The land-reform initiatives were significant but realising the benefits thereof was dependent on the successful operation of the island's underlying economy. As time went on, the island's fishing business virtually collapsed because of increased foreign competition and a 'protective tariff' of $1 per barrel imposed on imports of mackerel to the United States that caused fish prices to plummet. These forces eventually made it exceedingly difficult for the islanders to make a decent living from fishing, their primary trade.[3] Thus, the essential sustainability of the island as a cohesive functioning community was effectively compromised.

The three root causes of the erosion of the viability of the Great Blasket were: the lack of reliable communications, poor and inconsistent transportation to and from the island and, in large part as a result of these first two factors, a floundering economy. All three root causes were directly related to irreversible natural features of the island: its physical remoteness from the mainland and the adverse prevailing weather conditions.

Not surprisingly, the consequence of these multiple pressures on the island was the accelerating flow of emigration to the mainland and to the United States. This unremitting exodus of the island's youth and the inexorable ageing of the remaining adults further reduced the island's productive capacity and diminished its sense of community. Island women, in particular, insisted on a better lifestyle than the island could offer and they made their exit whenever the opportunity presented itself. The remaining island population was comprised mostly of older bachelors.

Ironically, it was the isolation of the island that originally attracted settlers from the mainland to the Great Blasket hundreds of years earlier. But, in a sad quirk of fate, the island's isolation eventually became an insurmountable obstacle.

Frankly, no King could have overcome these complex geographic, economic and demographic facts of life without direct and substantial assistance from the government. In the political environment prevailing in Ireland at the time, such assistance was not forthcoming.

It is not unreasonable to conclude, however, that Peats Mhicí's death in 1929, twenty-four years before the island's evacuation, and the absence of a strong successor King created a leadership vacuum on the island at the very time when the Great Blasket most needed an effective indigenous voice in dealing with the government on these fundamental issues.

One modest illustration of this vacuum is that the 1947 letter to Taoiseach Éamon de Valera demanding government action came from Mike Carney who had left the island ten years earlier and was living in Dublin. This pivotal letter accurately expressed the consensus sentiment of the islanders at that time. But it came from a former islander with no real current standing to speak for the community, other than that of a bereaved brother upset at the inaction of the government in the face of clearly deteriorating conditions on the island.

It seems that a more permanent and empowered 'kingship' on the Great Blasket coupled with an incumbent of the stature of Peats Mhicí might have better served the island's interests to at least some degree. A single strong community leader would probably have been in a better position to mount and sustain a more effective long-term political campaign on its behalf. While the island's core issues were physical in nature, they had an essential underlying political dimension.

The optimal time for the islanders to have pressed their communication and transportation issues with the government was during the 1930s, before conditions reached the point where the demise of the island community was almost a foregone conclusion. This was just after Peats Mhicí's death. Unfortunately, there was no apparent inclination on the part of the islanders to name a successor King. It may have been that there was no islander who, by comparison with Peats Mhicí, was suitable for the role. The old rundale system that may have historically led to the appointment of an island King was by then just a distant memory. In any event, the resulting gap in strong indigenous leadership may have been a contributing factor in determining the island's fate.

From a purely political point of view, and this is highly speculative, there might have been a brief window of opportunity during the decade of the 1930s to leverage the island's new-found stature for political advantage. This emergent level of fame was achieved as result of the publication of the five masterworks by Blasket authors during this period *(Island Cross-Talk, The Islandman, Twenty Years A-Growing, Peig* and *An Old Woman's Reflections)*. A well-orchestrated political campaign capitalising on the island's rising high profile might have generated broad-based political support for government action to ameliorate the root causes of the island's core problems. Such government action could and should have focused, not on the island's evacuation at this point, but on installing a consistently reliable communications system and instituting regular ferry service to and from the island. Instead, however, 'the golden age of Blasket literature ironically coincided with the imminent collapse of the island community'.[4]

Successfully mounting such a political campaign for government investment in the communications and transportation infrastructure of the Great Blasket would have required just the right spokesperson as well as the commitment and stamina to sustain the effort over an extended period of time. The example of the effective role of the King of Tory Island and his eventual successor, Patsy Dan Rogers, in opposing the government's plan to evacuate Tory in the mid-1970s underscores this point. The preservation of Tory as a viable island community occurred just twenty years after the evacuation of the Great Blasket. And it occurred, in large measure, because of the highly vocal and persistent indigenous leadership. It should be acknowledged, however, that the political climate in Ireland might have been more receptive to a plea for needed infrastructure improvements in the 1970s than in the 1940s and early 1950s when the fate of the Great Blasket hung in the balance.

At this point, however, such discussion of a successor King is nothing more than mere conjecture and maybe even unfair second-guessing. It should be clear that this observation about the impact of the passing of Peats Mhicí and the absence of a successor King is in no way a criticism of the islanders and the way in which they addressed the deteriorating conditions on the island. The Blasket Islanders did the very best they could with the scarce resources then at their disposal.

Eventually, the islanders confronted the reality that the government was not going to address the issues of providing regular transportation and reliable communication. They then changed their strategy and lobbied for relocation to the mainland. In pursuit of that objective, the islanders waged a very respectable political and public relations effort, including letters to the Taoiseach, securing support from the opposition party in the Dáil, sending the infamous distress telegram and more letters of pleading, and the issuance of a moving 'memorial'. The islanders even induced the Taoiseach himself to visit the island.

As well conceived and as well executed as these lobbying initiatives may have been, they were directed not at the preservation of the island, but the lesser goal of its evacuation.

Even then, the final government decision proved elusive for six long years of further deteriorating conditions. It appears that the narrow issue of the future of the Great Blasket raised larger policy and political issues having to do with the preservation of similar enclaves of cultural significance throughout Ireland. The government was ill equipped to deal with these issues at the time. And the rest is history.

Despite the eventual exodus of the remaining population of his beloved island kingdom, Peats Mhicí left behind a very proud and enduring legacy. One of the most important features of this legacy is the extensive body of literature that was generated on the island. While not an author himself, the King opened the figurative door to the island and put out the welcome mat for a succession of cultural visitors. He created the essential connections between the visitors and the future island authors that, over time, generated a robust library of Blasket literature. He was the principal facilitator who created the circumstances under which the latent potential of the island authors was unlocked and then fully realised. The extensive library of Irish folk literature from the Great Blasket is effectively a literary monument on which the last Blasket King, Peats Mhicí Ó Catháin, can stand proud along with the likes of islanders Ó Criomhthain, Ó Súilleabháin and Sayers.

Beyond the literary value of the Blasket literature itself, which is considerable, there is also the enormous impact of this body of work in terms of perpetuating the memory of the Great Blasket for posterity. The current prominence of the Blasket story began with the King and the island literature, but it has now been propagated far and wide through the worldwide popularity of that literature. The preservation of the memory of the Great Blasket is due in no small measure to the logistical support and enabling activities of last Blasket King.

On a more personal level, the King's children and their many descendants are also important features of his legacy. Each one of his immediate offspring was a true credit to the King and to the Great Blasket. His daughters Máire and Cáit were hosts to visitors on the island and enthusiastic goodwill ambassadors on behalf of the Great Blasket for years after they moved to Dunquin. His son Seán carried on his work as postman and he might, perhaps, have been a potential King in his own right, had his life not been unexpectedly cut short. His oldest son Mícheál (Mike 'The Fiddler') very ably represented the culture of the Great Blasket and Ireland in America.

As for the next generation of the King's family, the tradition of gracious Blasket hospitality was carried on by Máire (Ní Ghuithín) Uí Chiobháin, the King's granddaughter. She also wrote two books (*An tOileán a Bhí* and *Bean an Oileáin*) that themselves are important dimensions of the King's legacy. Other next-generation descendants of the King, whether they lived in Ireland, Britain or the United States, maintained a fierce passion for their heritage and were involved in numerous efforts to hand down the story of the Great Blasket.

Even in the current generation of the King's descendants, fervour for the Great Blasket still burns bright and will be perpetuated with creative expression through more contemporary media, including a documentary film as well as social media and blogs on the Internet. Indeed, the torch of the Great Blasket is now being passed to this generation of the Ó Catháins/Keanes/Kanes and the saga of the King continues.

Over the last twenty-plus years, Blasket descendants in Ireland and the United States, including those of the King, have collaborated with the Irish government and Fondúireacht an Bhlascaoid to establish the Great Blasket Centre in Dunquin. Furthermore, most of the land on the Great Blasket is now under government ownership and the preservation of the ruins and other much-needed visitor-oriented improvements are under way. Someday soon, one hopes, there will be a Great Blasket Island National Historical Park.

These permanent institutions will guarantee that the history of the Great Blasket and the legacy of its last King are celebrated forever. Yes, the King and his kingdom have passed into history, but their stories will continue to inspire all those who love Ireland, its language, its folklore and, of course, the Great Blasket Island itself.

In 1984, the King's granddaughter Máire (Ní Ghuithín) Uí Chiobháin wrote a fitting epitaph for the King that was included in Tim Enright's article in Cork's *Evening Echo* entitled 'Padraig Keane – King of the Blasket'. Máire's poignant words seems to capture the broad arc of the King's amazing life:

'*Fear déanta láidir, grámhar, macánta dob ea é, go raibh tréithe duchas na nglún a chuaidh roimis ann – uaisleacht na sean-Gheal ann, meas aige ar Dhia agus ar dhuine.*'

'He was a strong, loving and honest man, who carried the instinctive traits of the generations that went before him – he had the nobility of the Ancient Gaels, respect for God and for others.'[5]

As they say, 'Long live the King!'

Endnotes

Chapter 1. A Kingdom and A King

1 *The Blasket Islands – Next Parish America*, p. 63.
2 *Ibid.*, pp. 15 and 22 and *The Islands of Ireland*, p. 127.
3 *From the Great Blasket to America*, pp. 8 and 27.
4 *National Geographic Traveler*, p. 61.
5 *The Islands of Ireland, Their Scenery, People, Life and Antiquities*, pp. 102–103 and Wreck Site (http://www.wrecksite.eu/wreck.aspx?694460.
6 Irish Wrecks Online (http://www.irishwrecksonline.net/Lists/Kerry ListA.htm).
7 *The Blaskets – People and Literature*, p. 27.
8 *The Blasket Islands – Next Parish America*, pp. 23–24, *The Blasket Guide*, p. 18 and *The Western Island*, p. 32.
9 *Blasket Island Reflections*, Booklet Accompanying CD Set, p. 28.
10 *Blasket Memories*, pp. 7–8.
11 *The Ancient and Present State of the County of Kerry*, p. 183.
12 *The Blasket Islands – Next Parish America*, p. 82.
13 *The Loneliest Boy in the World*, p. 101.
14 *The Blaskets – People and Literature*, pp. 34–35 and *The Blasket Islands – Next Parish America*, p. 43.
15 Michael J. Carney, Springfield, Massachusetts.
16 *The Loneliest Boy in the World*, pp. 95–97.
17 *The Islandman*, pp. 233–235 and *The Blasket Islands – Next Parish America*, pp. 79–90.
18 *The Blaskets – People and Literature*, pp. 46–53.
19 *A Day in Our Life*, p. 7.
20 *On an Irish Island*, p. 59.
21 *Evening Echo*, Padraig Keane – King of the Blasket, p. 8.
22 *Blasket Island Reflections*, CD 1, Track 2, Máirín Nic Eoin.
23 *The Blasket Islands – Next Parish America*, p. 14.
24 Michael J. Carney, Springfield, Massachusetts.
25 *History of Ireland*, p. 11.

Endnotes

26 *Paradise Lost?*, pp. 202–203 and *From the Great Blasket to America*, p. 135.
27 Dáithí de Mórdha, the Great Blasket Centre, Dunquin, County Kerry.
28 *Ibid.*
29 *Blasket Lives*, Pádraig Peats Mhicí Ó Catháin.
30 *Island Home – The Blasket Heritage*, p. 23.
31 *The Islandman*, p. 30.
32 Dáithí de Mórdha, the Great Blasket Centre, Dunquin, County Kerry.
33 *Blasket Lives*, Pádraig Mhártain Ó Catháin.
34 *Ar Muir is ar Tír*, pp. 9–10.
35 *Blasket Lives*, Pádraig Peats Mhicí Ó Catháin.
36 Michael J. Carney, Springfield, Massachusetts.
37 *Ibid.*

Chapter 2. Kings in Irish and Blasket History

1 *Irish Kings and High Kings*, p. 7.
2 *Annals of the Four Masters*, Annal M379.1- and Annal M405.1.
3 *Irish Kings and High Kings*, p. 41, 42, 53 and 57.
4 *History of Ireland*, pp. 40–49.
5 *Irish Kings and High Kings*, p. 267.
6 *Ibid.*, p. 270.
7 *History of Ireland*, p. 43.
8 *Ibid.*, p. 48 and *Brian Bórú, The Greatest High King of Ireland*, pp. 4–10.
9 *Wars of the Irish Kings*, pp. xxii–xxiii.
10 *Ibid.*, pp. xxii-xxv and *History of Ireland*, pp. 50–55.
11 *Medieval Iveragh: Kingdoms and Dynasties*, pp. 148–150.
12 *An Rí [The King]: Example of Traditional Social Organisation.*
13 *Ibid.*
14 *What was Rundale and Where Did It Come From?*, p. 179.
15 *Ibid.*, p. 156.
16 *Studies of Field Systems in the British Isles*, pp. 584–586.
17 *What was Rundale and Where Did It Come From?*, p. 162.
18 *Ibid.* p. 186.
19 *Erris, in the 'Irish Highlands' and the 'Atlantic Railway'*, pp. 47–48.
20 *An Rí [The King]: Example of Traditional Social Organisation.*
21 *Observations on the Character, Customs and Superstitions of the Irish*, p. 164.
22 *A Topographical Dictionary of Ireland,* Cape Clear Island, A Parish.
23 *Rundale and its Social Concomitants*, p. 233.
24 *An Rí [The King]: Example of Traditional Social Organisation.*

25 *Ibid.*
26 *Erris, in the 'Irish Highlands' and the 'Atlantic Railway'*, p. 48.
27 *A Topographical Dictionary of Ireland*, Claddagh, A Village.
28 *The Ecological Dynamics of the Rundale Agrarian Commune*, p. 14.
29 *Ibid.*
30 *The Ecological Dynamics of the Rundale Agrarian Commune*, p. 14 and *Marx's Theory of Politics*, pp. 230–231.
31 *An Account of Ireland, Statistical and Political, Vol. 1*, p. 260.
32 *An Rí [The King]: Example of Traditional Social Organisation* and *The Blaskets, People and Literature*, p. 38.
33 *Tory Island: A Remote and Historic Outpost*, p. 4.
34 *Ibid.*
35 Patsy Dan Rogers, King, Tory Island, County Donegal.
36 Patsy Dan Rogers, King, Tory Island, County Donegal (http://patsydanrodgers.littleireland.ie).
37 Patsy Dan Rogers, King, Tory Island, County Donegal.
38 Dáithí de Mórdha, the Great Blasket Centre, Dunquin, County Kerry.
39 *Ibid.*
40 *Blasket Lives*, Pádraig Peats Mhicí Ó Catháin.
41 *Island Home – The Blasket Heritage*, pp. 23–24.
42 *The Western Island*, pp. 10–11.
43 *On an Irish Island*, pp. 19–20.
44 *Scéal agus Dán Oileáin*, p. 34.
45 *The Islandman*, p. 30.
46 *In Wicklow and West Kerry*, p. 41.
47 *An Caomhnóir, Rí an Oileáin*, 1990.
48 *An tOileánach Léannta*, p. 35.
49 *From the Great Blasket to America*, p. 18.
50 *Thar Bealach Isteach*, p. 29.

Chapter 3. *The Last Blasket King: A Profile*

1 *Ceiliúradh an Bhlascaoid # 14*, p. 9.
2 *The Islandman*, pp. 84 and 145.
3 *Ar Muir is ar Tír*, pp. 9–10.
4 *An Rí [The King]: Example of Traditional Social Organisation.*
5 *Blasket Lives*, Pádraig Peats Mhicí Ó Catháin.
6 *The Islandman*, p. 17.
7 *Allagar na hInise*, p. 42.
8 *Hungry for Home*, p. 22.
9 *Blasket Lives*, Pádraig Peats Mhicí Ó Catháin.

Endnotes

10   *Ibid.*

11   *The Blaskets – People and Literature*, p. 39.

12   *Island Cross-Talk*, p. 7 and 8.

13   *Island Home – The Blasket Heritage*, pp. 23–24.

14   *An Claidheamh Soluis*, 23 November 1908, p. 7.

15   *Oidhreacht an Bhlascaoid*, p. 211–212.

16   *An tOileán a Bhí*, p. 70.

17   *A Pity Youth Does Not Last*, p. 40.

18   *The Islands of Ireland*, p. 100.

19   *Thar Bealach Isteach*.

20   *The Lone Seagull*, p. 1.

21   Dáithí de Mórdha, the Great Blasket Centre, Dunquin, County Kerry.

22   *The Islandman*, p. 30.

23   *The Blaskets – People and Literature*, pp. 38–39.

24   *The Lone Seagull*, p. 5.

25   *Blasket Lives*, Pádraig Peats Mhicí Ó Catháin.

26   *An Caomhnóir*, Rí an Oileáin, 1990.

27   *Blasket Lives*, Pádraig Peats Mhicí Ó Catháin.

28   *Oidhreacht an Bhlascaoid*, p. 212.

29   *Allagar na hInise*, pp. 40–41.

30   *Island Cross-Talk*, p. 12.

31   *Oidhreacht an Bhlascaoid*, pp. 213–214.

32   *Blasket Lives*, Máire (Ní Chatháin) Uí Chriomhthain.

33   *Islandman Translated*, p. 191.

34   *Island Cross-Talk*, Spring, 1920, pp. 68–69.

35   *Ibid.*, Spring, 1920, p. 71.

36   *Seanchas ón Oileán Tiar*, p. 122.

37   *Méiní, The Blasket Nurse*, p. 59.

38   *Oidhreacht an Bhlascaoid*, pp. 208–221.

39   *Twenty Years A-Growing*, p. 20.

40   *Island Cross-Talk*, March, 1920, p. 74.

Chapter 4. The King's Lineage

1   *The Blasket Islands – Next Parish America*, p. 33.

2   Dáithí de Mórdha, the Great Blasket Centre, Dunquin, County Kerry.

3   *Blasket Memories*, pp. 33–34.

4   *Blasket Lives*, Pádraig Mhártain Ó Catháin.

5   *The Ancient and Present State of the County of Kerry*, p. 183.

6   *The Blasket Islands – Next Parish America*, p. 33

7   *Blasket Lives*, Pádraig Mhártain Ó Catháin.

8   *Ibid.*
9   *Ibid.*
10 *The Islandman*, p. 47.
11 *Ar Muir is ar Tír*, pp. 9–10.
12 *Ibid.*
13 Census of Ireland, 1901.
14 *Blasket Lives*, Pádraig Peats Mhicí Ó Catháin.
15 *The Blaskets – People and Literature*, p. 167.
16 Dáithí de Mórdha, the Great Blasket Centre, Dunquin, County Kerry.
17 *The Blaskets – People and Literature*, p. 167 and *The Lone Seagull*, p. 1.
18 *The Lone Seagull*, p. 5.
19 *Ibid.*, p. 3.
20 *Ibid.*, p. 5.
21 *The Islandman*, p. 47.
22 *Méiní, The Blasket Nurse*, p. 61.
23 Certificate of Baptism, Pádraig Ó Catháin, St Vincent's Church, Ballyferriter, County Kerry.
24 *The Islandman*, p. 145.
25 *Ibid.*, pp. 144–145.
26 *Ibid.*, p. 145.
27 *Ibid.*, p. 113.
28 *Blasket Lives*, Máire (Ní Chatháin) Uí Chriomhthain and *The Blaskets – People and Literature*, p. 130.
29 *Blasket Lives*, Máire (Ní Chatháin) Uí Chriomhthain.
30 *Blasket Island Reflections*, Booklet Accompanying CD Set, p. 9.
31 *Blasket Lives*, Máire (Ní Chatháin) Uí Chriomhthain.
32 *The Blaskets – People and Literature*, p. 131.
33 *Blasket Lives*, Máire (Ní Chatháin) Uí Chriomhthain.
34 *The Islandman*, p. 218.
35 *Blasket Lives*, Máire (Ní Chatháin) Uí Chriomhthain.
36 *Irish Tourism, Image, Culture and Identity*, p. 160.
37 *Blasket Lives*, Máire (Ní Chatháin) Uí Chriomhthain and *The Blaskets – People and Literature*, pp. 131–132.
38 *Letters from the Great Blasket*, p. 20.
39 *A Day in Our Life*, p. 27.
40 *Letters from the Great Blasket*, p. 33 and *Blasket Memories*, p. 116.
41 *Letters from the Great Blasket*, p. 7 and 11.
42 *Ibid.*, p. 7 and *A Day in Our Life*, p. 24.
43 *A Day in Our Life*, p 1 and pp. 28–30.
44 *Ibid.*, p. 28.
45 *Ibid.*, p. 14.
46 *Ibid.*, p. 3 and 9.

47   *Ibid.*, p. 12.
48   *Blasket Lives*, Mícheál 'Bofar' Ó Catháin.
49   Padraic Keane, County Sligo.
50   *Blasket Lives*, Mícheál 'Bofar Ó Catháin.
51   *Ibid.*
52   *Ibid.*
53   *Ibid.* and Padraic Keane, County Sligo.
54   *Blasket Lives*, Mícheál 'Bofar Ó Catháin.
55   *Ibid.*
56   *Ibid.*
57   *Méiní, The Blasket Nurse*, pp. 78–79.
58   *Blasket Lives*, Mícheál 'Bofar Ó Catháin.
59   *The Lone Seagull*, p. 58.
60   *Blasket Lives*, Mícheál 'Bofar Ó Catháin.
61   *Ibid.*
62   *Ibid.*
63   *The Lone Seagull*, p. 4.
64   *Blasket Lives*, Mícheál 'Bofar Ó Catháin.
65   *The Lone Seagull*, pp. 4–5.
66   *Ibid.*, p. 94.
67   *Ibid.*, p. 75.
68   *Ibid.*, p. 4.
69   Michael J. Carney of Springfield, Massachusetts was in attendance at this event.
70   *The Lone Seagull*, p. 75.
71   *Ibid.*, pp. 2, 71 and 76–77.
72   *Ibid.*, p.2 and p. 71.
73   *Ibid.*, pp. 97–99.
74   *Ibid.*, p. 113.
75   *Ibid.*, p. 121.
76   *Ibid.*, p. 123.
77   *Ibid.*, pp. 57–58.
78   *Ibid.*, p. 60.
79   *Ibid.*, p. 76.
80   *Ibid.*, p. 76.

Chapter 5. *The King's Youth*

1   Michael J. Carney, Springfield, Massachusetts.
2   *The Blaskets – People and Literature*, p. 39.
3   *Scéal agus Dán Oileáin*, p. 246.

4   *The Islandman*, p. 18.
5   *Scéal agus Dán Oileáin*, p. 246.
6   *The Islandman*, pp. 38–39.
7   *A Pity Youth Does Not Last*, p. 40 and *The Western Island*, pp. 10–11.
8   *The Islandman*, p. 18.
9   *Ibid.*, p. 21.
10 *Scéal agus Dán Oileáin*, p. 246.
11 *The Islandman*, p. 47.
12 *Ibid.*, p. 21.
13 *The Blaskets – People and Literature*, p. 39.
14 *Blasket Lives*, Pádraig Peats Mhicí Ó Catháin.
15 *The Islandman*, pp. 15–16.
16 *Ibid.*, p. 35.
17 *Ibid.*, p. 17.
18 *Blasket Lives*, Pádraig Peats Mhicí Ó Catháin.
19 *An tOileánach Léannta*, p. 11.
20 *The Islandman*, pp. 59–62.
21 *Evening Echo*, Padraig Keane – King of the Blaskets, p. 8.
22 *Blasket Lives*, Pádraig Peats Mhicí Ó Catháin.
23 Dáithí de Mórdha, the Great Blasket Centre, Dunquin, County Kerry.
24 *The Islandman*, pp. 47–49.
25 *Ibid.*, pp. 62–63.
26 *An tOileánach* (2002), pp. 45–46 and *Blasket Island Reflections*, Booklet Accompanying CD Set, pp. 36–37.
27 Michael J. Carney, Springfield, Massachusetts.
28 *Blasket Memories*, p. 33.
29 *Poets and Poetry of the Great Blasket*, p. 119.
30 *Seanchas ón Oileán Tiar*, p. 56.
31 *Poets and Poetry of the Great Blasket*, p. 15 and Dáithí de Mórdha, the Great Blasket Centre, Dunquin, County Kerry.
32 *Blasket Memories*, p. 34.
33 *Poets and Poetry of the Great Blasket*, p. 85.
34 Michael J. Carney, Springfield, Massachusetts.
35 *The Lone Seagull*, p. 1.

Chapter 6. The King's Family

1   *A Pity Youth Does Not Last*, p. 31.
2   *Méiní, The Blasket Nurse*, p. 161.
3   *The Islandman*, p. 84.
4   *Blasket Lives*, Pádraig Peats Mhicí Ó Catháin and *The Blaskets – People and Literature*, p. 167.

Endnotes

5   *The Islandman*, p. 84.
6   *Blasket Lives*: Cáit (Ní Chatháin) Uí Cathasa, Padraic Keane, County Sligo, and Census of Ireland, 1901.
7   *Island Cross-Talk*, p. 109.
8   Michael J. Carney, Springfield, Massachusetts.
9   SS *Celtic*, Passenger Ships and Images (www.ancestry.com).
10 *Blasket Lives*, Máire (Ní Chatháin) Uí Ghuithín.
11 *Blasket Lives*: Cáit (Ní Chatháin) Uí Cathasa.
12 *Blasket Lives*: Seán an Rí Ó Catháin.
13 *Blasket Lives*, Pádraig Peats Mhicí Ó Catháin.
14 Dáithí de Mórdha, the Great Blasket Centre, Dunquin, County Kerry.
15 *The Blaskets*, p. 26.
16 *On an Irish Island*, p. 46.

Chapter 7. The King's Stewardship

1   Dáithí de Mórdha, the Great Blasket Centre, Dunquin, County Kerry.
2   *An Baile, Highland History and Culture*.
3   *Island Cross-Talk*, p. 71.
4   *The Blasket Islands – Next Parish America*, pp. 87–89.
5   *Seanchas ón Oileán Tiar*, p. 140.
6   *Blasket Memories*, p. 18.
7   *A Day in Our Life*, p. 3 and *The Islandman*, pp. 233–235.
8   Michael J. Carney, Springfield, Massachusetts.
9   *The Blasket Islands – Next Parish America*, p. 18 and pp. 79–90.
10 *The Blasket Island Guide*, pp. 31–32.
11 Padraic Keane, County Sligo.
12 *A Galician in Ireland*, 16 September 1928, p. 35.
13 *The Islandman*, pp. 233–235.
14 *The Western Island*, pp. 37–38.
15 Padraic Keane, County Sligo.
16 *What was Rundale and Where Did It Come From?*, p. 166.
17 *Blasket Memories*, p. 78.
18 Dáithí de Mórdha, the Great Blasket Centre, Dunquin, County Kerry.
19 *Evening Echo*, Padraig Keane – King of the Blasket, p. 8.
20 *The Islandman*, pp. 201–204.
21 *Twenty Years A-Growing*, pp. 168–169.
22 *Blasket Memories*, p. 32.
23 *The Islandman*, pp. 154–155 and pp. 179–180.
24 Michael J. Carney, Springfield, Massachusetts.
25 *Méiní, The Blasket Nurse*, p. 138.

26   *Twenty Years A-Growing*, pp. 140–147.
27   *Méiní, The Blasket Nurse*, p. 139.
28   *Ibid.*, p. 139.
29   *Twenty Years A-Growing*, p. 142.
30   *An tOileán a Bhí*, pp.69–70.
31   *Blasket Memories*, p. 107.
32   *Blasket Lives*, Pádraig Peats Mhicí Ó Catháin.
33   *An Caomhnóir*, Rí an Oileáin, 1990.
34   *From the Great Blasket to America*, p. 47.
35   *Blasket Lives*, Pádraig Peats Mhicí Ó Catháin.
36   *The Western Island*, p. 11.
37   *Twenty Years A-Growing*, pp. 128–139.
38   *A Pity Youth Does Not Last*, pp. 40–41.
39   *An Old Woman's Reflections*, pp. 113–114.
40   *A Pity Youth Does Not Last*, pp. 52–54.
41   *Twenty Years A-Growing*, pp. 42–43.
42   *The Blaskets – People and Literature*, pp. 148–149.
43   *Twenty Years A-Growing*, pp. 19–23.
44   *Ibid.*, pp. 220–221.
45   *Allagar na hInise*, p. 74.
46   *Méiní, The Blasket Nurse*, pp. 23–25.
47   *Ibid.*, p. 47.
48   *Ibid.*, p. 52.
49   *Ibid.*, p. 53.
50   Dáithí de Mórdha, the Great Blasket Centre, Dunquin, County Kerry.
51   *Méiní, The Blasket Nurse*, pp. 88–99.
52   *Ibid.*, p. 91 and *The Blaskets – People and Literature*, p. 55.
53   *Méiní, The Blasket Nurse*, pp. 155–156.
54   *Ibid.*, p. 174.
55   *A Dark Day on the Blaskets*, p. 69 and *The Western Island*, pp. 15–16.
56   *An tOileánach Léannta*, p. 19.
57   *Méiní, The Blasket Nurse*, p. 85.
58   Michael J. Carney, Springfield, Massachusetts.
59   *From the Great Blasket to America*, p. 19.
60   Michael J. Carney, Springfield, Massachusetts, interview for *The Crest*.
61   *The Blaskets – People and Literature*, p. 39.
62   *The Kerryman*, 15 June 1929, Second Edition, p. 13.
63   *Blasket Lives*, Pádraig Peats Mhicí Ó Catháin.
64   *Island Cross-Talk*, Spring, 1920, p. 75.
65   *The Western Island*, p. 28. A rick is a rack for storing and drying turf.
66   *Blasket Lives*, Pádraig Peats Mhicí Ó Catháin.
67   *Island Cross-Talk*, p. 197.

68   View from the Pier, Interview with Dáithí de Mórdha (www.viewfrom
      thepier.com/2013/09/04/).

Chapter 8. Island Visitors and The King

1   *From the Great Blasket to America*, p. 68.
2   *Ibid.*, p. 68.
3   *Blasket Memories*, p. 78.
4   *An tOileánach Léannta*, p. 28.
5   *Allagar Na hInse*, p. 19–20.
6   *From the Great Blasket to America*, p. 69.
7   *Ibid.*, p. 68.
8   *Ibid.*, p. 69.
9   *On an Irish Island*, pp. 15–16.
10   *Hungry for Home*, p. 117.
11   *On an Irish Island*, p. 19.
12   *In Wicklow and West Kerry*, p. 39.
13   *Ceiliúradh an Bhlascaoid* # 14, pp. 112–113.
14   *In Wicklow and West Kerry*, p. 40–41.
15   *Ibid.*, pp. 41–42.
16   *Ibid.*, p. 42.
17   *Ibid.*, pp. 42–43.
18   *Ibid.*, p. 46.
19   *Ibid.*, p. 43.
20   *Ibid.*, p. 44.
21   *Ibid.*, p. 43.
22   *Ibid.*, p. 46.
23   *Ibid.*, p. 48.
24   *Ibid.*, p. 49.
25   *Hungry for Home*, p. 119.
26   *The Blaskets – People and Literature*, p. 134.
27   *On an Irish Island*, p. 23.
28   *Méiní, The Blasket Nurse*, p. 80.
29   *Blasket Lives*, Máire (Ní Chatháin) Uí Chatháin.
30   *Islandman* Translated, p. 38.
31   *On an Irish Island*, pp. 10–11.
32   *Islandman* Translated, p. 39.
33   *On an Irish Island*, p. 20.
34   *Blasket Memories*, p. 78.
35   *On an Irish Island*, p. 16.
36   *The Blaskets – People and Literature*, pp. 135–136.

37   *Blasket Memories*, p. 90.
38   *The Blaskets – People and Literature*, p. 135.
39   Michael J. Carney, Springfield, Massachusetts.
40   *Blasket Memories*, pp. 90–91.
41   *On an Irish Island* p. 34.
42   *The Islandman*, pp. 223–224.
43   *Orality and Agency*, p. 137.
44   *The Islandman*, pp. 224–225.
45   *Blasket Memories*, pp. 91–92.
46   *On an Irish Island*, p. 268.
47   *Blasket Memories*, p. 91.
48   *Islandman* Translated, p. 47.
49   *On an Irish Island*, p. 32.
50   *Ibid.*, pp. 38–39.
51   *A Day in Our Life*, p. 5.
52   Irish Biographies, Carl Marstrander (http://www.ainm.ie/Bio.aspx?ID=460).
53   *A Dark Day on the Blaskets*, pp. 121–125.
54   *Ibid.*, pp. 14–17.
55   *Ibid.*, p. 143.
56   *The Loneliest Boy in the World*, p. 65.
57   *The Irish Independent*, The Girl Who was Loved by Pearse, 17 September 1952.
58   *A Dark Day on the Blaskets*, pp. 68–75.
59   *Ibid.*, p. 85.
60   *Ibid.*, pp. 80–81.
61   *The Irish Independent*, The Girl Who was Loved by Pearse, 17 September 1952.
62   *A Dark Day on the Blaskets*, p. 87.
63   *Ibid.*, p. 88 and *Blasket Lives*, Cáit (Ní Chatháin) Uí Chathasa.
64   *A Dark Day on the Blaskets*, pp. 88–90.
65   *The Islandman*, pp. 197–198.
66   *A Dark Day on the Blaskets*, p. 97.
67   *Ibid.*, p. 102.
68   *Ibid.*, p. 104.
69   *Blasket Lives*, Máire (Ní Chatháin) Uí Ghuithín.
70   *A Dark Day on the Blaskets*, p. 109.
71   *Ibid.*, pp. 109–112.
72   *Ibid.*, pp. 112–117.
73   *Ibid.*, p. 113 and *The Irish Independent*, The Girl Who was Loved by Pearse, 17 September 1952.
74   *A Dark Day on the Blaskets*, p. 158.

Endnotes

75 *The Blaskets – People and Literature*, p. 137.

76 *Seanchas ón Oileán Tiar*, p. xxi.

77 *The Blaskets – People and Literature*, pp. 137–138.

78 *From the Great Blasket to America*, p. 69.

79 *Blasket Memories*, p. 92.

80 *On an Irish Island*, pp. 44–45.

81 *The Western Island*, pp. 10–11.

82 *On an Irish Island*, p. 42.

83 *In Wicklow and West Kerry*, p. 39 and *Blasket Lives*, Máire (Ní Chatháin) Uí Ghuithín.

84 *The Western Island*, p. 12.

85 *Ibid.*

86 *On an Irish Island*, p. 48.

87 *Blasket Lives*, Máire (Ní Chatháin) Uí Ghuithín.

88 *The Blaskets – People and Literature*, p. 138.

89 *The Western Island*, pp. 24–28.

90 *Ibid.*, pp. 84–85.

91 *The Blaskets – People and Literature*, p. 37.

92 *The Western Island*, pp. 108–109.

93 *Ibid.*, p. viii.

94 *The Blaskets – People and Literature*, p. 40.

95 *An tOileánach Léannta*, p. 40.

96 *Ibid.*, pp. 40–41.

97 *Ibid.*, p. 43.

98 *Ibid.*, p. 44.

99 *On an Irish Island*, p. 48.

100 *The Blaskets – People and Literature*, p. 139.

101 *Ibid.*, p. 139.

102 *On an Irish Island*, pp. 55–57.

103 *Blasket Lives*, Cáit (Ní Chatháin) Uí Chathasa.

104 *On an Irish Island*, pp. 55–56.

105 *Ibid.*, pp. 56–57.

106 Dáithí de Mórdha, the Great Blasket Centre, Dunquin, County Kerry.

107 *An tOileánach Léannta*, pp. 48–49.

108 *On an Irish Island*, pp. 58–59.

109 *An tOileánach Léannta*, p. 49.

110 *The Blaskets – People and Literature*, p. 140.

111 *Blasket Memories*, p. 114.

112 *On an Irish Island*, pp. 58–60 and *Blasket Memories*, p. 113.

113 *An tOileánach Léannta*, p. 59.

114 *On an Irish Island*, p. 58.

115 *Ibid.*, p. 62 and *Blasket Memories*, pp. 114–116.

116 *On an Irish Island*, pp. 137–143.
117 *Ibid.*, p. 50.
118 *The Blaskets – People and Literature*, p. 143.
119 *On an Irish Island*, p. 136.
120 *The Blaskets – People and Literature*, pp. 142–143.
121 *Ibid.*, p. 148.
122 *On an Irish Island*, p. 73.
123 *Island Home – The Blasket Heritage*, pp. 119–123.
124 *Blasket Lives*, Máire (Ní Chatháin) Uí Ghuithín.
125 *Island Home – Blasket Heritage*, p. 148.
126 *On an Irish Island*, p. 77.
127 *Ibid.*, pp. 105–106.
128 *Island Home – The Blasket Heritage*, p. 121.
129 *Ibid.*, p. 122.
130 *On an Irish Island*, p. 84.
131 *Ibid.*, p. 79.
132 *Ibid.*, p. 80.
133 *Ibid.*, pp. 85–91.
134 *Island Home – The Blasket Heritage*, p. 129.
135 *The Blaskets – People and Literature*, p. 153.
136 *Twenty Years A-Growing*, pp. 219–224.
137 *The Blaskets – People and Literature*, pp. 150–151.
138 *Blasket Island Reflections*, Booklet Accompanying CD Set, p. 23.
139 *The Blaskets – People and Literature*, p. 153.
140 *Island Home – The Blasket Heritage*, p. 134 and *On an Irish Island*, p. 205.
141 *Island Home – The Blasket Heritage*, p. 136.
142 *On an Irish Island*, p. 233.
143 *Island Home – The Blasket Heritage.*, pp. 148–149.
144 *The Blaskets – People and Literature*, p. 153.
145 *Ibid.* p. 154.
146 *On an Irish Island*, p. 111.
147 *Ibid.*, pp. 120–121.
148 *Ibid.*, pp. 119–120.
149 *Ibid.*, p. 126.
150 *Ibid.*, p. 125.
151 *An Irish Talk – Kerry*, p. ix.
152 *On an Irish Island*, pp. 121–125.
153 *Ibid.*, pp. 127–128.
154 *Ibid.*, p. 146.
155 *Ibid.*, p. 216.
156 *Ibid.*, p. 145.

Endnotes

157 *The Western Island*, pp. 80–81 and Do Dingle (www.dodingle.com/ Heritage/Armada_Wreck.html).
158 *A Galician in Ireland*, 9 September 1928, pp. 30–31.
159 Ibid, p. 31.
160 *A Galician in Ireland*, 21 September 1928, p. 47.
161 *Blasket Lives*, Mícheál 'Bofar' Ó Catháin.
162 *Blasket Lives*, Cáit (Ní Chatháin) Uí Cathasa and Dáithí de Mórdha, the Great Blasket Centre, Dunquin, County Kerry.
163 *On and Irish Island*, p. 8.
164 *A Day in Our Life*, p. 23.
165 *Irish Tourism, Image, Culture and Identity*, pp. 160–164.

Chapter 9. The King's Passing

1 *Island Cross-Talk*, March, 1921, p. 107.
2 *Blasket Lives*, Pádraig Peats Mhicí Ó Catháin.
3 *Island Cross-Talk*, p. 197.
4 *A Galician in Ireland*, 9 September 1928, p. 31.
5 *Ibid.*, 16 September 1928, p. 35.
6 *The Islandman*, p. 244.
7 *A Galician in Ireland*, 9 September 1928. p. 31.
8 *An tOileánach Léannta*, p. 19.
9 *The Blaskets – People and Literature*, p. 167.
10 *The Kerryman*, 15 June 1929, Second Edition, p. 13.
11 *The Kerry Champion*, 22 June 1929, p. 5.
12 *The Lone Seagull*, pp. 59–60.
13 *The Western Island*, p. viii.

Chapter 10. The Evacuation of the Great Blasket

1 *From the Great Blasket to America*, pp. 118–123.
2 View from the Pier, Interview with Dáithí de Mórdha (www.viewfrom thepier.com/2013/09/04/).
3 *The Blaskets – People and Literature*, p. 47.
4 *The Lone Seagull*, p. 59.
5 Dáithí de Mórdha, the Great Blasket Centre, Dunquin, County Kerry.
6 *The Irish Independent*, 10 July 2012.
7 Letter from Michael J. Carney to Éamon de Valera, 26 January 1947, the Great Blasket Centre, Dunquin, County Kerry.
8 Transcripts of the Proceedings of the Dáil Éireann on 25 February 1947 and 12 March 1947.

9 The Great Blasket Centre, Dunquin, County Kerry.
10 Dáithí de Mórdha, the Great Blasket Centre, Dunquin, County Kerry.
11 *The Irish Press*, 23 April 1947.
12 *The Kerryman*, 21 July 1947, p. 1.
13 *From the Great Blasket to America*, p. 128.
14 *Blasket Memories*, p. 163.
15 *The Irish Independent*, 17 September 1952, and *The Loneliest Boy in the World*, p. 84.
16 *Paradise Lost?*, pp. 190–204.
17 *Blasket Island Reflections*, CD 2, Track 37, Mícheál de Mórdha.
18 *Blasket Memories*, pp. 164–165.
19 *Paradise Lost?*, p. 203. and *The Kerryman*, 20 November 1953
20 *From the Great Blasket to America*, p. 136.
21 *Blasket Spirit*, p. 197.

Chapter 11. The King's Descendants In Ireland

1 *The Great Blasket – A Photographic Portrait*, pp. 138–139.
2 *An Caomhnóir*, Rí an Oileáin, 1990.
3 *Blasket Lives*, Máire (Ní Chatháin) Uí Ghuithín.
4 *In Wicklow and West Kerry*, p. 39.
5 *Blasket Lives*, Máire (Ní Chatháin) Uí Ghuithín.
6 *Ibid.*
7 *Ibid.*
8 *The Loneliest Boy in the World*, p. 17.
9 *The Lone Seagull*, p. 58.
10 *Bean an Oileáin*, p. 24.
11 *Ibid.* pp. 41–54, p. 71 and p. 64.
12 *Blasket Lives*, Máire (Ní Chatháin) Uí Ghuithín.
13 *Ibid.*
14 *Ibid.*
15 *Blasket Lives*, Cáit (Ní Chatháin) Uí Chathasa.
16 Irish Biographies, Máire (Ní Chatháin) Uí Chatháin (http://www.ainm.ie/Bio.aspx?ID=1702).
17 *Blasket Lives*, Cáit (Ní Chatháin) Uí Chathasa.
18 *A Dark Day on the Blaskets*, p. 166.
19 *The Irish Press*, Child of the Blasket, 25 December 1948, p.6, *The Irish Press*, The Future of Lone Blaskets Child, 4 August 1951, and *The Irish Times* Pictorial, The Loneliest Boy is Not Lonely Now, p. 1, 14 November, 1953.
20 *Blasket Lives*, Máire (Ní Chatháin) Uí Ghuithín.

Endnotes

21 *The Loneliest Boy in the World*, pp. 44–51.

22 *Blasket Lives*, Máire (Ní Chatháin) Uí Ghuithín.

23 *Blasket Memories*, p. 165 and Dáithí De Mórdha, the Great Blasket Centre, Dunquin, County Kerry.

24 *The Loneliest Boy in the World*, pp. 151–152.

25 *Blasket Lives*, Máire (Ní Chatháin) Uí Ghuithín.

26 *An tOileán a Bhí*, pp. 55–57.

27 *Evening Echo*, Padraig Keane – King of the Blasket, p. 8.

28 *Blasket Memories*, pp. 165–166.

29 *Ibid.*, p. 171 and *The Loneliest Boy in the World*, p. 92.

30 *Blasket Memories*, pp. 169–170.

31 *Ibid.*, pp. 166–167.

32 *Ibid.*, p. 170.

33 *From the Great Blasket to America*, pp. 16–17.

34 Michael J. Carney, Springfield, Massachusetts.

35 *The Kerryman*, 22 January 1999, p. 8.

36 *Blasket Memories*, p. 161.

37 *In Wicklow and West Kerry*, p. 39.

38 *Ibid.* p. 42.

39 *The Western Island*, p. 12.

40 *On an Irish Island*, p. 46.

41 *A Dark Day on the Blaskets*, p. 166.

42 *Ibid.*, p. 87.

43 *Ibid.*, p. 113 and *Blasket Lives*, Cáit (Ní Chatháin) Uí Chathasa.

44 *Blasket Lives*, Cáit (Ní Chatháin) Uí Chathasa.

45 *Ibid.*

46 *Ibid.*

47 *Ibid.*

48 *A Galician in Ireland*, p. 21.

49 *Blasket Lives*, Cáit (Ní Chatháin) Uí Chathasa.

50 *Béaloideas*, Volume XXV, Measgra ón Oileán Tiar, 22, 'Beó agus Marbh', p. 98.

51 *Blasket Lives*, Cáit (Ní Chatháin) Uí Chathasa.

52 *Riddled with Light*.

53 *Blasket Lives*, Cáit (Ní Chatháin) Uí Chathasa and Dáithí de Mórdha, the Great Blasket Centre, Dunquin, County Kerry.

54 *Blasket Lives*, Seán An Rí Ó Catháin.

55 *In Wicklow and West Kerry*, p. 39.

56 *Blasket Memories*, pp. 91–92.

57 *Blasket Lives*, Seán An Rí Ó Catháin.

58 *In Wicklow and West Kerry*, p. 46.

59 *Blasket Lives*, Seán An Rí Ó Catháin.

60 *Ibid.*
61 *Méiní, The Blasket Nurse*, p. 144.
62 *Ibid.* pp. 144–145.
63 Margaret Brosnan, Gortglas Scartlas, County Kerry.
64 *Evening Echo*, Padraig Keane – King of the Blasket, p. 8.
65 Margaret Brosnan, Gortglas Scartlas, County Kerry.
66 *Island Cross-Talk*, p. 109.
67 *Thar Bealach Isteach* and *Blasket Lives*, Seán An Rí Ó Catháin.
68 *Blasket Memories*, p. 152 and *Thar Bealach Isteach*, p. 29.
69 *An tOileán a Bhí*, p. 70.
70 *Méiní, The Blasket Nurse*, p. 156.
71 *Thar Bealach Isteach* and *Blasket Lives*, Seán An Rí Ó Catháin.
72 *Blasket Lives*, Seán An Rí Ó Catháin.
73 *Twenty Years A-Growing*, p. 218.
74 *On an Irish Island*, p. 113.
75 *Blasket Lives*, Seán An Rí Ó Catháin.
76 *Ibid.*
77 *The Irish Press*, 5 July 1934, p. 5.
78 *Letters from the Great Blasket*, 2 March 1934, p. 44.
79 *Blasket Lives*, Seán An Rí Ó Catháin.
80 Dáithí de Mórdha, the Great Blasket Centre, Dunquin, County Kerry.
81 *Blasket Lives*, Seán An Rí Ó Catháin.
82 *Evening Echo*, Letter to the Editor, Mairéad Bean Uí Choistealbha, March, 1984.
83 Margaret Brosnan, Gortglas Scartlas, County Kerry.
84 *The Kerryman*, 19 September 2012.
85 *Evening Echo*, Letter to the Editor, Mairéad Bean Uí Choistealbha, March, 1984.
86 *The Kerryman*, 20 November 1953, p. 1.

Chapter 12. The King's Descendants In America

1 Certificate of Baptism, Mícheál Ó Catháin, St Vincent's Church, Ballyferriter, County Kerry.
2 MET Éireann, the Irish Meteorological Service Online (www.met.ie).
3 *Evening Echo*, Padraig Keane – King of the Blasket, p. 8.
4 *The Islandman*, p. 186.
5 This account of Mícheál Ó Catháin's first trip to America is comprised of recollections of family friends; to date no documentation has been found of his presence in America prior to 1905. It is not uncommon, however, for such records to become lost over the years.

Endnotes

6   Keane later settled on the shorter spelling of his name, 'Kane,' a change that required no formalities at the time. He and his son John, however, would use 'Keane' when employed by the City of Springfield, to be consistent with Mike's immigration paperwork.

7   Immigration timeline (www.libertyellisfoundation.org/immigration-timeline#1880).

8   *Ibid.*

9   Blascaodaigh i Meiriceá.

10 Michael J. Carney, Springfield, Massachusetts.

11 *Ibid.*

12 *On an Irish Island*, p. 146.

13 Ellis Island: The Immigrant Experience (www.libertyellisfoundation.org/ellis-island-history).

14 Cobh Heritage Centre, Emigration & Famine (www.cobhheritage.com/emigration-famine).

15 Later re-named the Indian Motocycle Manufacturing Co.

16 Springfield Armory National History Website (http://www.nps.gov/spar/historyculture/index.htm).

17 *From the Great Blasket to America*, pp. 152–153.

18 *Ibid.*, p. 82.

19 *Ibid.*, p. 83.

20 *An Caomhnóir*, Sliocht Rí an Oileáin sna Stáit Aontaith, 1999.

21 SS *Celtic*, Passenger Ships and Images (www.ancestry.com).

22 Census of the City of Springfield, Massachusetts, 1930 and their marriage license; the exact date and ship of passage are unknown.

23 Joseph Kane, Springfield, Massachusetts.

24 Mary Foley probably only helped Mike Kane to improve his English; he very likely learned some English in school on the Great Blasket. Mike's sister Cáit (the Princess) spoke English but their sister Máire did not.

25 *Springfield Present and Prospective: The City of Homes*, p 145.

26 Peared Creation, Liberty Brewing Company of Springfield, Massachusetts (www.pearedcreation.com/shop/liberty-brewing-co/).

27 Believing he had no middle name, John Kane used Francis, his chosen confirmation name. Only later did he learn that he was actually baptised John Patrick Kane.

28 Mike 'The Fiddler' Keane was naturalised 19 June 1911 in Springfield at the Superior Court Ward 1 Precinct E; citizenship registration noted as 25 September 1914. Source: original document of petition for citizenship. As this took place prior to the ratification of the 19th Amendment to the US Constitution, Mary Kane's citizenship was established through her husband's citizenship. Listed as 'Substituted

Witnesses' on his Petition for Naturalization paperwork were presumed fellow islander Mike Kearney, Michael J. Carney's uncle, and Thomas Crohan, son of the famed Blasket author Tomás Ó Criomhthain, who had also emigrated to Springfield where he worked as a butcher.

29 This and all insights from John P. Kane were taken from an interview recorded 20 April 1987 by his son Jack; transcript courtesy of the Kane family.

30 Dorothy always thought her name was 'Dorothy Agnes,' but the family bible shows it the other way around.

31 The family lived at 34 Linden until they were forced out for the 1925 school expansion. As per the demolition permit, 14 Everett was torn down on 25 July 1974 (well after the Kanes had relocated), for the construction of Interstate 291 (a major highway).

32 This and all insights from Ronald Anthony Bencevenni were taken from a 16 June 2013 interview conducted for the documentary *The Crest*; transcript courtesy of Butter Flavored Films.

33 Residential information aggregated from Springfield City Directories, 1906–1945 and John P. Kane interview.

34 Ronald Anthony Bencevenni, Springfield, Massachusetts.

35 This and all insights from Joseph Kane were taken from a 16 June 2013 interview conducted for the documentary *The Crest*; transcript courtesy of Butter Flavored Films.

36 Census of the City of Springfield, Massachusetts, 1940.

37 Joseph Kane, Springfield, Massachusetts.

38 *Blasket Memories*, p. 82.

39 Michael J. Carney, Springfield, Massachusetts.

40 *An Irish Fiddle Finds its Way Home*.

41 *An Caomhnóir*, Sliocht Rí an Oileáin sna Stáit Aontaith, 1999.

42 *Blasket Memories*, p. 82.

43 *Ibid.*

44 *A Dark Day on the Blaskets*, p. 142.

45 Joseph Kane, Springfield, Massachusetts.

46 This and all insights by Mary Fitzgerald (née Kane) were taken from a 15 June 2013 interview conducted for the documentary *The Crest*; transcript courtesy of Butter Flavored Films.

47 John P. Kane also quipped that, sometime later, younger brothers Mike and Jim attempted to share this paper route as his replacement, but they quit after only one week on the job.

48 John P. Kane, Springfield, Massachusetts.

49 *Ibid.*

50 Commonly spelled Eileen, but spelled Ilene in the Kane family bible.

51 Joseph Kane, Springfield, Massachusetts.

52 Ronald Anthony Bencevenni, Springfield, Massachusetts.
53 *Springfield Union*, Michael P. Kane Dies in Hospital, 18 October 1949, p. 2.
54 Mary Fitzgerald, Springfield, Massachusetts.
55 Letter from Joanne 'Kandy' Kane to Eliza Kane dated 26 February 2013.
56 *Springfield Union*, Woman's Death in Forest Park Ruled Suicide, 21 June 1959 p. 1 and 12A.
57 Normally it was Mary the younger's husband, Jack Fitzgerald, who would make the Kane clan perform some impromptu Irish songs.
58 Letter to Eliza C. Kane from Dennis Kane, Sr, dated 31 March 2014.
59 *Springfield Union*, Mary Foley Kane Obituary, 2 December 1982, p.8.
60 *Ibid.*
61 *Blasket Memories*, p. 82.
62 *Ibid.*, pp. 79–80.
63 Michael J. Carney, Springfield, Massachusetts.
64 *Blasket Memories*, pp. 82–83.
65 *Ibid.*, p. 82.
66 *Ibid.*
67 *A Dark Day on the Blaskets*, p. 142.
68 *An Irish Fiddle Finds its Way Home*. See also note 5 above.
69 Michael J. Carney, Springfield, Massachusetts.
70 *Blasket Memories*, p. 82.
71 *A Dark Day on the Blaskets*, p. 142.
72 *Ibid.*, p. 143.
73 *Ibid.*
74 *Ibid.*
75 *An Caomhnóir*, Thar Moladh Beirte, 2006.
76 *Ibid.*
77 Edna Uí Chinnéide, Moorestown, County Kerry.
78 *An Caomhnóir*, Thar Moladh Beirte, 2006.
79 *Ibid.*
80 *Ibid.*
81 Edna Uí Chinnéide, Moorestown, County Kerry.
82 *An Caomhnóir*, Sliocht Rí an Oileáin sna Stáit Aontaith, 1999.
83 Edna Uí Chinnéide, Moorestown, County Kerry.
84 *Ibid.*
85 Behind the Crest, Blog Post by Jack Kane, 12 December 2013 (http://crestmovie.com/buzz).
86 *Ibid.*
87 Dennis Kane's father, also named Dennis Kane, was born to Michael Thomas Kane and his wife Mabel.

88   Behind the Crest (http://crestmovie.com/buzz).
88   *Nuacht* TG4, *Blasket Surf Kings*, Seán Mac an tSithigh, Episode 151 aired 31 May 2013.
90   *The Irish Times*, Islandmen Reborn — Capturing a Blasket Gathering, 22 June 2013.
91   *Ibid.*
92   Michael J. Carney is referencing the trend of seal overpopulation on the Great Blasket since its 1953 evacuation, courtesy of Butter Flavored Films.

Chapter 13. The King's Legacy

1   *Blasket Memories*, p. 75.
2   *The Blaskets – People and Literature*, p. 46.
3   *Blasket Island Reflections*, CD 2, Track 30, Críostóir MacCárthaigh.
4   *The Great Blasket – A Photographic Portrait*, p. 45.
5   *Evening Echo*, Padraig Keane – King of the Blasket, p. 8.

Acknowledgements

First and foremost, we gratefully acknowledge the enormous contribution of Dáithí de Mórdha, the chief archivist at the Great Blasket Centre in Dunquin, County Kerry. Dáithí is a genuine scholar of all things Blasket. Without his constant help and encouragement, his regular infusions of detailed background information and his painstaking review of the draft manuscript, this book would have been an impossible undertaking.

Profuse thanks as well to Mícheál de Mórdha, the soon-to-be retiring long-time director of the Great Blasket Centre for mentoring this project and for providing highly constructive feedback. Thanks also to Mícheál Ó Cinnéide, currently of County Wexford and a passionate Blasket activist for over thirty years, for his wise advice and counsel.

We also express our appreciation to: John 'Jack' Anthony Kane Sr, the great-grandson of the last Blasket King, for information on the Kane family in Ireland and the United States and for his enthusiastic support for the overall undertaking; Padraic Keane of Sligo, a descendant of the King himself, for access to his extensive and detailed genealogical research; Bosco O'Connor on information on the descendants of the King's sister Cáit (Ní Chatháin) Uí Conchúir of Muiríoch, Maurice Brick of Gorta Dubh, West Kerry and New Rochelle, New York for information on the Kane family in Muiríoch and New York; Andrea Makin for information on the Kane family in the United States; Edna Uí Chinnéide of Moorestown, West Kerry for information of the history of the famous Kane fiddle; Declan Malone, editor of *The Kerryman*, for guidance and permissions; Mike Lynch, archivist at the County Kerry Library, for documentary and bibliographic research on the King and his family and, finally, Maggie Humberston, Head of Library and Archives at the Lyman & Merrie Wood Museum of Springfield History, for background information about Mike 'The Fiddler' Kane and his family.

The Last Blasket King

A special and very warm thanks to Patsy Dan Rodgers, King of Tory Island, for his enthusiastic assistance in connection with the tradition of local Kings in Ireland.

We appreciate permission to use copyrighted material from the following sources: Oxford University Press (*Island Cross-Talk* and *The Islandman* both by Tomas O'Crohan, *The Western Island* by Robin Flower, *An Old Woman's Reflections* by Peig Sayers and *A Pity Youth Does Not Last* by Micheál O'Guiheen), Mercier Press (*Méiní, The Blasket Nurse* by Leslie Matson and *Blasket Memories*, edited by Padraig Tyers), Alfred A. Knopf, an imprint of Knopf Doubleday Publishing Group, a division of Random House LLC (*On An Irish Island* by Robert Kanigel), An Clóchomhar Tta. (*An Oileáin a Bhí* and *An tOileánach Léannta* by Mairéad Nic Craith), Maura Llewelyn O'Sullivan Kavanagh (*Twenty Years A-Growing* by Maurice O'Sullivan), Plácido Castro Foundation (*Articles in the Galician Town* by Plácido Ramón Castro del Rio) and Coiscéim (*Bean an Oileáin* by Máire Ní Ghuithín).

We are grateful to the following sources for permission to use copyrighted and other photographs that illustrate this story: the Board of Trinity College Dublin, the National Folklore Collection at University College Dublin, the Great Blasket Centre, the MacMonagle Archive, Oxford University Press, the Plácido Castro Foundation, the Kane family, Liam Blake, Leslie Matson, the Ross family, Patrick Langan, Patsy Dan Rogers, Ray Stagles, Maura Llewelyn O'Sullivan Kavanagh and the University of Oslo.

Thanks to Síobhra Aiken of Ardee, County Louth, then a Fulbright Language Scholar and Teaching Assistant of Irish at Elms College in Chicopee, Massachusetts for her skillful translation of background literature from Irish to English and to Samalid Hogan of Chicopee, Massachusetts for translation from Spanish to English.

Special thanks also to our distinguished panel of expert 'readers', including Michael J. Carney, Mícheál Ó Cinnéide, Lorcan Ó Cinnéide, Edna Uí Chinnéide and Jack Kane, for their insightful review of the manuscript as well as their invaluable comments and suggestions.

And, of course, we extend our heartfelt appreciation to Joe Spurr for his encouragement and generosity as well as our 'editor-in-chief', Maureen Carney Hayes, for patience and guidance beyond measure.

GERALD HAYES
ELIZA KANE

Photo Credits

Photographs incorporated herein are presented courtesy of the following:

Gerald Hayes: pp. 4, 215, 271 and 296
The Great Blasket Centre: cover, pp. 10, 13, 63, 77, 84, 94, 116 (George Thompson), 153, 178, 185 (Ida Streeter Flower), 189, 220, 227, 229, 231, 232, 233, 235, 246, 252, 253, 257 and 261(Ned Fitzgerald)
National Monuments Service/Department of Arts, Heritage and the Gaeltacht: p. 10
Board of Trinity College Dublin:
• Charles R. Browne Collection: p. 21 (TCD MS 10961/3 fol 22v)
• John Millington Synge Collection: pp. 29 (TCD MS 11332/47) and 52 (TCD MS 11332/48)
Patsy Dan Rogers: p. 27
National Folklore Collection, University College Dublin:
• George Chambers: pp. 61, 256 and 260
• Carl von Sydow: pp. 65, 67, 149 and 205
• Thomas Waddicor: pp. 145, 206 and 254
• Other: p. 193
The Mason Family (photos by Thomas Mason): pp. 64 and 182
The MacMonagle Archive: pp. 71, 224, 226 and 244
Oxford University Press: p. 95
Coiscéim: pp. 98, 240, 245 and 247
Plácido Castro Foundation: pp. 111 and 202; inside front cover
Leslie Matson: p. 136
University of Oslo: p. 169
Maura Llewelyn O'Sullivan Kavanagh: p. 197
The Ross Family (photos by John Ross): p. 222
Patrick Langan: p. 228
Ray Stagles: p. 234

Liam Blake: p. 243

The Kane Family: pp. 265, 269, 275, 280 (Kimberly F. Kane), 288 and
    293 (John A. Kane Jr)

Every effort has been made to secure permission from the copyright
holders of photographs and other material presented in this book. We
apologise and regret any error or oversight. Please advise the publisher
of any corrections that should be made in future editions of this book.

Bibliography

Books

Baker, Alan R.H. and Butlin, Robin A. (eds), *Studies of Field Systems in the British Isles* (Cambridge University Press, Cambridge, 1973)

Byrne, Francis J., *Irish Kings and High Kings* (Four Courts Press, Dublin, 2001, first published 1973)

Carney, Michael with Hayes, Gerald, *From the Great Blasket to America – The Last Memoir by an Islander* (The Collins Press, Cork, 2013)

Coohill, Joseph, *Ireland: A Short History,* third edition (Oneworld Publications, London, 2008, first published 2000)

Cronin, Michael and O'Connor, Barbara (eds), *Irish Tourism – Image, Culture and Identity* (Channel View Publications, Clevedon, 2003)

De Mórdha, Dáithí and De Mórdha, Mícheál, *the Great Blasket – A Photographic Portrait* (The Collins Press, Cork, 2013)

De Mórdha, Mícheál (ed.), Ceiliúradh an Bhlascaoid #14 – Celebration of the Blasket # 14: John Millington Synge (Coiscéim, Dublin, 2012)

De Mórdha, Mícheál, *Scéal agus Dán Oileáin – The Story and Fate of an Island* (Coiscéim, Dublin, 2012)

Dewar, Rev. LL.O. Daniel, *Observations on the Character, Customs, and Superstitions of the Irish* (Gale and Curtis, London, 1812)

Fennelly, Anita, *Blasket Spirit, Stories from the Islands* (The Collins Press, Cork, 2009)

Flower, Robin, *The Western Island – the Great Blasket* (Oxford University Press, Oxford, 2000, first published 1944)

Gardner, Eugene Clarence, *Springfield Present and Prospective: the City of Homes* (Pond and Campbell Publishers, Springfield, Massachusetts, 1905)

Kanigel, Robert, *On an Irish Island* (Alfred A. Knopf, New York, 2012)

King, Jeremiah, *County Kerry Past and Present – A Handbook to the Local and Family History of the County* (Mercier Press, Cork and Dublin, 1931 and 1986)

Knight, Philip, *Erris, in the 'Irish Highlands,' and the 'Atlantic Railway'* (Martin Keene and Son, Dublin, 1836)

Lewis, Samuel, *A Topographical Dictionary of Ireland* (S. Lewis & Company, London, 1837)

Mac Conghail, Muiris, *The Blaskets – People and Literature, A Kerry Island Library* (TownHouse, Dublin, 2006, first published 1987)

McCourt, Malachy, *History of Ireland* (MJF Books, New York, 2004)

McCullough, David Willis, *Wars of the Irish Kings* (Three Rivers Press, New York, 2002)

MacLochlainn, Cóilín, *Toraigh: Oileán Iargúlta, Stairiúl – Tory Island: A Remote and Historic Outpost* (Comharchumann Thoraí Teoranta, Derrybeg, County Donegal, 2003)

McNally, Kenneth, *The Islands of Ireland* (W. W. Norton & Company, Inc., New York, 1978)

Maguire, John M., *Marx's Theory of Politics* (Cambridge University Press, Cambridge, 2009)

Mason, Thomas H., *The Islands of Ireland – Their Scenery, People, Life and Antiquities* (Mercier Press, Cork, 1967, first published 1936)

Matson, Leslie, *Méiní – The Blasket Nurse* (Mercier Press, Dublin, 1996)

Moreton, Cole, *Hungry for Home – Leaving the Blaskets: A Journey to America from the Edge of Ireland* (Viking Penguin, New York, 2000)

Nic Craith, Mairéad, *An tOileánach Léannta – The Learned Islandman* (An Clóchomhar Tta, Dublin, 1988)

Ní Ghaoithín, Máire, *An tOileán a Bhí – The Island that Was* (An Clóchomhar Tta, Dublin, 1978)

Ní Ghuithín, Máire, *Bean an Oileáin – Woman of the Island* (Coiscéim, Dublin, 1986)

Ní Shéaghdha, Nóra, *Thar Bealach Isteach – Beyond the Sound* (Oifig an tSoláthair, Dublin, 1940)

Ní Shúilleabháin, Eibhlís, *Letters from the Great Blasket* (Mercier Press, Irish American Book Company, Boulder, Colorado, undated)

Ó Catháin, Gearóid Cheaist with Ahern, Patricia, *The Loneliest Boy in the World – The Last Child of the Great Blasket Island* (The Collins Press, Cork, 2014)

Ó Catháin, Muiris, *Ar Muir is ar Tír – On Land and Sea* (Foras na Gaeilge, Dingle, 2010)

Ó Conaire, Breandán, *Tomás an Bhlascaoid – Tomás of the Blasket* (Comhar Teoranta, Dublin, 1977)

Bibliography

Ó Criomhthain, Tomás with Flower, Robin, *Seanchas ón Oileán Tiar –*
Lore of the Western Island (Comhlucht Oideachais na h-Éireann,
Tta, Dublin, 1956)

— edited by Ua Maoileoin, Pádraig, *Allagar na hInise – Island Cross-*
Talk (Oifig an tSoláthair, An Gúm, Dublin, 1997)

— edited by Ó Coileáin, Seán, *An tOileánach – The Islandman* (Cló
Talbóid, Dublin, 2002)

O'Crohan, Seán, translated from Irish by Enright, Tim, *A Day in Our*
Life – The Last of the Blasket Islanders – Lá Dár Saol (Oxford
University Press, Oxford, 1993)

O'Crohan, Tomás, translated from Irish by Flower, Robin, *The*
Islandman – An tOileánach (Oxford University Press, Oxford,
2000, first published 1937)

— translated from Irish by Enright, Tim, *Island Cross-Talk – Pages from*
a Blasket Island Diary – Allagar na hInise (Oxford University Press,
Oxford, 1986, first published 1928)

O'Dowd, Anne, *Meitheal – A Study in Co-Operative Labour in Rural*
Ireland (Comhairle Bhéaloideas Éireann, Dublin, 1981)

O'Dowd, Kate Keane, translated from Irish by Ó Dúshláine, Tadhg,
The Lone Seagull (Cuallacht Cholm Cille, National University of
Ireland, Maynooth, 2011)

Ó Dubhshláine, Mícheál, *A Dark Day on the Blaskets* (Brandon Press,
Dingle, 2005, first published 2003)

O'Guiheen, Mícheál, translated from Irish by Enright, Tim, *A Pity Youth*
Does Not Last – Reminiscences of the Last of the Great Blasket Island's
Poets and Storytellers (Oxford University Press, Oxford, 1982)

Ó Muircheartaigh, Aogán (ed.), *Oidhreacht an Bhlascaoid – Blasket*
Heritage (Coiscéim, Dublin, 1989)

Ó Scannláin, Séamas (ed. and trans.), *Poets and Poetry of the Great Blasket*
– Filí agus Filíocht an Bhlascaoid Mhóir (Mercier Press, Cork, 2003)

O'Sullivan Maurice, translated from Irish by Llewelyn Davies, Moya
and Thomson, George, *Twenty Years A-Growing* (J. S. Sanders &
Company, Nashville, Tennessee 1998)

Sayers, Peig, translated from Irish by Ennis, Séamus, *An Old Woman's*
Reflections – The Life of a Blasket Island Storyteller – Machnamh
Seanamhná (Oxford University Press, Oxford, 1962)

— translated from Irish by MacMahon, Bryan, *Peig, The Autobiography*
of Peig Sayers of the Great Blasket Island (Syracuse University Press,
Syracuse, 1974)

The Last Blasket King

Sigerson, George, *History of the Land Tenures and Land Classes of Ireland* (Longmans, Green, Reader and Dyer, London, 1871)

Sjoestedt-Jonval, Marie-Louise, *An Irish Talk, Kerry* (French Ministry of Education, Paris, France, 1938) Smith, Charles, *The Ancient and Present State of the County of Kerry* (Gale ECCO Print Editions, Hampshire, first published 1756)

Stagles, Joan & Ray, *The Blasket Islands – Next Parish America* (The O'Brien Press, Dublin, 2006, first published 1980)

Stagles, Ray and Redican, Sue, *The Blasket Island Guide* (The O'Brien Press, Dublin, 2011)

Synge, John Millington, *In Wicklow and West Kerry* (Dodo Press, Gloucestershire, first published 1912)

— *Playboy of the Western World and Riders to the Sea* (Dover Publications, Inc., New York, 1993, first published by Maunsel & Co., Ltd, Dublin, 1907)

Thomson, George, *Island Home – The Blasket Heritage* (originally published in a shorter form as *The Island that Was)* (Brandon Press, Dingle, 1998, first published 1988)

Tyers, Pádraig, *Blasket Memories – The Life of an Irish Island Community* (Mercier Press, Cork, 1998)

— *West Kerry Camera* (The Collins Press, Cork, 2006)

Wakefield, Edward, *An Account of Ireland, Statistical and Political* (Longman, Hurst, Rees, Orhe and Brown, London, 1882)

Walsh, Clarán and de Mórdha, Dáithí, *The Irish Headhunter, The Photograph Albums of Charles R. Browne* (The Stationery Office, Dublin, 2012)

Journals, Newspapers and Periodicals

An Caomhnóir, 'Sliocht Rí an Oileáin sna Stáit Aontaith – The Island King's Descendants in the United States', Uí Cinnéide, Edna (Dunquin, 1999)

— 'Rí an Oileáin – The King of the Island', Ó Glaisne, Risteárd (Dunquin, 1990)

— 'Thar Moladh Beirte – Worthy of Praise', Uí Cinnéide, Edna (Dunquin, 2006)

— '*Tír na nÓg* – Land of the Young', Ó Catháin, Pádraic (Dunquin, 2012)

Bibliography

An Claidheamh Soluis, Mac Milidh, Donn (pseudonym for Séamas Ó Súilleabháin) (23 November 1908)

Béaloideas, 'Measgra ón Oileán Tiar – Stories from the West Island', Flower, Robin, including 'Beó agus Marbh – The Living and the Dead', Cáit (Ní Chatháin) Uí Chathasa (*The Folklore of Ireland Society,* Volume 25, Dublin, 1957)

— 'Paradise Lost? Leaving the Great Blasket', Lysaght, Patricia (The Folklore of Ireland Society, Volume 74, Dublin, 2006)

— 'What was Rundale and Where Did It Come From?', Yager, Tom (Volume 70, The Folklore of Ireland Society, Dublin, 2002)

Blascaodaigh i Meiriceá – Blasket Islanders in America (Fondúireacht an Bhlascaoid, Dunquin, 1989)

A Galician in Ireland, Plácido Castro Foundation, Vigo, Galicia, 2013 (Originally published in *El Pueblo Gallego*, Vigo, Spain, 1928)

Dublin Review of Books, Riddled with Light, Lillis, Michael (Royal Irish Academy, Issue 42, Dublin, 7 October 2013)

Eastlake, John, *Orality and Agency: Reading an Irish Autobiography from the Great Blasket Island* (National University of Ireland, Galway, 2009)

Evening Echo, Letter to the Editor, Uí Choistealbha (Ní Chatháin), Mairéad, (Cork, 1984)

Evening Echo, 'Padraig Keane – King of the Blasket' Enright, Tim (Cork, 25 February 1984)

Ireland of the Welcomes, 'Brian Bórú, The Greatest High King of Ireland', Volume 63, No. 3 (Dublin, May/June 2014)

Irish Independent, 'The Girl Who Was Loved by Pearse', Hallahan, Imelda, (Dublin, 21 May 1974)

— 'Islanders Plead for New Life on the Mainland' (Dublin, 17 September 1952)

— 'Lovelorn Islanders Wanted "Boatload of Women" and Food', O'Sullivan, Majella (Dublin, 9 July 2012)

The Irish Press, 'Blasket Postman, Death of Well-Known Island Figure – Seán An Rí Ó Catháin's Obituary' (Dublin, 5 July 1934)

The Irish Press, 'Child of the Blasket', Robinson, Liam and MacMonagle, Donal (Dublin, 25 December 1948)

— 'Future of Lone Blaskets Child – Island Without School' (Dublin, 4 August 1951)

— 'Storms and High Seas Isolate the Blaskets' (Dublin, 23 April 1947)

The Irish Times, 'The Blaskets Gathering – Dún Chaoin, Dingle Peninsula', Gordon, Yvonne, Boland, Rosita, and Quinn, Gary (Dublin, 22 June 2013)

The Irish Times Pictorial, '"Loneliest Boy" is Not Lonely Now' (Dublin, week ending 14 November 1953)

The Journal of the Royal Society of Antiquaries of Ireland, 'An Rí (The King) Example of Traditional Social Organisation', Ó Danachair, Caoimthín (Volume 111, Dublin, 1981)

The Kerry Champion, 'Death Lays His Icy Hand on King', (Tralee, 22 June 1929)

The Kerryman, 'Blasket Evacuation Impeded by Heavy Seas on Tuesday' (Tralee, 21 November 1953)

— 'Blasket Islanders Greet An Taoiseach' (Tralee, 19 July 1947)

— 'Evacuation' (Tralee, 21 November 1953)

— 'Evacuation Marks End of Era as Last Families Leave the Blaskets' (Tralee, 28 November 1953)

— 'King of Blaskets, Pádraig Ó Catháin's Obituary (Tralee, 15 June 1929, Second Edition)

— 'One of Last Islandmen Passes Away – Seán Ó Guithín' (Tralee, 22 January 1999)

— 'One of the Last Remaining Blasket Natives Passes Away – Pádraig Ó Catháin', Marian O'Flaherty *(Tralee, 19 September 2012)*

Lucchitti, Irene, *Islandman Translated: Thomas O'Crohan, Autobiography & the Politics of Culture* (PhD thesis, University of Wollongong, New South Wales, Australia, 2005)

MacCotter, Paul and Sheehan, John, *Medieval Iveragh: Kingdoms and Dynasties* (Cork University Press, Cork, 2009)

McCourt, Desmond, 'Rundale and its Social Concomitants' (Queens University of Belfast, Belfast unpublished MA thesis, 1947)

National Geographic Traveler, 'Dingle – Ireland, Country Style' (The National Geographic Society, Washington, DC, summer 1986)

The Shanachie – An Irish Miscellany Illustrated, In West Kerry: The Blasket Islands, Synge, John Millington (Second Number, Volume 2, Maunsel & Co. Ltd, Dublin, 1907)

The Springfield Union, Springfield, Massachusetts, 'Mary Kane Obituary' (2 December 1982)

— 'Michael P. Kane – Had Organized Kerry Dances' (18 October 1949)

— 'Woman's Death in Forest Park Ruled Suicide' (21 June 1959)

Bibliography

Slater, Eamonn and Flaherty, Eoin, *The Ecological Dynamics of the Rundale Agrarian Commune* (National University of Ireland, Maynooth, Kildare, 2009)

Archives, Websites and Other Sources

An Baile, The Gaelic Village, The St Kilda Parliament (www.gaelic village.co.uk/en/item/item_photograph.jsp?item_id=22632)

Annals of the Four Masters, Annal 279.1-405.1 (http:/ucc.ie/celt/ published/T100005A/text031.html)

Behind the Crest (http://crestmovie.com/buzz)

Census of the City of Springfield, Massachusetts, 1930 and 1940

Clans and Chieftains in Ireland (www.heraldry.ws/info/article06.html)

Cobh Heritage Centre, Emigration & Famine (www.cobhheritage. com/emigration-famine/)

Dodingle.com, Dingle Peninsula Armada Wreck (www.dodingle.com/ Heritage/Armada_Wreck.html)

Ellis Island: The Immigrant Experience (http://www.libertyellis foundation.org/)

The Great Blasket Centre Archives (Dunquin, County Kerry)

Griffith's Valuation, County Kerry (July 1853)

Houses of the Oireachtas, Transcripts of the Proceedings of the Dáil Éireann (Volume 104, 25 February 1947 – Ceisteanna – Questions. Oral Answers – Blasket Islander's Death, Dublin)

Houses of the Oireachtas, Transcripts of the Proceedings of the Dáil Éireann (Volume 104, 12 March 1947 – Ceisteanna – Questions. Oral Answers – Telephone Communication with Blasket Islands, Dublin)

Immigration timeline (www.libertyellisfoundation.org/immigration-timeline#1880)

Irish Biographies, Máire (Ní Chatháin) Uí Chatháin (www.ainm.ie/ Bio.aspx?ID=1702)

Irish Wrecks Online (irishwrecksonline.net/Lists/KerryListA.htm)

Kane, Larry, An Irish Fiddle Finds Its Way Home (http://lasttrain. wordpress.com/2008/02/24/)

Keane, Padraic, the Ó Catháin Family Tree (unpublished genealogical research, Sligo, 2014)

Mac an tSithigh, Seán, Blasket Surf Kings (*Nuacht TG4*, Dublin, Episode 151 televised 31 May 2013)

Matson, Leslie, Blasket Lives: Biographical Accounts of 125 Blasket People: Cáit (Ní Chatháin) Uí Chathasa; Máire (Ní Chatháin) Uí Ghuithín; Mícheál 'Bofar' Ó Catháin; Pádraig Mhártain Ó Catháin; Pádraig Peats Mhicí Ó Catháin; and Seán An Rí Ó Catháin (unpublished research, the Great Blasket Centre, Dunquin, 2005)

Minister of Education, Submission to the Government: Migration of the Population of the Great Blasket Island to the Mainland (Dublin, 5 November 1952)

National Archives of Ireland, Census of Ireland, 1901 and 1911 (www.census.nationalarchives.ie)

National Archives of Ireland, History (www.nationalarchives.ie/about-us/history/)

Office of Public Works, The Blaskets/Na Blascaodaí (Government of Ireland, Stationery Office, Dublin, undated)

Peared Creation, Liberty Brewing Company of Springfield, Massachusetts (http://www.pearedcreation.com/shop/liberty-brewing-co/)

Póirtéir, Cathal, Blasket Island Reflections (RTÉ Radio Documentary, Compact Disk Set and Booklet, Dublin, 2003)

Rogers, Patsy Dan, Patsy Dan Rogers, King of Tory Island – Patsy Dan Mac Ruaíri, Rí an Oileáin (http://patsydanrodgers.littleireland.ie/index.htm)

Springfield Armory National History Site (http://www.nps.gov/spar/historyculture/index.htm)

Springfield City Directories, 1906–1945 (Price & Lee Co., Springfield, Massachusetts)

SS *Celtic*, Passenger Ships and Images (Provo, Utah, www.ancestry.com)

View from the Pier, Ireland Peer to Pier – interview with Dáithí de Mórdha (http://www.http://viewfromthepier.com/2013/09/04/daithi-de-mordha_-archivist_great-blasket-centre/)

Wreck Site (wrecksite.eu/wreck.aspx?694460)

Index

Note: illustrations are indicated by page numbers in **bold**. Women are listed under their married names, with maiden names in brackets.

Almqvist, Bo 171
America 6, 10–11, 34, 55, 59, 62, 66, 68–9, 91–2, 133, 196, 201, 211, 225, 230, 260, 262–94, 297, 302
Anderson, Eileen Kane **269**
Andrew, Maura 112
Annals of Inisfallen 20
Annals of the Four Masters 20
Ar Muir is ar Tír (Ó Catháin) 14, 54
Aran Islands (*Oileáin Árann*) 26, 149
Atkinson, Henry 121–2

Baile, An (island village) 2–3, 7, **10**, 11, 55, 58, 62, 70, 85, **92**, 93–6, 166, 179, 182, 221, 226, 230–31
Baile an Teampaill 60, 135, 176, 215, 237, 245–6, 259
Baile na Rátha 131, 236, 241
Baile Loiscithe 259
Ballydavid 68
Ballyferriter (*Baile an Fheirtéaraigh*) 5, 57, 90, 100, 122, 134, 156–7, 167, 259, 260
Ballykeen 133, 135, 255
Bean an Oileáin (*Woman of the Island*) (Uí Chiobháin) 233, 238–9, 302
Beauty (*naomhóg*) 86–8, 137
beehive huts (*clocháns*) 4, 184
Beginish (*Beiginis*) 1, 48, 109–10
Bencevenni, Kathryn Kane **269**, 270, 272, 278
Bencevenni, Ronnie **269**, 272, 276, 277, 278–9

'"*Bheauty*" Deas an Oileáin' (Ó Duinnshléibhe) 87, 137, 256
Biuso, Tom 264
Blasket Lives (Matson) 51–2
Blasket Sound (*An Bealach*) 3, **4**, 40, 90, 115, 127, 138, 151–2, 160, 172, 176, 213, 255–6
Boland, Máire 56
Boland, Seán Eoghain 56
Bórú, Brian (Brian Bóroimhe) 18–19
Boyle, Sir Richard 7
Brosnan, Michael 225
Buchanan, Ronald H. 21
Byrne, Francis J. 19
Byrne, Theresa Kane **269**, 278

Cahersiveen 34
Caladh an Oileáin 3, **116**
Cape Clear Island (*Chléire*) 23, 26
Caramazza, Dorothy Kane **269**
Carna 66
Carney, Helena P. 'Lena' 277, 279
Carney, John 124
Carney, Mike 9–10, 15, 34, **71**, 140, 144, 147–8, 177, 217, 219, 221, 225, 242–3, 264, 266–7, 292, 298
Casement, Roger 191
Casey, John (Seán Ó Cathasa) 90, 200, 245–6, 248
Cashel 18
Castlegregory 86
Castro del Rio, Plácido Ramón 102, 105, 201–3, **202**, 210–12, 247

Chambers, George 60, 205, 258, 259
Chicago 260
Chicopee, Massachusetts 133, 264, 270
Civil War 45, 51, 119
Claddagh (*Chladaigh*) 24, 25, 26
Cloghane 69
Clontarf, Battle of 19
Congested Districts Board 7, 25, 62,
    100, 102, 103, 104, 105, 106,
    226, 296
Corca Dhuibhne, Kings of 19–20
Corcoran, John 106, **185**
Cork 119
Cork, Earl of 5, 14, 43, 99, 100
Costelloe, Máiréad (Ní Chatháin) 253,
    259, 260
Costelloe, Thomas 260
Coumeenole (*Com Dhineoil*) 54, 59
Cousins, James H. 175
Covino, Mark 291
Crest, The (film) 291
Crow, the (*An Cró*) 2, 146
Cullen, John 66
Cullen, Peig Bofar (Ní Chatháin) 63,
    65, 66, **67**
Curtin, Jeremiah 163, 164

Dáil, An 55, 88, 93, 118, 230
Day in Our Life, A (*Lá Dár Saol*)
    (Ó Criomhthain) 60
de Mórdha, Dáithí 105, 143, 218
de Mórdha, Mícheál 32
de Mórdha, Willie Devin **228**
de Valera, Éamon 16, 219–22, **222**,
    298, 300
Desmond, Earl of 7
Desmond Rebellion 7
Dewar, Daniel 22
Dingle (*An Daingean*) 54, 55–6, 73,
    106, 127, 131, 134, 155, 166, 176,
    180, 190, 198, 241, 260, 261, 264,
    283, 285–7, 289, 292–4
Dowling, Cáit (Ní Chatháin) 253, 260
Dowling, Jerh 260
Dublin 116, 123–5, 131, 171, 176, 196,
    197, 198, 219, 235
Dunleavy's Point 81
Dunquin (*Dún Chaoin*) 3, 5, 6, 11, 60,
    62, 69, 90, 93, 99, 115, 120, 121,
    132, 133, 135–6, 137, 155, 161,
    166, 176, 195, 200, 202, 213, 214,
    215, 220, 223–6, 228, 229–30,
    232, 234, 235, 237–8, 240–44,
    245–9, 302

Easter Rising 46, 116, 118, 123–6
England 125, 259, 260, 302
Enright, Tim 79, 105, 194, 240, 303
Erris 22, 25

Famine 5–6
Ferriter, Bríd 52
Ferriter, Eibhlín (Ní Chatháin) 253,
    259–60
Ferriter, Jack 259
Fhaill Mhór, An 3
First World War 10, 45, 116, 118,
    119–23, 181, 188, 191
Flaherty, Eoin 25
Flower, Ann 292
Flower, Barbara 182
Flower, Ida 96, 138–9, 180, 182, 188,
    210, 212, 247
Flower, Jean 182
Flower, Patrick 182, 248, 251, 256
Flower, Robin 31, 42, 45, 49, 73, 96,
    103, 119, 138, 142, 146, 147,
    166–7, 170, 177–191, **178**, **182**,
    185, **189**, 194, 195, 202, 203, 210,
    215–16, 244, 247, 248, 251
Flower, Síle 182
Foley, Maura 271
Foley, Pat 271
Fondúireacht an Bhlascaoid (Blasket
    Foundation) 45, 287, 302
Forest Park, Springfield 280–81
Fort, the (*An Dún*) 4, 147, 191

Galway 198, 199, 235
Gorky, Maxim 192
Graigue 52
Great Blasket (*An Blascaod Mór*)
    American Wakes 130, 264
    communications with mainland
        218, 219, 223, 297,
        298–300
    culture 8–9, 144–5, 146, 171,
        177–9, 207–8

Index

Great Blasket (*An Blascaod Mór*)
(*continued*)
decision-making 97–9
economy 7–8, 296–7
emigration from 6, 10–11, 55, 59,
62, 66, 68, 91–2, 130, 133,
196, 201, 211, 225, 230,
259–60, 262–94, 297
evacuation 11, 16, 26, 190, 217–28,
224, **226**, 234, 236–7, 261,
300–301
fishing 4, 7–8, 65–6, 109–11, 155,
210–11, 223, 296, 297
The Gathering (2013) 291–4
history 4–6
Irish language 8–9, 144–8, 165–71,
190, 191, 195, 199, 201
Kings 12–16, 28–35, 43
land organisation 7, 13, 15, 29,
100–106, 296, 297
literature 1, 9, 60, 148–9, 190,
191–4, 197–8, 299, 301
living conditions 6–7, 9–11,
217–21, 223
lobstering 65–6, 109–11, **111**
maps **2**, **6**, **92**
ownership 7, 100–101, 296, 302–3
population 5–6, 16, 218, 259
preservation 11–12, 227–8, 302–3
religion 8, 132–3
rent collection 99–101
school 8, 60, 70–79, **71**, 182,
217–18
settlement 4–5
shipwrecks 3, 111–14, 202
slipway **185**, 186
sports 85–8
telegram to de Valera 219–20, **220**,
300
topography 1–3
transport to and from mainland
3–4, 127–31, 138, 160,
195, 218, 219, 255–6, 297,
298–300
visitors to 9, 11, 31, 40, 93, 115,
137–9, 144–208, 227, 236,
295, 301, 302
yellow meal provided by
government 106–9

Great Blasket Centre (*Ionad Bhlascaoid
Mhóir*) 11, 105, 228, 287, 288,
289, 290, 291, 302
Green, David H. 161–2
Gregory, Augusta, Lady 31–2
Gweedore (*Gaoth Dobhair*) 26

Hartford, Connecticut 62, 66, 133, 264
Holyoke, Massachusetts 196, 264
Home Rule 45
Humphries, Richard 205
Humphries, Síle 205
Hungry Hill, Springfield 266–7,
270–71
Hussey, Clara 104

In the World (Gorky) 192
In Wicklow and West Kerry (Synge)
152–61
Inishark (*Inis Airc*) 26
Inishkea (*Inis Gé*) 24, 26, 104
Inishmurray (*Inis Muireadheach*) 24, 26
Inishnabro (*Inis na Bró*) 1, 66, 251
Inishtooskert (*Inis Tuaisceart*) 1
Inishtrahull (*Inis trá Tholl*) 26
Inishvickillane (*Inis Mhic Uileáin*) 1,
57–8, 66, 186, 251
Irish Republican Army (IRA) 274
Irish Talk – Kerry, An (Sjoestedt-
Jonval) 200
Island Cross-Talk (*Allagar ne hInise*)
(Ó Criomhthain) 9, 44, 45–6, 47,
79, 132–3, 192–4, 299
Islandman, The (*An tOileánach*)
(Ó Criomhthain) 9, 44, 45–6,
70, 79, 80–85, 100, 103, 106–8,
167–8, 192–4, 197, 208, 299

Jackson, Kenneth **189**, 205, **206**
Jacob, Andrew AnRi 'Drew' 294
Jacob, Lawrence Andrew 'Andy' 291–4

Kane, Agnes Dorothy 'Dotty' 270, 278
Kane, Dennis 'DK' 290–94
Kane, Eileen Shirley 278
Kane, Helen Elizabeth 270
Kane, James 'Jim' 270, 282
Kane, Joanne 'Kandy' 280, **288**
Kane, John A., Jr 290–91, 294

Kane, John 'Jack' Anthony, Sr 281, **288**, 289–90, 293–4

Kane, John Patrick **269**, 269, 270, 276–8, 279–81, **280**, 282, 287

Kane, Joseph 'Joe' Roland **269**, 272, 273–4, 275, 276, 277, 278, 279, 281, 282

Kane, Larry **288**

Kane, Mary (daughter of Mike 'The Fiddler') 270, 274–5, 278, 279, 282, 286

Kane, Mary (granddaughter of Mike 'The Fiddler') **288**

Kane, Mary Foley (wife of Mike 'The Fiddler') 268–70, **269**, 274–6, **275**, 278, 281–2

Kane, Michael 'Mike' (son of Mike 'The Fiddler') 270, 277–8, 281, 282

Kane, Mike (boarder) 271

Kane, Mike 'The Fiddler' *see* Ó Catháin, Mícheál (Mike 'The Fiddler' Kane)

Kanigel, Robert 96, 150, 161–2, 164, 166–7, 171, 179, 190, 192, 199, 201, 207

Keane, Bede 286

Keane, Martin (Mártan Ó Catháin) 285–6

Keane, Padraic 101, 293–4

Kelly, Brian (Brian Ó Ceallaigh) 191–4

Kilmalkedar (*Cill Maoilchéadair*) 66, 68

Kinsale 119

Knight, Peter 22, 25, 28

Land Commission 223, 241

Landers, Máire (Ní Chonchúir) 61

Landers, Patrick 62

Leeson-Marshall, Mary 235

Leoithne Aniar (*Westerly Breeze*) (Ó Criomhthain) 60

Letters from the Great Blasket (Uí Chriomhthain) 60

Lewis, Samuel 23

Lillis, Michael 248–50

Lochie (ship) 3

London 190, 259

Lone Seagull, The (O'Dowd) 42, 69

Loneliest Boy in the World (Ó Catháin) 236

Loti, Pierre 192

Lucchitti, Irene 47–8, 163

Lusitania 119–22

Mac Cárthaigh, Críostóir 236

Mac Chriomhthain, Máire 54

Mac Clúin, Seoirse 205

Mac Conghail, Muiris 75, 205–6

McCourt, Desmond 24

McCourt, Malachy 10

mac Domnaill, Máel Sechnaill (Malachy II) 18, 19

McGeever, Nell (Ní Chatháin) 68

McGeever, Paddy 68

Mac Milidh, Donn 41

mac Murchada, Máel Mórda 19

Mac Riocaird, Mark (Mark Crickard) 286–7, 292, **293**

Maguire, John M. 25

Marstrander, Carl 45, 96, 138, 146, 147, 165–71, **169**, 177–8, 180, 251

Mason, Thomas H. 42

Matson, Leslie 38, 45, 47, 51–2, 54, 56, 65, 77, 79, 90, 114, 117–19, 139, 141, 142, 162, 248, 255

Measgra ón Oileán Tiar (*Collection from the West Island*) (Flower) 248

Meyer, Kuno 171, 181

Mistéal, Pádraig 'An Fíogach' **226**

Moibhi College, Glasnevin 235

Moran, Ulick 225

Moreton, Cole 38, 150

Moriarty, Tom 236

Moriarty, Éilís (Ní Chinnéide) 292

Moriarty, John Benny 292

Muiríoch 55, 60, 61, 62, 66, 67–8, 88

Mulcahy, Richard 219

My Childhood (Gorky) 192

Nantasket Beach, Massachusetts 276–7

Nantucket, Massachusetts 69

New York City 68–9

Ní Ceárna, Máire 196

Ní Chatháin, Cáit 63, 66, **67**

Ní Chatháin, Eibhlín 63, 66

Ní Chatháin, Eibhlís 55

Ní Chatháin, Éilís 63, 66

Index

Ní Chatháin, Joan 63, 66
Ní Chatháin, Mary 253, 259
Ní Chatháin, Nóirín 253, 260
Ní Chiobháin, Caitlín 236, **247**, 248
Ní Chiobháin, Máirín 236
Ní Chriomhthain, Eibhlín 59
Ní Chriomhthain, Niamh 60, **61**
Ní Dhálaigh, Cáit 57–8
Ní Dhonnchú, Áine 72–3
Ní Dhonnchú, Cáit 73–4
Ní Ghuithín, Eibhlín 230, 233–4, 238, 246, **257**
Ní Shéaghdha, Nóra 34–5, 42, 254–6, 257
Ní Shúilleabháin, Cáit 'Lís' 255–6
Ní Shúilleabháin, Eibhlín 234
Nic Craith, Mairéad 146–7, 212
Nic Gearailt, Máirín **71**
Nic Niocaill, Eibhlín 59, 171–7, **172**, 231, 245, 285, 288
Noígíallach, Niall 17

Ó Caomhánaigh, Seán 'an Chóta' 200
Ó Catháin, Gearóid 'Cheaist' 173, 225, 236, 237
Ó Catháin, Maraisín Mharas Mhuiris **224**
Ó Catháin, Mártan (great-grandfather of King) 51, 52–3
Ó Catháin, Mártan (uncle of King) 58
Ó Catháin, Mícheál (Mike 'The Fiddler' Kane) (son of King) 91–2, 93, 173, 213, 255, 230, 254, 262–79, **265**, **269**, 282, 283–6, 289, 292, 302
Ó Catháin, Mícheál (son of Muiris) 68
Ó Catháin, Mícheál 'Bofar' (brother of King) **52**, 62–7, **63**, 182, 203–4, **205**
Ó Catháin, Mícheál 'Micí' (father of King) 54, 55–6
Ó Catháin, Mícheál Muiris (cousin of King) 87
Ó Catháin, Muiris (son of Mícheál 'Bofar') 63, 66
Ó Catháin, Muiris (uncle of King) 54
Ó Catháin, Muiris 'Gog' (son of Muiris Mhicí) 68

Ó Catháin, Muiris 'Maras Mhuiris' (cousin of king) 14, 16, 36, 54, 65–6, 114, 221, 223, 225
Ó Catháin, Muiris Mhicí (brother of King) **52**, 55, 67–8, 88
Ó Catháin, Pádraig (son of Mícheál 'Bofar') 63, 66, **67**
Ó Catháin, Pádraig (son of Seán An Rí) **253**, 253, 259, **261**
Ó Catháin, Pádraig (uncle of King) 55
Ó Catháin, Pádraig Mhártain (second Blasket King) 14–15, 36, 43, 52, 53–4
Ó Catháin, Pádraig Peats Mhicí (last Blasket King)
  as adviser and counsellor 40, 132–7
  as arbitrator 40, 140–41
  baptism 15, 57
  bed-and-breakfast business 33, 43, 138–9, 147, 230, 295
  birth 56–7
  character 12, 39, 41–2, 295
  children 91–3, 229–61, 262–94, 302
  death and funeral 34–5, 69, 212–16, 298
  descendents in America 262–94, 302
  descendants in Ireland 229–61, 302
  education 70–79
  family grave **215**
  family home 'the palace' 33, 93–6, **94**, **95**, 106, 139–40, **145**, 147, 152, 169–70, 173, 179, 188, 192, **229**, 232, **253**, **257**, **296**
  as fisherman 33, 43, 295
  as host-in-chief 40, 137–40, 295
  as intermediary 40, 117–27, 295
  as leader 13, 32–3, 38, 40, 97–114, 295
  legacy 295–303
  lineage 51–6
  marriage 36, 89–91
  named as King 15, 36–9
  obituaries 213–14
  old age 209–12
  oratorical skill 38, 49–50
  physique 39, 41, 50, 212, 295
  pictured **13**, **29**, **37**, **52**, **98**, **229**, **253**

Ó Catháin, Pádraig Peats Mhicí (last
    Blasket King) (*continued*)
    political views 33, 45–6
    as postman 30, 34, 38–9, 40, 43, 56,
        114–17, **116**, 295
    religion 132–3
    role as King 12–13, 30–35, 39–41,
        97–143, 295–6
    siblings 55, 56–69
    and Tomás Ó Criomhthain 44–7,
        70–85
    as transporter 40, 117, 127–31, 138,
        160, 195
    and visitors to the island 33, 40, 43,
        137–9, 144–208, 295, 301
    voice 38, 47–50, 295
    wealth 43
    youth 54, 55–6, 70–88
Ó Catháin, Páidín **228**
Ó Catháin, Peats 68, 69
Ó Catháin, Séamusín Bofar 63, **65**,
    66, **67**
Ó Catháin, Seán (son of Seán An Rí)
    253, 253
Ó Catháin, Seán An Rí 15, 30, 93,
    115–16, 137, 139, 169, 173, 181,
    186, 195, 204, **206**, 209, 213, 214,
    225, 229, 232, 250–61, **252**, **253**,
    254, **256**, 301
Ó Catháin, Seán Cheaist 225
Ó Catháin, Seán Mharas Mhuiris 'Faelí'
    223, **226**, **228**
Ó Ceárna, Peats Tom 66, 175, 176
Ó Ceárna, Seán 'Filí' **226**
Ó Ceárna, Seán 'Sheáisi' 220, **226**, 261
Ó Ceárna, Seán Tom 221, **222**, 263,
    267
Ó Ceárna, Seánín 190, 217, 218–19
Ó Ceárna, Tomás 127
Ó Ceárna, Tomás 'An Poncán' 55, 112,
    118, 121
Ó Ceárnaigh, Seán Peats Tom **228**, 255
Ó Ciobháin, Labhrás (Larry Kavanagh)
    236, 240, **247**
Ó Coileáin, Seán 194
Ó Conchúir, Muiris 61–2
Ó Conchúir, Peats 61–2
Ó Conchúir, Seán 61
Ó Conchúir, T.P. 286

O'Connor, Catherine Veronica 'Katie'
    279–80
O'Connor, Rory (Ruaidhrí Ua
    Conchubhair) 19
Ó Criomhthain, Dómhnall 59, 174,
    175–6, 231, **245**, 245, 285, 288
Ó Criomhthain, Muiris 59
Ó Criomhthain, Seán 5, 52, 59–61,
    104–5, 146, **149**, 164–5, 166,
    169, 177–8, 192, 207–8, 251,
    260, 283
Ó Criomhthain, Tomás (father) 5, 8,
    9, 14, 31–3, 36, 38, 43, 44–8, 54,
    55–60, 70–85, 77, 86, 90, 95,
    98–9, 100, 103, 105–8, 132–3,
    138–9, 141–3, 146–8, 166,
    167–8, 170, 175, 176, 180–81,
    182, **185**, 187, 188–90, 191–4,
    197, 200, 201, 204, 209–12, 216,
    253–4, 262–3, 295, 299, 301
Ó Criomhthain, Tomás (son) 59
Ó Dálaigh, Peaidí Beag **224**
Ó Danachair, Caoimthín 20, 22–3, 24
O'Dowd, John 69
O'Dowd, Kate Keane (Cáit Ní
    Chatháin) 42, 66, 68–9, 88, 114,
    215, 218, 232–3
Ó Dubhshláine, Mícheál 138, 173–4
Ó Duinnshelé, Séamas **52**
Ó Duinnshelé, Tomás **52**
Ó Duinnshléibhe, Séamus 218, 252
Ó Duinnshléibhe, Seán Eoghain 'Seán
    Fada' 46, 47, 48, 49, 62, 87, 95,
    109–10, 120, 122–3, 124, 126,
    130–31, 134–7, 141–2, 252, 256
Ó Glaisne, Risteárd 44–5, 117, 230,
    236
Ó Guithín, Mícheál (son of Peig Sayers)
    42, 45, 73, 89, 122–3, 124–5, 195,
    200, 234
Ó Guithín, Micheál (son of Máire
    Pheats Mhicí) 230, 235
Ó Guithín, Mícheál Mhaidhc Léan
    (husband of Máire Pheats Mhicí)
    157, 173, 230, 234, 238, 251
Ó Guithín, Muiris Mhaidhc Léan **206**,
    223, **224**, 225, **228**, **229**, 230,
    233, 234, 237, 240–44, **242**, **243**,
    289–90

Index

Ó Guithín, Pádraig (first Blasket King)
  14, 43
Ó Guithín, Pádraig (son of Máire
  Pheats Mhicí) 230
Ó Guithín, Peatsaí 87, 125
Ó Guithín, Seán Mhaidhc Léan **206**,
  221–2, 223, 224–5, **226**, 230,
  233, 234, **235**, 237, 240–44, **243**,
  290
Ó hAiniféin, Mícheál 75
Oidhreacht an Bhlascaoid (Ua
  Maoileoin) 41, 46
Old Woman's Reflections, An
  (*Machnamh Seanamhná*) (Sayers)
  9, 123–4, 299
Ó Loinsigh, Mícheál 66
Ó Maoileoin, Tomás 59
Ó Raithile, Áine 205
Ó Raithile, Tomás 205
Ó Rathaille, Aogán 250
Ó Sé, Diarmuid 57
O'Shea, Kathleen 291
O'Shea, Máire Keating 133–6
Ó Siochfhradha, Pádraig 191, **193**,
  193–4, 247
Ó Súilleabháin, Mícheál 95
Ó Súilleabháin, Muiris 9, 49, 59, 86,
  95, 109–10, 112–13, 119–22,
  126–31, 148, 196–8, **197**, 199,
  256–7, 295, 299, 301
Ó Súilleabháin, Peaidí Mhicil **224**
Ó Súilleabháin, Seámas 41
Ó Súilleabháin, Seánín Mhicí **226**, **228**
O'Sullivan, Hannah 261

Pearse, Patrick 125, 171–2, 285
Pêcheur d'Islande (*An Iceland
  Fisherman*) (Loti) 192
Peig (Sayers) 9, 299
Pender, Ian Moffat 236
Pity Youth Does Not Last (Ó Guithín)
  122–3, 124–5
Playboy of the Western World (Synge)
  157, 161–2
Port Urlainn *(Port Durlainne)* 24, 26
Potts, Sr Kevin 286

Quebra (ship) 3, 111–14
Queenstown (Cobh) 201, 265

Redican, Sue 101, 227
Redmond, John 45
Rice, Bess 104
Rinn an Chaisleáin (Castle Point) 186
Rogers, Patsy Dan (Patsaí Dan Mac
  Ruaidhrí) 26–8, **27**, 300
Russell, Connor 287
Ruth, George Annesley 235

Sacred Heart Church, Springfield 268,
  269, **271**
St Kilda 97–8
Santa Maria de la Rosa (ship) 3, 202
Sayers, Peig 9, 95, 123–4, 148, 200,
  205, 227, 295, 299, 301
Seal's Cove 114
Seanchas ón Oileán Tiar
  (Ó Criomhthain) 86
Sinn Féin 45, 118
Sjoestedt-Jonval, Marie-Louise
  199–201, **200**, 247, 265
Slater, Eamonn 25
Slea Head (*Ceann Sléibhe*) 3, 108, 289
Slinneán Bán 62–3, 182
Smith, Charles 5, 53
Smith, Robert 74
Smyth, Thomas 268
Springfield, Massachusetts 92, 225, 230,
  263–4, 266–82, 284, 286, 287
Stagles, Joan 53, 101, 206, **234**
Stagles, Ray 53, 101, 206
Sullivan, Pat 273
Synge, John Millington 31–2, 33, 36,
  93, 96, 149–65, **150**, 170, 173–4,
  230, 244, 251, 267

Tara 17
Tearaght (*An Tiaracht*) 1, 66
Thomson, Mrs D.P. 163, 164
Thomson, George 12, 30–31, 131,
  194–9, **197**, 207, 256–7
Three Sisters (*An Triúr Deirfiúr*) 3
tOileán a Bhí, An (*The Island that Was*)
  (Uí Chiobháin) 41–2, 238, 302
Tory Island (*Toraigh*) 23, 26–8, 300
Tráigh Bháin, An 2, **84**, 174–5, 291
Tráigh Ghearraí 114
Tralee 260
Trehiou, Pierre 110

Twenty Years A-Growing (Fiche Bliain ag Fás) (Ó Súilleabháin) 9, 127–31, 197, 198, 299

Tyers, Padraig 243–4

Ua Maoileoin, Pádraig 41, 46, 47, 49, 59, 194

Uí Ceárna, Máire (Ní Scannláin) 55

Uí Chatháin, Eibhlín (Ní Dhálaigh) 55

Uí Chatháin, Eibhlín (Ní Ghairbhia) 90–93, 212

Uí Chatháin, Máire (Ní Chriomhthain) 57–8

Uí Chatháin, Máire Mháire Eoghain (Ní Dhuinnshléibhe) 62–7, **64**, 67

Uí Chatháin, Máiréad 'Mag An Rí' (Ní Chiobháin) 252–3, **253**, **254**, **257**, 258–9, 260

Uí Chatháin, Siobháin (Ní Chonchúir) 67–8, 88

Uí Chathasa, Cáit an Rí 'The Princess' (Ní Chatháin) 32, **52**, 55, 69, 90, 93, 139, 152, 156, 158, 164, 173, 174–5, 176, 178, 180, 200, 209, 213, 225, 229, 232, 233–4, 235, 244–50, **245**, **246**, **247**, 283, 285, 302

Uí Chinnéide, Edna 287, 292

Uí Chiobháin, Máire Mhaidhc Léan (Ní Ghuithín) 41–2, 114, 115, 173, 174, **189**, **206**, 230, **231**, 233, 235–6, 237, 238–40, **240**, 246, **247**, 248, 255, **257**, 302, 303

Uí Chriomhthain, Eibhlís (Ní Shúilleabháin) 59–61, **61**, 258–9, **260**

Uí Chriomhthain, Maire (Ní Chatháin) 44, 55, 56, 57–61

Uí Conchúir, Cáit Mhicí (Ní Chatháin) 55, 61–2

Uí Dhuinnshléibhe, Méiní (Ní Shé) 47, 49, 133–7, **136**, 139, 162, 175, 252, 255

Uí Ghuithín, Máire Pheats Mhicí (Ní Chatháin) 93, 139, 152–4, **153**, 157–9, 160, 161–2, 173–4, 176, 180, 182, **189**, 195, 199, 200, **206**, 213, 221, **222**, 225, 229, 230–38, **231**, **232**, **233**, **234**, 247–8, 283, 302

Uí hAiniféin, Siobhán (Ní Scannláin) 75

Uí Loinsigh, Máire (Ní Chatháin) 63, 66, **67**

Uí Mhaoileoin, Cáit (Ní Chriomhthain) 59, 174–6, 231, 245

Uí Néill clan 17, 18

United States *see* America

Ventry (*Ceann Trá*) 5, 69, 238, 249, 250, 252, 260, 268

Ventry Regatta 85–8, 126–7, 137

von Sydow, Carl Wilhelm 64, 205

Wakefield, Edward 25

Western Island, The (Flower) 103, 216

Westfield, Massachusetts 282

Yager, Tom 37

Yank's Well (*Tobar an Phoncáin*) 55, 94, 231

Yeats, William Butler 150